HOW TO BEAT

Internet Casinos
&
Poker Rooms

ABOUT THE AUTHOR

Arnold Snyder, one of the world's foremost gambling authorities, is a high-stakes professional player who has been writing about casino gambling and beating casinos at their own games for well over two decades. He is the author of ten books and advanced strategies including *The Blackjack Formula*, the groundbreaking work which revolutionized the ways professional card counters attacked the games, and of course, the best-selling classic, *Blackbelt in Blackjack*. For 25 years, Snyder has been the publisher and editor of *Blackjack Forum*, a quarterly journal for professional players now published online at BlackjackForumOnline.com. In January 2003, Snyder was elected one of the seven charter members of the Blackjack Hall of Fame.

HOW TO BEAT
Internet Casinos
&
Poker Rooms

Cardoza Publishing is the foremost gaming and gambling publisher in the world with a library of more than175 up-to-date and easy-to-read books and strategies. These authoritative works are written by the top experts in their fields and with more than 8,500,000 books in print, represent the best-selling and most popular gaming books anywhere.

FIRST EDITION

Visit us at www.cardozapub.com or write to the address below for a full list of Cardoza books, advanced, and computer strategies.

CARDOZA PUBLISHING

P.O. Box 1500 Cooper Station, New York, NY 10276
Phone (800)577-WINS
email: cardozapub@aol.com
www.cardozapub.com

TABLE OF CONTENTS

PART I
Beating Online Casinos

PART II
Making Money in Internet
Poker Rooms

PART III
End Matter

INTRODUCTION

The Internet today is providing the greatest opportunities for aspiring professional gamblers in the history of gambling, a chance to take $500 to $1,000 and turn it into a real bankroll. No matter where you are in the world, you have hundreds of Internet casinos ready to take your bets at any hour of the night or day.

Gambling in online casinos and poker rooms is the single most accessible form of gambling available. You not only don't need to dress up to go out, you can enjoy a greater variety of games than you'll find in brick-and-mortar casinos. Even better, you don't need a whole lot of money to play. In fact, in addition to blackjack games with $1 minimum bets and poker games for five and ten cents, most online casinos also offer free games if you simply want to learn how to play.

For players who know how to figure the odds, the bets they place in these online casino games can be made with advantages over the house only dreamed of by the most skilled professional gamblers in the past. I know kids in their early 20s making six-digit incomes from exploiting the online casino bonus offers. Never has the simple ability to do math paid so well, so fast, to so many.

And there has never before been as good an opportunity for poker players to learn the game as exists online today. You can begin your poker education with online poker room deposit bonuses that will cover the cost of your blinds, with a smaller house rake than exists in live poker rooms, and no dealer tipping expense. You can study the best players for hours on end, and as you progress in your skills, you can increase your hourly win rate by playing multiple tables simultaneously. There are smart kids who have never even been in a live casino poker room making six-digit incomes online. Many of these kids leave the online casinos after a few years and enter the world of high stakes poker tournaments, and compete on equal footing with world class professionals who have spent decades learning the game.

How long these opportunities will last is anybody's guess. Historically, these types of situations have always disappeared within a few years. Those who get in on them reap a financial gain that can finance any dream.

Far be it from me to encourage anyone to take up professional gambling as a career. The fact that it's fun to make your living playing games, matching wits with other gamblers, soaking casinos for thousands of dollars, traveling when you want to travel, never having to punch a time clock or say "Yes, sir," to a boss—professional gambling is a tough life indeed.

But for those few depraved souls who might happen to find this lifestyle, full-time or part-time, intriguing, don't pass up the opportunity that's sitting right there on your laptop. The time is now. The opportunity is vast. The money is waiting.

If that appeals to you, read on!

OVERVIEW

This is really two books in one:
1. *Beating Internet Casinos*
2. *Making Money in Internet Poker Rooms.*

There are significant differences between the two. Both of these activities involve gambling by connecting to the Internet and playing games on a computer screen. But that's about as far as the similarities go.

On the Internet, just as in live casinos, playing **house games** (like blackjack, craps, or slot machines) in which you play against the casinos, and playing against other players in a poker game are two very different activities.

When you play blackjack, you are either going to win the house's money or lose your own money to the casino. And you are usually bucking a built-in **house edge**. When you play poker, there is no house edge. The house takes a small percentage of each pot to cover its expenses, which is called the house **rake**, but essentially, in a poker game, you are putting your money and your skills up against the players around your table—players just like you. Your advantage or disadvantage in a poker game is primarily determined by your skill compared to the other players at your table, not the house rake. So whether you play in live casinos or online, the approach to beating a casino game like blackjack is very different from your approach to beating a poker game.

BEATING INTERNET CASINOS

To beat Internet casino games, you'll need to learn how to take advantage of the lucrative bonus offers online casinos make to entice new players into their games. These bonuses turn the house edge that normally exists in these casino games into a player edge over the house. The rules for beating the Internet casino games are fairly straightforward and nearly foolproof.

In my opinion, just about any intelligent person can beat online casinos, provided they follow a few simple techniques. It's my job to provide you with those techniques. If you can follow instructions, you'll get the money. And you'll be amazed at how easy it is.

MAKING MONEY IN THE INTERNET POKER ROOMS

Some of the techniques for making money in Internet casino games can also be used to profit in online poker rooms, which also offer bonuses to entice new players. But making money at poker—whether you are in live games or on the Internet—requires that you be a capable poker player to start with. The game of poker is far more complex than any casino game because it is based as much on psychology and strategic maneuvering as mathematics.

It's easy to figure out the house edge at blackjack or craps. So it's pretty easy to figure out the value of a bonus offer, and to calculate the average profit in dollars. You can't estimate your advantage or disadvantage at poker so easily. It depends on how good you are, and how good the other players at your table are. If they're much better players than you, you may not have any advantage at all.

This is not a book on how to play poker, or how to win at poker. However, if you are new to poker, I will steer you in the right direction and help you find the best games for beginners. I'll also provide you with guidelines for selecting the best online tournaments for your skill level.

The Internet is a fantastic learning ground for the game of poker and your education need not be expensive. All of the reputable Internet poker rooms offer free games for beginners, and the limits in the real money games online are lower than you'll ever find in a live casino. You can play poker for pennies on the Internet, as opposed to dollars in live casinos.

THE LEGAL ISSUE

I'm not going to spend much ink discussing the legality of gambling on the Internet. The U.S. government has been threatening for years to pass laws that would make Internet gambling illegal. There are federal laws against setting up an Internet casino in the U.S., but no federal laws that make gambling in online casinos illegal for private citizens. A few states, spurred on by morality crusaders who lump gambling in with pornography and drug addiction, have passed laws that prohibit its citizens from gambling on the Internet. But most states completely ignore the issue. They have, after all, virtually no ability to enforce such laws. With many of the big Internet poker rooms now advertising on television and in national magazines, and with many of the big tournament winners bragging that they earned their seats in the tournaments by winning online tournaments, it's obvious that there isn't a whole lot of legal action being taken against Internet gamblers.

You may have noticed, however, that most online casinos and poker rooms now emphasize the free games they offer players in their TV and magazine advertising. This is specifically to avoid being prosecuted for encouraging illegal activities, should the government suddenly decide that Internet gambling is a crime. To cover my own ass, so to speak, let me state emphatically once again: you can play all the Internet casino games for free, and if gambling is illegal where you live, then consider this book just an education in the ways that professional gamblers today are beating online casinos.

The situation with Internet gambling today is similar to the pre-Playboy magazine 1950s, when any magazine, book, or film that showed nudity protected itself from prosecution by including statements from psychiatrists, medical doctors, or art historians, justifying the "redeeming social value" of the material. This old stuff is a real hoot. Here's Doctor Siegfried Zambuzi claiming on page one that the photos within are meant to be studied by students of advanced psychology only for the purpose of delving into the primal mysteries of human nature. And inside the mag, we see Bettie Page on all fours in a leather corset. Somehow, Hugh Hefner and Larry Flynt managed to get the government out of our bedrooms for the most part, but it's unlikely Mike Sexton and Howard Lederer will ever get the government out of our wallets.

So, my advice is to check your local laws to see if Internet gambling is legal in your state or country. As neither I nor my publisher are attorneys, we cannot provide you with legal advice on this matter. But I will say this: if you make money gambling on the Internet, do not neglect to declare that income on your tax forms, and pay those taxes. Gambling income is taxable in the U.S., and the IRS wants its cut of your profits.

Now, as for those profits...

PART I

Beating Online
Casinos

1. INTRODUCTION

There's a lot of money in online casinos that's pretty easy to pick up. In fact, it's such a nice little piece of change—$5,000 to $10,000— and so much easier to get than the money that can be earned in most other forms of gambling, it's kind of weird that the situation even exists.

I feel like one of those late-night TV hucksters telling you to call their 800 number with your MasterCard at the ready and they'll tell you where piles of cash are just laying around waiting for you to grab—only I'm telling you the truth. Making money from online casinos is not quite as easy as just asking for it. You've got to jump through a few hoops to get it, and there is some risk involved. But it's there, the risk is minimal, and it's available to just about anyone who has a computer with an Internet connection and a thousand bucks or so to invest in this venture.

I've been writing about casino blackjack for twenty-five years, so until now most of my approach to helping players beat casinos has been related to card counting in live casino games. Compared to card counting in Vegas, making money in online casinos is child's play. You'll risk a lot less of your money on the Internet and you'll have a much bigger advantage over the house.

If you start flipping through this book, you'll no doubt notice a few mathematical analyses and god-awful formulas. Don't fret, because you only have to do a small amount of the math yourself. I've already worked out the important stuff for you, and I give clear instructions on the things you have to figure out for yourself. This is pocket calculator math, not advanced statistical analysis. I'm including all the math in this book because if you eventually want to gamble on the Internet at higher stakes, long-term, and at a professional level, you'll need to know where the player's edge comes from, how big of an edge it is, and most importantly, how to recognize when it disappears.

Most readers will probably take the quick and easy route to beating online casinos. They'll go in, pick up the easy cash, and get out. After they've picked up $5,000 to $10,000 in the first month or so—and yes, that's quite easily attainable—they never go back. That may strike you as strange, since it isn't all that easy for many people to just pick up $5,000 to $10,000 in a month or so. Why don't they keep going, month after month, year after year? It sounds like a pretty good gig, doesn't it? Sitting at home in your underwear, playing video games and getting paid for it? Sounds like a lifestyle, not a one-shot deal. But let me tell you what you're up against.

1) Gambling in online casinos is one of the easiest ways for an average person, with no professional gambling experience, to start making money right from the start.

2) Gambling in online casinos is one of the most mathematically complex forms of gambling, and one of the most difficult to pursue profitably as a career.

Believe it or not, these statements are not contradictory. The first statement addresses the ease of getting into games with a strong advantage over the house. The second statement addresses what happens after that initial entry into the world of Internet gaming, how the games and casino offerings change, the complexities of game analysis, and the unusual strategies that must be employed to continue with an expectation of winning.

What it comes down to is that online casinos offer very big profit opportunities to novices because they are attempting to entice new players into their games. If you are selective about which casinos you play at based on their enticements, you will not have to do much of anything to get an edge over the house as a new player in an online casino. As a new player—that is, unknown to them—you will already have an edge over the house. They hand you that edge on a golden platter!

But like everything else on the Internet, your status as a new player in an online casino changes quickly. Your edge over the house can change overnight, and in many cases, within your first hour of play. If you don't know what you're doing, if you don't quit when your edge is gone, you're going to give back everything that you earned when the casino was courting you with a juicy profit opportunity.

So, this part of the book is really about choosing the casinos where you play, choosing which games to play in those casinos, devising your least risky and most profitable betting strategy, and knowing when to get out. The rankest amateur can make money gambling in online casinos provided he's careful about getting into the strongest opportunities and getting out fast when the party's over.

My advice to most players who enter online casinos is to resign yourself from the start to taking the easy money and then getting out. As in every other form of professional gambling, there are potential dangers. Pay very close attention to details if you take on this project, and you will be rewarded.

THE LOOT-AND-SCOOT APPROACH

Throughout this book, I will provide two strategies for beating online casinos. The first perspective, and the most important for the players I'm aiming at, I call "Loot-and-scoot" (L&S). This is the easiest approach that should be of interest to most players. If you follow the L&S approach to choosing casinos, getting in, and getting out, you will not have to do any major mathematical analyses. You can take the $5,000 to $10,000 that's easy for you to pick up, then go your merry way.

If you feel intimidated by even the simple math involved in this approach, please stick with me. Just follow along with a pocket calculator and a notepad if necessary. All you have to do is plug in a few numbers and let the book do the rest.

THE PROFESSIONAL APPROACH

The second strategy will be for the serious player who will take the time to do more complex mathematical analyses, then take the measures necessary to play with a calculable profit. The professional player will take advantage of special bonuses online casinos offer to their VIP customers, which is to say, the big bettors. Many of these bonuses require buy-ins of $1,000 or more, and the bonuses offered at these levels generally give the players less of a percentage advantage over the house, but a greater dollar return. The pro who can calculate the advantage, and who has the bankroll to withstand the fluctuations that are inevitable with big bets, will often find the lower percentage edges more than justified by the greater dollar-per-hour expectation. If you intend to play at this higher level, then I will assume that you are fully aware of other facets of gambling that professional players must be familiar with—in particular, estimating risk based on your bankroll, calculating your advantage, and recognizing the variance of the games. I repeat: this book is not a primer for gambling as a profession. If you don't already have a handle on these facets, then don't fool yourself into thinking that this book will turn you into a gambling pro. For broader information on gambling as a profession, you should start with my book, *Blackbelt in Blackjack,* and visit the free online library at my website, www.blackjackforumonline.com.

WHICH METHOD IS RIGHT FOR YOU?

I highly recommend the loot & scoot approach to both new and experienced players who already play in live casino games and know blackjack basic strategy. I also recommend it for low-stakes card counters, to quickly crank up their playing bankroll by thousands of bucks. Skilled card counters may also find value in sticking with Internet gambling a bit longer than the average L&S player, as the advantages available through Internet casino bonuses are often quite a bit higher than those available from card counting, and often with less risk. This is not meant to imply that blackjack card counting is a skill you will use online. It's not.

The L&S approach is also an excellent method for college students who want to earn some quick cash, and it pays better than most summer jobs. Retired people can supplement their incomes with this method. Anyone with some free time and the ability to understand math concepts on the level of, say, credit card interest rates can profit from this approach.

A BIT OF THE HISTORY

The enticements offered by online casinos to lure in customers are nothing new to the casino industry. Live casinos have been giving freebies to their customers by serving them free drinks since day one. Depending on the level of a player's action, casinos comp rooms, meals, and airfare, and even make loss rebate deals with high rollers. Online casinos can't serve drinks or give you a room. And you don't need airfare to get online. So, online casinos have only one enticement to offer their customers, but it's a great one: money.

I first learned that professional gamblers were making money in online casinos by picking up bonus money about six years ago. A player writing under the name "Yikes!" submitted an article to *Blackjack Forum* magazine—a trade journal for professional gamblers that I have been editing for twenty-five years—briefly describing a technique for making money in the online casinos that he called "milking the matchplays." This technique, which basically consists of going from online casino to online casino and picking up the bonus money—without giving them any action once the bonus has been collected and the house edge kicks in—is the foundation of the loot & scoot approach described in this book.

I was fascinated by this new opportunity for players and began a correspondence with the author. In the fall of 1999, he and I attended an International conference for the Internet casino industry that was held in Vancouver, Canada, in order to collect information on Internet casinos from the perspective of those who were operating them. We also visited StarNet, a major Internet casino software provider whose offices were located in Vancouver.

In January of 2000, I edited and published a book by "Yikes," who was now writing under the name of "Bill Haywood," titled *BeatWebCasinos.Com*. It was the first book ever written on this subject, and it described the basic techniques of making money online. Haywood's book was to Internet gambling what Edward O. Thorp's *Beat the Dealer* was to card counting at blackjack in 1961. But although *BeatWebCasinos.Com* provides all of the basic techniques for beating online casinos, in just five year's time the book has become outdated. The Internet changes that fast.

In 2003, Barry Meadow—a highly respected gambling author who writes primarily on horse racing—wrote a 63-page technical report titled *Crushing the Internet Casinos,* which I had the honor of publishing as a *Blackjack Forum Professional Report*. Barry did an excellent job of updating many of the changes that had occurred in online casinos since Bill Haywood's book.

SO WHY THIS BOOK?

Another three years have passed and the online casino scene has continued to change. I also know a lot more now about making money online than Haywood or Meadow reveal in their books. Neither author provides any simple techniques for estimating the percentage advantage available from the different types of bonuses, nor do they provide much guidance on the best betting strategies for players on limited bankrolls. For players with small bankrolls—who should target only the strongest profit opportunities—knowing the percentage advantage is the single best tool for selecting games. Knowing the least risky betting strategy is of equal importance once your money is on the line.

When Avery Cardoza asked me if I could write a book on Internet gambling for Cardoza Publishing, the timing couldn't have been better. I had recently launched my Internet site, BlackjackForumOnline.com, and a group of professional Internet gamblers—all longtime professional casino gamblers I had known for years—were monitoring one of my discussion forums on Internet gambling. My wife and I had just finished six weeks of playing an hour a day on the Internet, with a profit of about $9,000 on a starting test bankroll of $1,000. In the course of our play, I developed my own simple methods for players to estimate the dollar value of the various bonuses, while lowering their risk to comfortable levels, and maximizing profits based on their bankrolls. I was impressed with the ease with which a player on a small bankroll—minuscule by professional gamblers' standards—could extract $9,000 from these games so quickly.

So, with a tip of my sombrero to the forerunners in this field, notably Bill Haywood and Barry Meadow, I'm excited about leading you into this cyber-adventure.

As you read and study the methods we use to extract bonus money from casinos, you will probably note that many of our examples show bonuses with dollar amounts of $100 or less, sometimes only $40 or $50. This may lead you to believe that I am exaggerating about the amount you can collect from these bonuses in a month or two. Before you go on to the methods, flip to the end of the Odds and Ends chapter, and check out the list of online casinos, taken from the list on my website, that are currently offering bonus programs. (The details in this list will have changes by the time you read this, but if you go to BlackjackForumOnline.com, you will find a current list as good or better. Just start adding up the bonus money, and see if you think it might be worth your time and effort.

Now... let's go get the money!

2. THE BASICS

The basic premise is simple. You deposit money in an Internet casino account—let's say it's $100. Because you are a new customer, the casino adds a bonus of $100, so your account now reads $200. Hey, that's great! Let's cash out now!

Yeah, right. It's not quite that simple.

If it was that easy to make $100, online casinos would have all gone broke long ago. The casino requires you play a certain amount before you can withdraw your funds. We call this the **wagering requirement**, which you'll find on the terms and conditions page of each online casino's home page. Let's say that at this particular casino you have to wager five times the amount of your deposit and the bonus money combined before you can withdraw any money from your account. This means you must place a total of $1,000 in bets before you can withdraw any funds. That wagering requirement is strictly enforced. If you withdraw any funds prior to meeting this requirement, you will usually lose the full amount of the bonus and any winnings from your play.

You may wager this $1,000 any way you want. You may place ten $100 bets, or two hundred $5 bets, or a thousand $1 bets—whatever you prefer, so long as you put a total of $1,000 into action.

Is this a good deal? Yes, it is, since this casino allows you to play their six-deck blackjack games, where the house advantage over a basic strategy player is only one-half of one percent (0.5%).

One-half of one percent of $1,000 is only $5. So, if you play perfect basic strategy until you've given them a total of $1,000 of action, you can expect to have $195 remaining of your starting balance of $200. That's a $95 profit on your $100 investment. Not bad!

Now I don't want to lose you here because you didn't know what the house advantage was on six-deck blackjack and how to figure out the "cost" of playing based on this. I'm going to provide you with the house edges for all the games you'll find online, and I'll teach you the simple way that pro gamblers figure out the overall expectation based on this action. All you'll need to do is press a few buttons on a pocket calculator. It's not brain surgery.

So, you play through your $1,000 in action at their blackjack tables, but unfortunately, you have a bad run of cards, and you wind up with only $165 in your account at the end of your session. Well, a $65 profit is still a profit, and you know that in the next casino you may have a good run of cards, leaving you with more than your $95 expectation. Sometimes you'll win more than your expectation and sometimes less, but for every time you play a bonus like this, you'll average a $95 profit.

THE TEN-STEP L&S PROCESS IN A NUTSHELL

I've given you an example of the loot-and-scoot method; now let me show you the process, step-by-step. Here it is, from getting in to getting out:

1) Go to the casino's home page to see what bonuses they offer.

2) If you see one that looks good, you click on it to get the details. How do you determine if it's "good?" Just follow my advice for estimating the dollar value of a bonus in Chapter 4: Free Cash Bonuses. It's easy.

3) Then you go to the casino's terms and conditions page and find the wagering requirement for the bonus. If it's not too big, the bonus is still looking good. What's "too big?" That's all part of the Free Cash Bonus chapter, where we get into the simple math of bonus analysis.

4) The next step is to check the terms and conditions to find what games you may play in order to meet the wagering requirement, and multiply the wagering requirement times the house percentage against you on that game to find the cost of playing the game to earn the bonus.

5) Now you have to decide if the profit looks reasonable based on the amount of time you estimate it will take you to meet the wagering requirement. This is pretty easy to do, and it doesn't really require much more than common sense. If you have a wagering requirement of $50,000, that you have to achieve with $10 bets, in order to get a $15 profit, it's not worth your time. Even if you can play blackjack faster than most people, it would take you way too many hours to place 5,000 $10 bets for a puny $15 return. Either the bonus is too small, or the WR is too big, but the fact is your time is worth more than that. On the other hand, if you have to meet a $3,000 WR, in order to get a $150 profit, that's looking a lot better. Online games are fast, and a lot of players can play 300-500 hands per hour in Web casinos. This bonus could be worth going for. (This is also covered in more depth in Chapter 3.)

6) So, you check the terms and conditions to see whether the bonus is automatically entered into your account, or whether you have to jump through any other hoops to get that bonus. For instance, some casinos specify that you must enter a code to apply for the bonus after depositing your funds. Others may require you to email a request for the bonus. Or you may be required to bet a small amount of your own money before the bonus funds are added. Some may state that the bonus will automatically be added to your account, but that it will not appear in your account for some number of hours.

7) If the hoops aren't unreasonable, enter all of the details into your **Play Log**, a record book in which you will write down all of the important details of your online casino play. (I will discuss setting up this log in the next chapter.)

8) Deposit funds with the casino cashier and follow the instructions for getting the bonus credited to your account.

9) Enter the casino and play your game of choice, keeping track of the total amount of money you bet, so that you know when you have met the wagering requirement.

10) Withdraw your funds and celebrate—but only after entering the details in your Play Log.

TYPICAL BONUS OFFERS

Here are a couple of online casino banner ads that have appeared recently on the Internet. Note that the ads say very little about the terms, but simply state a bonus amount in percentage and/or dollars. If you click on the ad, it will take you to the casino's website, where you can get more information about the bonus.

And this is what you get when you click on a typical bonus banner such as above. (I've reproduced the online casino's text verbatim here but changed the name):

50% MATCH PLAY BONUS

At the TripleGoldX Casino we run many regular promotions. Our current promotion is a 50% match bonus up to $500 for new players. This means for every $1 you put into your account, we will give you 50 cents absolutely free—deposit $1,000 and we will give you $500 Free.

Download the casino software, install it and register a new account, and you are automatically eligible for our signup promotion.

How to claim your Sign-On Bonus:
1) Login to the TripleGoldX Casino Software, click on CASHIER and then on REDEEM Coupon.
2) Enter your exclusive 50% Bonus code.
3) Make your first deposit with the TripleGoldX Casino of $20 or greater!
4) Your bonus will be instantly credited to your casino account on making your first deposit.

Click here for details relating to this promotion.

Note that the bonus is exactly 50% of our deposit amount, with a maximum bonus of $500 for a $1,000 deposit. You can redeem the bonus by entering a "bonus code number" with the cashier at the time of your deposit, and the bonus amount will be instantly credited to your account—no waiting period, email requests, etc. So, is it a good deal? We don't know until we read the terms and conditions.

BONUS TERMS & CONDITIONS

This is what you get when you click on the typical bonus offer terms and conditions page, reproduced verbatim from a different Internet casino offer, this one with a 20%/$50 maximum bonus offer (and again with the casino name changed):

TripleSilverX Bonus Policy states that:
All new members will receive a welcome bonus on their first deposit to their TripleSilverX account. The welcome bonus is limited to one bonus per household. This welcome bonus may be cashed out only after an amount totaling no less than 10 times the welcome bonus has been wagered—for example, a member must wager $500 before being able to cash out a welcome bonus of $50.

All other TripleSilverX bonuses may be cashed out only after an amount totaling no less than two (2) times the bonus amount received has been wagered—for example a member must wager $100 before being able to cash out a $50 bonus.

** Bonus points accumulated via roulette and craps bets will not be eligible for any of our events and will not count as a wager for our bonus policy.

There is a 20% bonus of up to a maximum value of $50 for trying a new deposit method. This bonus does not apply to deposits via credit card.

TripleSilverX bonus policy applies to all event or promotion funds received in excess of regular payouts.

All bonuses must be wagered at TripleSilverX within three months of being credited to a member's account.

> *TripleSilverX reserves the right at a time of its choosing to revoke any bonuses not used within the aforementioned time period. Any promotional offers extended to members (whether of bonuses or otherwise) must be claimed by the member within three months of the date of notification of the offer.*
>
> *TripleSilverX reserves the right to withhold the amount of any bonus from a member's cash out.*
>
> *In the event of abuse, TripleSilverX reserves the right to discontinue the member's TripleSilverX membership and to prevent the member from accessing the casino in the future.*
>
> *For assistance with this, or any other matter, please email us at: support@TripleSilverX.com*
>
> *Or call us toll-free from U.S./Canada at: +1-800-xxx-xxxx.*

If you're like me, you get a headache just wading through all that verbiage. So, now is the time to reveal the deepest darkest secret of the professional online gamblers. What separates the winners from the losers is one simple but powerful strategy the winners apply: *they read the terms and conditions.*

The vast majority of online players don't even click on the link to the terms and conditions page. They just download the casino software, sign up, deposit their money, and start gambling. At some point in the future, when the bonus disappears from their account, or they go to cash out and discover that they're not getting the bonus money—or any of their winnings—they contact the casino's support line to ask about it. Here's what they hear:

"Oh, you played roulette and that's not allowed for the bonus," or,

"You didn't enter the bonus code with the cashier when you made your deposit," or,

"You lost the bonus and your winnings because you made a cash withdrawal before you completed your wagering requirement."

There's an old proverb: "If all else fails, read the instructions."

THE BASICS

Most often, we don't read instructions. I got a 64-page manual with my coffee maker. Never cracked it. A 140-page manual with my Casio digital watch in case I need to know the barometric pressure in Guam. We don't read instructions because it's usually a waste of time. I've never been in your kitchen, but I'll bet I could heat up a TV dinner in your microwave without referring to the 96-page user's manual that came with it.

The first online bonus hustlers were simply the players who read the instructions. With very basic math skills, they realized the Web casinos were giving away money—if the player abided by their terms. And every Web casino has different bonus terms—different dollar amounts, different excluded games, different wagering requirements, different procedures for claiming and withdrawing funds—one false step and you lose it—the bonus and your winnings.

The online casinos draw millions of players to their games with banner ads that say, "Free Money!" or "$100 Free!" or "200% Deposit Bonus!" But they really give away very little of what they offer. Because if you don't read the terms and conditions, your chances of not violating the casino's bonus policies are pretty slim.

But, this laziness is plain crazy. These online casinos are giving away money, not 2-for-1 buffet passes. Lots of money—$50, $100, $200 and more—on plays that will all take you less than an hour.

If you've gotten this far into this book, you may have what it takes to make money online. I'm simply providing you with an instruction book on how to read instructions. Provided you're willing to learn a few basic concepts of gambling math—that are not difficult, and which I will explain in full—you are on your way to the money.

So, stick with me. We all hate instruction manuals. But think of it this way: if you knew that the 148-page owner's manual you got with your toaster had a few lines that explained how to extract a $100 bill from the side panel, would you read that damn manual? You've got a hundred virtual toasters on the Web, and every one of them has money inside. *Don't burn the money!*

In the above sample terms and conditions page, smart players skim the text looking for the important details. This particular bonus is for *20% of the deposit* amount, with a *maximum bonus of $50.* The wagering requirement is *10 times the bonus amount,* or 10B, in our shorthand. Roulette and craps are *not eligible* for bonus play, and we have a *three* *month time limit* on fulfilling the wagering requirement.

Is all of this good or bad? We still don't know until we do the math, which I'll show you in the Free Cash Bonus chapter. The important thing right now is that we've taken their bonus terms and reduced them to the few important details that explain how we qualify for the bonus. The math is easy, but let's just take one step at a time. At this point, you're already far ahead of the average online player. You at least know which games you can play and how much you have to wager on them.

THE "GENERAL" TERMS AND CONDITIONS

In addition to a terms and conditions page for each bonus the casino offers—and have I mentioned that many casinos offer more than one type of bonus?—every Web casino also has a "general" terms and conditions page that usually consists of three or more pages of fine print. Stop. Take an aspirin. Okay, let's go on...

You have to look at these general terms and conditions, which explain casino policies that apply to all games and all bonuses, as these policies may also affect your decision to play at a casino.

Some of the terms you should keep an eye out for include:

1. Money in accounts that stay inactive for three months (or some other period of time) will be deemed *abandoned* by casino management.

2. Players may request a withdrawal from their account at any time but the maximum withdrawal by any one player is $5,000 (or some other amount) per calendar week.

The general terms and conditions are composed of a lot more verbiage to wade through, *but you've got to do it*. Look for clauses that are not included in the bonus offer description. The general terms and conditions pages might specify other disallowed games or disclose transaction charges for withdrawals. You might even find a policy that states that certain types of deposits will add 10% or 20% more to the bonus, or may have greater wagering requirements. Some specify that players from certain countries, or states, are disallowed from bonus play. Some casinos specify that large wins (and this amount will be defined differently by every casino) will be paid in installments. And some specify that there may be a minimum withdrawal amount, such as $20 or $50. Some of the wording will drive you nuts. Here's an example: "No withdrawal will be honored for an amount less than the player's original deposit plus twice the bonus awarded." In other words, if you don't make a killing here, you can't withdraw any of your money!

Most of the general Terms & Conditions will be legalistic technicalities that won't affect you. Only one active account per player, or per household. A player must be an adult as legally defined in his home state or country. A player is responsible for protecting his password from use by others. Hacking into the casino's computer to alter games or results is disallowed.

In my opinion, it would be a great service to their customers if the online casinos posted all of their terms and conditions in one place, rather than have separate links to specific bonus terms that don't include the general terms. But just because an online casino organizes its information in an illogical or cumbersome way doesn't mean they won't hold you responsible for knowing it. For instance, you might read on the bonus page that craps and baccarat are disallowed. If you then go in and play video poker, you might find the casino refusing to pay you the bonus because on the general terms and conditions page, their policy says no video poker is allowed for *any* bonus play.

In the following chapters, we're going to look at all of the above in much greater detail. You have to be careful which online casinos you go to, and I'll tell you everything you need to know to choose the right ones. There are more factors than the bonus offers and the terms and conditions to consider, such as a casino's reputation. There are lots of crooks on the Internet, but it's not hard to avoid them if you know what to look out for.

I'll also explain how to keep records of every session, including records of bonus offers, wagering requirements, excluded games, and casino contact information. In fact, in the next chapter, I'll provide a form that will help you keep all of the records you need.

FREQUENTLY ASKED QUESTIONS ON BONUS PLAY

Q: How much money do I need to do this?
A: Anyone with $500 that they can afford to gamble with can afford to get into this venture. $1,000 would be better, but $500 will get you started. Most of the deposits you'll make will be smaller than this, usually $50 to $200. You need the extra funds because you will sometimes have money on deposit at numerous online casinos simultaneously, and it can take days (or even weeks in some cases) to withdraw your funds. It would be best to have $5,000 to $6,000 in order to take advantage of some of the more lucrative bonus offers that allow larger deposits and pay bigger bonuses. But you can build up your bankroll as you play and take advantage of these bigger bonuses when you have the funds.

Q: How do I deposit my money, and how do I withdraw it?
A: There are many ways to deposit funds. Most U.S. banks do not allow credit card transactions or wire transfers of funds directly to online casinos. In some other countries these types of transactions are allowed, but gambling debts are not legally collectible in the U.S., so both the banks and online casinos disallow these transactions to eliminate fraud by players. These transactions were allowed up until a few years ago, but some players abused the system by withdrawing funds on their winning plays, but canceling the transactions as "illegal gambling debt collections" when they lost.

It is easy to set up an Internet bank account with an online Canadian bank called Neteller, which makes both deposits to and withdrawals from online casinos safe and efficient.

The process of withdrawing funds differs from casino to casino. At some, you simply request that the cashier transfer your account balance back to your Neteller account, and that's it. Clean and simple. Others may require you to fax or email them scans of your driver's license or passport, sometimes with a copy of a utility bill (as proof of your residence address), before they will process your first withdrawal. They will usually contact you by email to request this ID. Other online casinos mail you a personal identification number (PIN) that you must use to make withdrawals. This can slow the withdrawal process down by a couple of weeks. Is this worth it? At first, it's kind of scary. You wonder if you'll really get your money. But if you follow the procedures, within a few hours to a week you'll generally get the full amount owed you. Is it worth it to get paid a few hundred bucks for 20 minutes of work if you have to wait a week till the money is paid? The pros just put up with it as one of the hassles of beating the casinos. You'll find the withdrawal terms in the casino's terms and conditions.

Q: Are these games honest?
A: Not all of them. But I will steer you to the trusted casinos and describe easy ways for you to identify the good guys from the bad guys. You will primarily rely on the advice of a few reliable watchdog Internet sites where burn joints are identified and players describe their experiences, good and bad. You should have few problems if you're careful.

Q: Do I need to know any special strategies for the games?
A: Absolutely, but the strategies are not that difficult. One nice feature about gambling on the Internet is that you can have your strategy right out on your desk as you play. For blackjack, you simply need to know basic strategy. I have included in this book simple charts that detail basic strategies for the most common blackjack games. I have also provided basic strategies for other common Internet games that you don't often find in live casinos, like pontoon and blackjack switch.

Q: How much time is required for this?
A: That's another nice feature about Internet gambling. Online casinos are all open 24/7, and you can play sessions of any length you desire, from a few minutes to a few hours. The actual amount of time it will take you to earn your bonuses will depend on various factors. If you have a dial-up modem, the games will be slower than if you have a DSL connection. If you already know the basic strategy for a game, you will play faster than someone who must consult a chart to make decisions. Some casinos' software is fast, and some software is slow. How much you are betting per hand to meet your wagering requirement is also a factor. Depending on all of these factors, you may spend from a few minutes to many hours playing for each bonus you collect.

Q: How much will my hourly win rate be?
A: Your rate of profit will likely be between $20 and $100 per hour,

depending on your bankroll and all of the time factors listed above. We will discuss these factors in detail, so that you can estimate your hourly return precisely, as this will be an important consideration when you are choosing casinos and games. Much of the time required for bonus plays will be spent on the clerical chores of reading the bonus offers and terms and conditions, figuring out the bonus values, copying the necessary information, and bookkeeping. The actual time spent playing the games will be minimal. Players with greater skill and bigger bankrolls will often make more per hour, as they will be able to take advantage of some of the bigger bonuses that require larger deposits.

Q: If I have exactly $1,000 to try this out, what are the chances that I will lose my entire $1,000 just due to bad luck?
A: Slim to none, providing you are careful about choosing reputable casinos and bonus offers, use the accurate basic strategy for the games you play and follow my advice on sizing your bets according to your bankroll and the type of bonus you are playing. With a small bankroll, you must play more conservatively—which will lower your hourly win rate—in order to protect yourself from simple bad runs of cards that occur in all casino games. One of the reasons you would be unlikely to lose your whole bankroll is that you will never deposit it all in one casino. You will make many small deposits and withdrawals at numerous online casinos over time.

But players do lose money on individual bonus plays, even when the bonus provides them with a significant advantage over the house. If you avoid playing in online casinos that use crooked software, and you use an extremely conservative betting strategy—say, making bets of only $1 to $2—then the chance of losing all of your money would be close to zero. With such small bets you would be extremely unlikely not to show a decent profit for your dollar investment, assuming you are playing for the most generous bonuses. The bonuses really are that advantageous. If you play at a higher level, you will earn more per hour, *but with greater risk.*

Think of it this way: if you have $1,000, and you stick to bonuses that require deposits of $50 to $100, most of the time you will make money on your plays, but here and there you will lose your deposit just due to a bad swing. Since you're winning much more often than you're losing, you end up making money despite the bad swings that occur.

But if you start making bonus plays that require a $1,000 deposit, you could lose your whole bankroll on one bad swing. That's too risky. The better plan is to stick with the smaller bonuses while your bankroll is small, and go for the bigger bonuses as you build your bankroll. Resign yourself to a small hourly return when you first start out, so that you'll have the bankroll to increase this hourly return in the near future.

A player who has $5,000 right now to play with would not have to stick to the $50 and $100 deposit bonuses. He could afford to take a negative swing on a bigger bonus play, and still keep going. Because of this, his hourly return will be bigger right from the start than the player who is starting on a much smaller bankroll.

Many people don't realize that professional gamblers rarely take big risks, if ever. One of the first things a professional gambler learns is how to survive on his bankroll, no matter what size it is. Gambling, at the pro level, is about building your bankroll, not risking it. In fact, professional gamblers know quite a bit more about risk aversion than most stock investors. You must take this attitude if you want to make money gambling, and that's what I'm going to show you how to do—at least insofar as making money in the lucrative online casino opportunities.

I would advise any person considering this venture to not play with money that is dear to them. Do not gamble with the rent money. If you have only $500 or $1,000 that you can afford to gamble with, then I suggest starting out very conservatively. Go ahead and play with $2 bets for your first few bonuses. Just spend the hours it takes to do this and keep your peace of mind while you're learning and building confidence. When your bankroll gets up to $1,500 or $2,000, and you can see the process is working for you, then get a bit more aggressive. Make bets of $4 or $5. Always play at your own comfort level.

For conservative players on small bankrolls, there are certain types of bonuses, called "sticky" bonuses, that have little value. These bonuses must be played more aggressively in order to extract their value, and aggressive play is always more risky. The traditional cashable bonuses, however, will still have value for you, and you need not take the risk of big fluctuations.

Before we look at these different types of bonuses, however, let's get prepared for the whole process of beating Internet casinos by setting up a Play Log where we can begin recording information on casinos, bonuses, the value of these bonuses, and our play results. Let's not jump the gun and start throwing our money into online casinos until we're ready to take care of business.

3. THE BUSINESS END

Internet gambling involves record keeping, filing, and following through on collections. It's not difficult. You just have to be careful. If you take your time and do it right, you'll save yourself a lot of headaches.

READ THE TERMS AND CONDITIONS

Every Internet casino has a bonus terms and conditions page. After reading the bonus offer, this is the very next place you must visit on the casino's website. If the terms and conditions meet with your approval, and you decide that you will play in this casino, you must copy the full terms and conditions page onto your computer for future reference. Casinos often change their terms and conditions, so you want a copy that describes the exact bonus offer you signed up for in case there is ever any dispute.

Most of the misunderstandings between players and online casinos arise when a player misreads a casino's Terms & Conditions. Read them carefully! Also, the applicable Terms & Conditions are sometimes listed in several areas of the casino's website. Be sure to look for Promotional or Bonus Terms & Conditions, as well as the general casino Terms & Conditions. Make sure you can live with a casino's terms and conditions before you deposit money or accept any bonus money.

SAVING SCREEN SHOTS

It's not difficult to save the terms and conditions. The best way, on either PCs or Macs, is to use the "Print Screen" button on your keyboard. This way you have an exact copy of a casino's terms and conditions page as it appeared on your computer screen when you signed up. Since most terms and conditions go on for several pages, you will have to keep scrolling down to the next section of each terms and conditions page, and saving multiple screen shots.

If you've never done this before, here's what to do. Let's just save a screen shot right now for practice. Pull up any document, or just leave your computer showing the desktop icons, then hit the Print Screen button, located on most keyboards on the top row of keys on the right side. Although nothing visible will occur, your clipboard will now have a full-color picture of whatever is on your computer screen, even if it's just the desktop icons.

Now open any word processing program to a fresh page and hold down the Control key on your keyboard while you hit the letter V key. With most word processing software on a PC, this Control-V is a command to paste whatever is on the clipboard to whatever document or page is open (on a Mac it is Command-V). You may use any other valid pasting method that may apply to your specific word processing software. That is, you could also just pull down the edit menu and click on Paste. Within a second or two you should see an exact picture of whatever was on your computer screen pasted onto the document. The picture will be small, but if you zoom in on it, you should be able to read it easily. You may also enlarge it, if you know how your software does this, but it's not necessary.

That's all there is to it. You simply save this file and you've got what you need. To save the complete terms and conditions, you simply do this as many times as necessary to get the full text of the terms and conditions onto a file. You will find it most convenient to create folders with the names of the casinos where you play, and save the terms and conditions for each casino in its own folder. Do not just save these files onto your hard drive as many terms and conditions have similar file names, which fail to identify the casino they are for. Creating separate folders for information on the casinos where you play will make it easy for you to find documents if and when you need them later.

Also, do not just highlight the text of the terms and conditions and copy and paste it onto a page as text. This is not as good as saving the screen shots because text can be easily altered after the fact. If you have a dispute with an Internet casino about the terms and conditions you signed up for, your arguments will have more weight if you send them the screen shots of their terms and conditions pages in support of your position. If you find the screen shot terms and conditions difficult to read because of small print and poorly chosen colors, then go ahead and highlight the text to create a text file for your own reading convenience.

But always get the screen shots. You will be surprised at how many online casinos make their terms and conditions very unpleasant to read by using small print and colors that do not contrast. I have even seen dark blue print on a black background. For some casinos, it is almost impossible to read their terms and conditions as displayed on your screen without highlighting the text. In these cases, highlight the text before making your screen shot.

Saving screen shots is important for another reason. If you are playing a casino game and suddenly something goes wrong (the screen freezes or you lose your connection) you must make a screen shot that shows all of the current details, such as the amount in your account, the amount of your bet, the hand on the table, and the result of that hand if it has already been determined. Save that screen shot, then reconnect to the casino and see what the status of your account is. If the account balance is inaccurate, or if there is some other problem with the result of the hand you were playing when your computer crashed, then take another screen shot and save it as well. Now you can contact the casino via their phone or email and file your complaint with proof of your claim.

I have encountered such problems half a dozen times, but I never had any trouble getting my account corrected after I provided screen shots that supported my claim.

DEPOSIT METHODS

Not too many years ago, you could make deposits in online casinos via credit cards, but as I've already explained, this is no longer possible for players in the U.S. In addition to the problems U.S. banks and online casinos have had with players who took advantage of the laws that make it illegal to collect gambling debts, the feds have also pressured the banking industry to discontinue Internet casino transactions. Despite the fact that there are no federal laws against gambling in online casinos, the U.S. government has been staunchly opposed to them for years, and banks have voluntarily complied with federal requests under threat of fines and penalties.

Most online casinos offer credit card deposits to their customers, but these deposits are only for customers who are not living in the U.S.

If you live in the U.S., you must use a different deposit method. I recommend the Canada-based Neteller as the best banking option for U.S. players involved in online gaming. It is reliable, convenient, and fast. Online casinos also seem to like Neteller because some offer additional bonuses if you make your deposit through Neteller. Many of the other options have extra charges that Neteller doesn't have. In addition, Neteller is very serious about protecting access to your account. You will want to link a real bank account to your Neteller account for ease of transferring funds and to avoid service charges. For complete information, go to www.neteller.com.

Two other common online banking options are FirePay and Citadel. You will occasionally find an online casino that offers better bonus terms or a lower wagering requirement if you use one of these other deposit options. All of these online banks work similarly to Neteller, so if you find a bonus that has exceptional value only if you use, say, FirePay, then it may be worth the hassle to open another online bank account. But for beginners, just start with Neteller, the most widely used and accepted online bank.

BE PREPARED TO WIN

If you play, you might win. That's the plan, isn't it? If you win and you're like me, you might want to withdraw your money. Some online casinos require that you send them proof of who you are before they send you money. You can fax this info but it's easier to email it to them. So have the following ready:

- A scan of your driver's license (front and back), or passport;
- A scan of a recent utility bill (just the top portion with your address);
- A scan of a bank statement (again, just the top portion with your address).

If you have a scanner, this is no problem. If you don't, most copy centers provide scanning services for a minimal charge. Ask them to scan each document separately, and save the scans onto a floppy disk or CD that you can take home. Make sure that the name and address are the same on all of these documents and that they are the same name and address as the ones on your Neteller and casino account. You can then attach the necessary files to an email in order to collect your winnings. Not all online casinos require this, but it's best to be prepared. Casinos specify this requirement in their terms and conditions and usually will notify you by email at the time of your first withdrawal if they require you to send proof of your identity.

KEEP CAREFUL RECORDS

Some players have reported occasions where money was improperly deducted from their accounts at an Internet casino, either during play or between visits. It has happened to me as well.

To protect yourself from such glitches, you should play only at reputable online casinos and always record your balance at the end of a session, whether you logged out deliberately or accidentally got disconnected. Then check to make sure that your balance is what it should be when you return to the casino. Notify customer support before resuming play if there is any discrepancy.

KEEP A COMPLETE LOG OF YOUR PLAY

Before you ever deposit a single dollar in any Internet casino account, create a log book that you can use to record all details. You do not need a paper copy of this log. You will probably find it more convenient to keep your records on a file you create with a word processing program or a spread sheet program like Excel or Quatro. The spreadsheet is nice because it will automatically add and subtract entries as needed and total columns for your results. If you're good with spreadsheets, you can set one up to not only record the data on your bonus plays and results, but to calculate bonus values, wagering requirements, and even your advantage over the casinos based on the simple formulas provided in the next chapter.

SAMPLE ENTRY

You need at least a separate page or two for each casino. Be sure to set up your log to record information for the following categories (and information on calculating some of these entries will be included in the next chapter):

INTERNET CASINO LOG BOOK

1. Casino:	Nero's Palace	
2. Group:	Unlucky Lounge	
3. Software:	Microgaming	
4. Link:	blackjackforumonline.com	
5. Phone:	800-012-3456	
6. email:	support@nerospalace.com	
7. website:	www.nerospalace.com	
8. User Name:	big21guy	
9. Password:	21skidoo	
10. Acct. Number:	N/A	
11. Bonus Offer:	$150 match, cashable	$100 for $200, cashable
12. Wager Req:	12DB (3600)	12DB (3600)
13. Games Excluded:	craps, bac, roul	same
14. House Edge:	0.50% on BJ	same
15. Bonus Value ($):	$132	$82
16. Bonus Value (%):	+7.33%	+3.41%
17. Buyin Date:	3/12/04	3/29/04
18. Amount:	$150	$200
19. Payment Method:	neteller	neteller
20. Bonus Added:	yes	yes
21. Session Date(s):	3/12/04	3/31/04
22. Game Played:	BJ	BJ
23. Session $ Bet:	3980	4050
24. Bet Size:	$10-$30	$10-$50
25. Session Result:	-$65	+325
26. Wager Req Complete?	yes	yes
27. Profit/Loss:	+85	+425
28. Cashout Date:	3/13/04	needed
29. Cashout Amount:	$235	—
30. $ Due:	paid	$625
31. Date Cashout Paid:	3/21/04	—
32. Current Balance:	$625	
33. Cum. Win/Loss:	$510	
34. Problems/Comments:		

emailed scan of passport on 3/14, called 3/20, paid 3/21.
Software crashed twice on 3/12, support (Gary) helpful.

EXPLANATION OF THE LOG ENTRIES

1. Casino: *Nero's Palace*
The name of the Internet casino.

2. Group: *Unlucky Lounge*
Many online casinos, just like casinos on land, share common owner-ship. This is the name of the casino's management or marketing group, if any.

3. Software: *Microgaming*
The brand of software being used, if known (and you should never play without knowing the software brand, as the major software brands are known to be reliable and honest).

4. Link: *blackjackforumonline.com*
The Internet site where you found the link to this casino. This may have been a banner ad on the website of a "sister" casino in the same group, or it may have been a **portal site**, a site with no casino that acts as a gateway for online casinos. Casinos pay portals a commission for each click-through that brings a customer to them. It's a good idea to keep a list of the link you used to first go to a casino's website, because a reputable portal will assist you in resolving any dispute.

5. Phone: *800-123-4567*
Always get the casino's phone number from its website. You will find this on its support page.

6. email: *support@nerospalace.com*
Ditto.

7. website: *www.nerospalace.com*
The casino's URL.

8. User Name: *big21guy*
You will register in each casino with a username or login ID. It's all right to use the same username in all online casinos, if you are allowed to select the username yourself. Often, however, your username will be assigned by the casino when you first sign up for an account.

9. Password: *21skidoo*
Every casino requires you to have a password in order to access your funds and play games. Virtually all online casinos allow you to select your own password.

10. Acct. Number: *N/A*
In some casinos, you will be assigned an account number instead of or in addition to your username. If so, record it because you may need it to log in or cash out later.

11. Bonus Offer: *$150 match, cashable*   *$100 for $200, cashable*
Note that there are two different bonuses recorded here. If you look down the page, you'll note that these bonuses are associated with different buyin dates. If you are using a computer spreadsheet as your play log, it's a good idea to record all of your play in one casino in different columns on the same page. If you are keeping your records on paper, use a columnar pad, but if you play many sessions in the same casino, you may require more than one page. You might also note that both bonuses are described as "cashable." We will define the different types of bonuses in the next chapter.

12. Wager Req.: *12DB (3600)*   *12DB (3600)*
This is the Wagering Requirement for the casino's bonus offer. Note that the wagering requirement is recorded both as defined in the casino's terms and conditions (12 x the deposit and bonus), and the actual dollar total this amounts to for our buy-ins, or $3,600 in both cases.

13. Games Excluded: *craps, roul, bac*   *same*
Again, this information is taken from the casino's terms and conditions. If you use abbreviations, be sure you know what they stand for. In the above example, "roul" is roulette, and "bac" is baccarat. With lots of abbreviations, make a list at the end of your Play Log with explanations. It is very important that you list these, as you do not want to play a game that is not authorized for bonus play. In some cases, play on excluded games simply won't be counted toward your wagering requirement, but in other casinos, playing disallowed games will actually void the bonus and any winnings you may have acquired during your bonus play. Craps, roulette, and baccarat are typically excluded from Internet casino bonus programs because players can bet on both sides (pass/

don't-pass, red/black, or player/banker), thus removing all fluctuation and simply giving up the house edge on every bet. Online casinos try to prevent such strategies, as they are attempting to target regular gamblers, not bonus hustlers. Your biggest concern will be casinos that disallow blackjack and/or video poker, as these games typically have the lowest house edge against smart players.

14. House Edge: *0.50% on 6D BJ*   *same*
Here you record the house edge on the game you are playing. At this casino, you played six-deck blackjack where the house edge was 0.50%. (You'll find a chart that has these values for the various games in the Appendix.)

15. Bonus Value ($): *$132*   *$82*
The total dollar value of the bonus, estimated by multiplying the wagering requirement by the house edge to figure out your expected loss on the play, then subtracting the amount left from the starting total, then subtracting your initial deposit from this amount. We'll go through this process in the next chapter with simple examples.

16. Bonus Value (percent): *+ 7.33%*   *+3.41%*
This is your calculated advantage over the house on your bonus play. It is simply the expected profit divided by the total amount of your money that you must bet to get it. Note that each of the two different bonus offers above have different percentage advantages. Again, we'll go through this process in the next chapter, with examples.

17. Buy-in Date: *3/12/04*   *3/29/04*
Self explanatory.

18. Amount: *$150*   *$200*
Self explanatory.

19. Payment Method:*Neteller*   *Neteller*
Self explanatory.

20. Bonus Added?   *yes*   *yes*
Here you verify that the bonus offered has been added to your account. In some casinos, the bonus is automatically added to your account bal-

ance as soon as you make your deposit. Some will state that the bonus will be added within three, twelve, twenty-four, or forty-eight hours of your deposit. Some will require you to email them or submit a claim form requesting the bonus after you make your deposit. Some will require that you play some specified amount before adding the bonus to your account. It is important to fill in this item with a "yes" when the bonus has been added so that you know you may begin your wagering requirement play, especially when you are juggling bonus plays with numerous casinos simultaneously.

21. Session Date(s): *3/12/04*   *3/31/04*
Self explanatory.

22. Game Played: *BJ*   *BJ*
Self explanatory.

23. Session $ Bet: *3980*   *4050*
Note that in these examples you completed your bonus plays for each of the bonus offers in a single session. In reality, you might play numerous sessions over a few days to complete a bonus play. In this case, you simply record the details of each play separately. This is very easy to do on a computer spread sheet, since you can add columns as needed. On paper, you may require multiple pages of data on each casino, especially if you take advantage of several return offers, using numerous play sessions to complete each one. The important thing is to record the exact dollar amount wagered in each play session.

24. Bet Size: *$10-$30*   *$10-$50*
Always record the minimum and maximum amounts you bet while playing for a bonus.

25. Session Result: *-$65*   *+325*
This is the actual amount won or lost on each play session.

26. Wager Req Complete?   *yes*   *yes*
Self explanatory.

27. Profit/Loss: *+85*   *+425*
This item is filled in at the very end of a bonus play. On the first bonus,

item 25 shows that you lost $65 on the play but your Profit/Loss entry shows an $85 profit since you started with a $150 bonus. This is something that will occur frequently in your bonus plays. Even when you lose on your play result, the bonus will still show you had a profit for the overall play because the bonus amount exceeds the loss.

28. Cashout Date: *3/13/04*   *needed*
Note that no cashout is recorded for the second bonus play. That is because you completed your play, but have not yet cashed out.

29. Cashout Amount: *$235*   —
Self explanatory.

30. $ Due: *paid*   *$625*
This is the money you are owed by the casino, either because you have not yet cashed out, or you have made the withdrawal but the funds have not yet appeared in your Neteller account.

31. Date Cashout Paid: *3/21/04*   —
This is the date that the funds withdrawn from the casino appeared in your Neteller account.

32. Current Balance: *$625*
If you have no money remaining on deposit at a casino, this will read zero. If you still have play to do in order to fulfill a wagering requirement, or you have completed a play but have not yet cashed out, or you have cashed out but have not yet been paid, this entry tells you how much money is still in your account at the casino.

33. Cum. Profit/Loss: *$510*
This is the cumulative result of all play at this casino. You simply add all of the totals from the Line 27 Profit/Loss entries (in this case, $85 + $425 = $510).

34. Problems/Comments: *emailed scan of passport on 3/14, called 3/ 20, paid 3/21*
                    software crashed twice on 3/12, support (Gary) helpful
This is where we record any notes on the bonus plays that may be of interest when we have to decide whether to play at this casino again.

I cannot overstate the importance of keeping a play log and updating it play-by-play, casino-by-casino. Once you have played in more than half a dozen online casinos, the plays and the results, the bonus offers and the problems, will all start to run together in your mind. Once you've played in a couple dozen or more casinos, your play log will provide a history of your Internet gambling experiences that will be invaluable to you. With money on deposit in half a dozen or more casinos simultaneously, this play log will be a reminder of exactly how much you must play in casinos where you have not yet completed your wagering requirement. It will remind you of cashout dates so that you can stay on top of casinos that owe you money, and it will be a convenient source of the casinos' 800-numbers and email addresses if you have to deal with a problem.

The last thing you want to do is remember that you cashed out at a particular casino "about a week or so ago," for an amount of "around $140 or so," and then have to find the casino's website and look for an 800-number buried on some support page just to call and talk to someone about where your money is when you don't even have the exact details.

So, before you ever play for real money in an online casino, either set up a spread sheet play log on your computer, or go to any office supply store and get yourself a standard columnar pad to use for this purpose.

Keeping a play log is important whether you are hoping to make a career of Internet gambling or just planning to loot-and-scoot. Even a loot-and-scoot player will play in somewhere between fifty and one hundred online casinos before he burns out the best bonus offers. So, take this seriously, and do it right from the start.

KEEPING TRACK OF YOUR BETS

It is absolutely necessary that you keep track of the total amount you have bet while you are in the process of meeting a wagering requirement. This is not something you should attempt to do in your head. If you're trying to get $2,000 or $3,000 of action in on a blackjack game with bets of $2, $5, $10, or even $20, forget about trying to keep track of this mentally.

THE BUSINESS END

All you need is a pen or pencil and a piece of notebook paper. If you make bets of a specific size, say $10 per hand, you make a notch on the paper each time you make a bet. Do it just like a guy on a deserted island counting down the days. Make four notches, then cross them with the fifth. Every group of five equals $50 in action. If you make four groups on each line, then each line is $200. If your wagering requirement is $2,000, number the lines from 1 to 10 before you start, and just play until you finish the tenth line. Some players use a "tally clicker"—which is a small, inexpensive, hand-held counter that you can purchase at any office supply store—to keep track of their bets.

For some bonuses, you might place different size bets at certain times. In this case, you must clearly mark the groups according to bet size. The important thing is that you keep an accurate record that works for you.

At the end of each session, total your bets. Always write down your action in dollars from each play session, and be sure to enter the session data in your play log.

4. FREE CASH BONUSES

Internet casino owners have always offered cash bonuses to entice players to try out their games. Traditionally, a player's deposit was matched by the casino with a bonus that could be withdrawn in full after the player fulfilled the minimum wagering requirement specified by the terms and conditions of the bonus offer.

Even novice players soon realized that the dollar value of many of these bonuses gave them a pretty healthy edge over the house, provided they quit playing and withdrew the bonus money immediately after meeting the wagering requirement. Within a few years, online casinos wised up and started employing countermeasures against these tactics. There were four basic actions the online casinos took:

1) Online casinos started requiring greater amounts of play before the bonus could be collected. In the early days, players only had to play through their deposit and bonus one or two times before cashing out. Casinos realized that many players, the original loot-and-scoot pros, were simply taking the bonus money and running. Today, bonus offers commonly have wagering requirements of anywhere from four times to seventy-five times the deposit plus bonus, or 4DB to 75DB.

This increase in the wagering requirement does not necessarily make the bonuses valueless. It just lowers the bonus value and adds a hoop players must jump through to get it. In some cases, the wagering requirement is so high compared to the bonus that the bonus may be worthless for most players. No one wants to work for $2 per hour! That's why you have to learn how to calculate the real value of the bonuses that are offered.

2) Online casinos started disallowing some games from qualifying for the wagering requirement on their bonus offers. Only a few online casinos today allow bonus play on roulette, baccarat, or craps for their wagering requirements, because these games offer bets that cancel each other out, eliminating fluctuations if a player were to bet on both sides. For example, a roulette player who bets the same amount on every number will lose on every spin of the wheel, but he will lose exactly the house edge, with no flux. Likewise for a baccarat player who bets on both the banker and player bets, or a craps player who bets on both pass and don't pass.

Some online casinos now disallow blackjack. Although a player cannot take both sides of a blackjack bet, as in these other games, the casinos know that many smart players prefer blackjack, despite the flux, because the house advantage is so low against a solid basic strategy player. Some online casinos that once disallowed blackjack, however, are again allowing blackjack play for their wagering requirements because it is quite simply the most popular table game. Online casinos that disallow blackjack from their bonus offers lose a lot of good customers who are not bonus hustlers, but just gamblers who prefer blackjack to other casino games. There are still many online casinos that disallow blackjack from the wagering requirement qualifying play, but you should always look at which games these casinos do allow, and play only if the house edge will be small enough on the allowed games to provide good dollar value for the bonus.

3) Online casinos started watching for obvious bonus hustlers, which the casinos termed "bonus abusers," and barring these players from further play. And, just as in the live casinos of Las Vegas and Atlantic City, online casinos started sharing information with each other on these blacklisted players. As a loot-and-scoot amateur, you need not be overly concerned with this countermeasure. You're planning to take your initial sign-up bonuses, which are the most lucrative, then get out of the game. I will give you a few camouflage tactics you can use to keep the welcome mat out at the casinos where you play, as some of these casinos will email follow-up offers to you with bonuses that will be valuable, though usually not as valuable as the initial sign-up bonuses. But essentially, you're looking for some quick cash, not a career.

4) And finally, the casinos created a new type of bonus that the pros quickly labeled the **sticky** bonus, which could not be cashed out—*ever*. It was simply money added to a player's account for wagering purposes only. You could keep any money you won betting with the bonus money, but you couldn't cash out the bonus money itself. If you win money using a sticky bonus, you may withdraw your winnings, assuming you have met the casino's wagering requirement, but you may not withdraw the bonus itself. A bonus is sticky if the casino's terms and conditions statement describes it as **non-cashable** or **for wagering purposes only.** (The online casinos do not use the term "sticky." That's player's slang for a bonus that "sticks" with the casino.)

The traditional bonus that is fully cashable soon became known as a **non-sticky bonus**, which "comes loose" from the casino once you have met your wagering requirement. In other words, this bonus money is yours to keep once you have given them the action specified in their terms and conditions.

It is important for you to understand the difference between play before and after you have met the casino's wagering requirement. Before you meet the wagering requirement, however, a non-sticky bonus is simply money that you are allowed to play with, just like a sticky bonus. If you lose a non-sticky bonus prior to meeting the wagering requirement, you lose the casino's money, as it is not yet yours to withdraw. If you lose a non-sticky bonus or any portion of it *after* meeting the wagering requirement, however, you are losing your own money.

In this chapter, we're going to describe the strategies required for playing with sticky versus non-sticky bonuses, as well as a hybrid type of bonus we call the **semi-sticky bonus**. It's very important that you understand whether a bonus is sticky, non-sticky, or semi-sticky. You will employ different betting strategies for each, and each has a different real dollar value depending on how you play them. At the end of this chapter, I'll explain what makes a bonus semi-sticky, and I'll describe a few other less-common types of bonus variations.

But for now, lets start by analyzing the comparative dollar values of the traditional non-sticky bonus and the newer sticky bonus, assuming they have otherwise identical wagering requirements.

THE NON-STICKY BONUS

The bonus offer says, "Deposit $100 and get a $100 bonus!"

Sounds good. Let's look at the terms and conditions. The fine print specifically tells us that the bonus is **cashable** after we meet the wagering requirement, or this is implied because it is not stated that the bonus is "for wagering purposes only." That is how we know that this is a "cashable" (or non-sticky) bonus, and not a sticky bonus. The terms and conditions state that the wagering requirement is ten times the deposit plus bonus, and that only craps, baccarat and roulette are disallowed for meeting the wagering requirement. That means that playing blackjack is allowed, and that is our game of choice.

If you decide to play at this casino, in your play log you will record the following entries:

> $100 deposit.for $100 bonus, *non-sticky*
> Wagering requirement = 10DB ($2,000)
> Game: BJ
> House edge: 0.50%

Note that you compute the total wagering requirement by adding the deposit and bonus ($100 + $100), then multiplying the $200 total by 10. So, you must play through $2,000 in order to meet the wagering requirement. After meeting that play requirement, any amount of the balance that's left in your account is yours to keep, including the bonus.

> **WARNING:**
> Most Internet casino bonus offers specify that if you withdraw any funds from your account before you meet the wagering requirement, you will lose the bonus and all winnings. Never withdraw funds from your account while you are in the middle of a bonus play. Finish the wagering requirement first.

Before you make your deposit, however, you want to figure out the **exact dollar value** of this bonus. Here's how to do it.

1) Figure out your expected loss from playing $2,000 at the game you choose. When played according to the basic strategy defined in this book, blackjack gives the house an advantage of only one half of one percent, so we must multiply 0.50% by $2,000, which comes to $10.

Note that 0.50% is expressed decimally as 0.005. To express a percentage as a decimal, move the decimal two places to the left. Examples:

1% is 0.01. 2% is 0.02. 3.5% is 0.035. So, one-half percent, which is 0.50%, is .005.

This means that with this low 0.005 house edge, you expect to lose only $10 over the long run for every $2,000 you bet.

2) Subtract the estimated loss ($10) from the starting amount ($200), and you get $190.

Of your $200 you would expect to have $190 left, all of which is now cashable. Since your initial deposit was only $100, that means you would expect to profit $90 on this $100 investment. It is possible that you'll net more or less than $90, but if you were to play this same bonus offer with these same terms over and over, you would earn, on average, $90 for every time you played it.

Blackjack is a good game for bonus plays because players can calculate the house edge on the game precisely—assuming they play according to correct basic strategy—and the house edge at blackjack is very small.

> **Tip for Players on Small Bankrolls:**
> Always look for these traditional, non-sticky, cashable bonuses when you first start playing in online casinos. This type of bonus can be played with the least amount of fluctuations, and it is nearly impossible to lose money with them if you have a strong advantage and you keep your bets small.

THE STICKY BONUS

You can tell when a bonus is a sticky bonus because the casino's terms and conditions will specify that it is "for wagering purposes only." Though many Internet gamblers do not realize it, a sticky bonus may be as valuable to a knowledgeable player as a traditional non-sticky bonus of the same amount, even though the actual sticky bonus cannot be withdrawn. But you have to play a sticky bonus differently than a regular bonus to extract its value.

First, let's assume you have the same terms and conditions as in the non-sticky example already described. The only difference is that, instead of being cashable after meeting the wagering requirement, this bonus is for wagering purposes only.

If you decide to play at this casino, in your play log you will write:

> $100 deposit for $100 bonus, *sticky*
> Wagering requirement = 10DB ($2,000)
> Game: BJ
> House edge: 0.50%

The only change to your play log entry is that this bonus is defined as sticky instead of non-sticky.

Next, since you'll be playing blackjack again, you follow through with the exact same mathematical analysis that was used to determine the result on $2,000 of action—the wagering requirement—when the house has a half-percent advantage. And again, you determine that you'll wind up with $190 remaining.

So far, everything is the same, but here's the difference: with the traditional non-sticky bonus, you were allowed to withdraw the remaining $190, showing a $90 profit. But with a sticky (non-cashable) bonus, if you withdraw your funds now, you will only get $90 total. Since you cannot remove the $100 bonus, you will show a $10 loss on the play, instead of a $90 win.

When sticky bonuses were first introduced in online casinos about five years ago, many players thought they were worthless. Since you expect to lose on the game itself due to the built-in house edge, and since you cannot withdraw the bonus from your account, where's the profit?

The profit comes from the fact that you can gamble with the house's money and keep your winnings.

Here's an oversimplified example to illustrate this point. Let's assume that after meeting your wagering requirement on this bonus play, you are allowed to flip a coin and call heads or tails, with even money payouts. So, you are sitting there with your $190, having played through your wagering requirement. If you do not withdraw the $90 remaining of your deposit at this point, but instead place a single bet of $190 on a coin flip, you will have one of two results.

If you win the flip, you will have $380 in your account. If you decide to quit at this point, you can withdraw the $380 minus the $100 sticky bonus. This means you can withdraw $280, for a win of $180 on your $100 deposit.

If you lose, your account will be zero, but all you will have lost is the $100 you initially deposited.

Since you will win 50% of the time and lose 50% of the time on a coin flip, you will win $180 half the time and lose $100 half the time.

$180 win - $100 loss = $80 profit for two plays

So if your betting strategy with a sticky bonus like this was to play through the wagering requirement, then place one coin-flip bet and quit the game, win or lose, in the long run your $100 sticky bonuses would be worth $40 to you—an average of $80 for every two plays.

But, what if you don't withdraw your money right after you win that first flip? What if you flip a coin once more?

You now have $380 in your account. Of this total, $280 belongs to you—only the $100 sticky bonus may not be withdrawn. If you bet all $380 on your next coin flip and win, you will now have $760 in your account. If you bet the $380 and lose, you lose $280—your $100 deposit plus the prior $180 win. Note that the $100 sticky bonus is not considered your loss, since it was not cashable. It was never yours, except to gamble with.

Now, stay with me here. Assuming you win half the time and lose half the time when you flip a coin, you will win two hands in a row only one out of four times. One time you'll win twice, one time you'll win the first time and lose the second time, and twice you'll lose the first time and never get to the second bet. Therefore, if your betting strategy is to bet it all twice in a row, three out of four times you will lose your $100 deposit, and one out of four times you will turn it into $760.

Of that $760 in your account, you may withdraw only $660, since the $100 bonus is not cashable. Of that $660 you can withdraw, $100 is your initial deposit, so one out of four times you use this strategy, you'll have a $560 profit. Three out of four times, you will lose your initial $100 deposit.

$560 - $300 = $260, so you have a $260 expectation on four plays, for $65 per play.

This means that the bonus is worth roughly $65 to you if you use the two-coin-flip strategy, to try to double up twice—roughly $25 more win than with the one-flip strategy.

In any case, you should be able to see that it would be a mistake to cash out without flipping the coin, because just one flip turns an average $10 loss into an average $40 win. And it may also be a mistake to cash out after only one flip, since the two-flip strategy turns an average $40 win into an average $65 win.

But you may recall that I said that the sticky bonus could actually have about the same dollar value as the non-sticky bonus. There's still quite a difference between $65 and $90. So, how do you get this sticky bonus to be worth $90?

If you just keep betting on another coin flip, the value gradually approaches, but never quite gets to, $90. In fact, you may have noticed that the first coin flip with the house's $100 had a $50 value, turning the $10 loss into a $40 win. And the second coin flip turned the house's $100 bonus into an extra $25, bringing our average win from $40 to $65. Each succeeding flip, in fact, just keeps adding to our average overall win exactly half of what the preceding win added. That is, the next flip will add $12.50. Here's how the $100 sticky bonus value rises with each flip of the coin, assuming the above conditions:

# Flips	Value	Cum. Value	Avg. Win/Loss
0	$0	$0.00	-$10.00
1	$50	$50.00	+$40.00
2	$25	$75.00	+$65.00
3	$12.50	$87.50	+$77.50
4	$6.25	$93.75	+$83.75
5	$3.12	$96.87	+$86.87
6	$1.56	$98.43	+$88.43
7	$0.78	$99.21	+$89.21
8	$0.39	$99.60	+$89.60
9	$0.20	$99.80	+$89.80
10	$0.10	$99.90	+$89.90

The problem, however, is that with each subsequent bet you have to keep betting more of your own money to win ever-decreasing amounts of bonus value. In fact, even if a casino had a coin flip option, instead of a blackjack game, the above strategy to extract $89.90 would be impossible. Look at what happens to your bet size with each succeeding bet:

Flip #	Bet
1	$190
2	$380
3	$760
4	$1520
5	$3040
6	$6080
7	$12,160
8	$24,320
9	$48,640
10	$97,280

So on that tenth coin flip, assuming the casino would accept your bet, you'd be betting $97,280 in order to win 10 cents. Not exactly an intelligent strategy, even for a billionaire. So the real dollar value of a sticky bonus depends on your tolerance for risking money you've already won in order to get smaller and smaller increments of the bonus value.

Obviously, there is a point where it is foolish to keep betting in an attempt to get it all. Note that as early as the fifth double-up bet, you would be betting $3,040 in order to extract just $3.12. This is an advantage over the house of only one-tenth of one percent (0.1%). So from a practical perspective, we have to view the dollar value of a sticky bonus as less than the value of a non-sticky cashable bonus.

Professional players tend to play sticky bonuses aggressively. In the above example, they might look at the third flip data and see that they would be risking $760 to win $25, which is an advantage over the house of 3.3%, still a very healthy edge. So they may play this bonus until they achieve a total win of about $1,500 before deciding that there is no longer a strong enough edge to keep betting. This would make the sticky bonus worth about $77.50 on average to a knowledgeable player who has a sizable bankroll and can afford the risk. This means the sticky bonus is worth about 86% of the value of an otherwise equivalent non-sticky bonus to this player.

But casinos don't offer coin-flipping as a house game. The above example was just meant to illustrate why a non-cashable bonus has real dollar value if you gamble with it. And whether you are flipping a coin or playing blackjack, the theory is the same. Even though you can't cash out the bonus, you can use it to win money that you can cash out.

In real Internet games, the exact value of a bonus and the best strategy for extracting that value is complicated by such things as the house edge, the variance on the game you play, the wagering requirement for the bonus, the casino's betting limits, and other factors. In fact, in a game like blackjack, you might not want to risk your entire account even if you could, because you may need funds in order to double down or split a pair.

Also, it is not the best time management tactic to grind through your whole wagering requirement before making big bets to try and extract the value from the sticky bonus. I used this example simply to describe how we figure out the value of the bonus. It's a better strategy to bet big and try to get this result early. If you have a number of big wins early, and you're satisfied with your results on the bonus play, you can always cut back your bets and grind out the rest of the wagering requirement with smaller bets in order to protect your winnings from that point on. If you bet big right off the top and lose your deposit and bonus early, then you have saved yourself the time and trouble of grinding out a few hundred more hands. The only problem with this strategy is that the casino may recognize that you are using an intelligent strategy to keep from risking your winnings, and they may not send you any more bonus offers.

THE BASIC DIFFERENCE BETWEEN NON-STICKY AND STICKY BONUSES

The major difference between these two types of bonuses is that the closer you are to meeting the wagering requirement, the more conservatively you should play the non-sticky, cashable bonuses. That bonus money all belongs to the house at first. But as you progress through the wagering requirement, it keeps getting closer and closer to being your money. The secret to extracting value from bonuses is in betting with the house's money. With a cashable bonus, once that money is almost in your pocket, aggressive play loses value.

The sticky bonus, on the other hand, will always be the house's money. You can never withdraw it. You want to play very aggressively when you are playing on any sizable amount of the house's money. Consider the sticky versus non-sticky examples above, when on both plays you had finished the wagering requirement, and had $190 in your account. With the non-sticky bonus, you do not want to play at all. You've locked in a $90 profit and that money is all yours. If you play, you're just giving up the house edge on your own money on every bet. On the other hand, with the sticky bonus, only $90 is yours and $100 belongs to the house. But you're allowed to play with the house's money, so, you want to bang it out big time. Otherwise, there's no value to it.

What this means to you as a player is that sticky bonuses have more variance than non-sticky bonuses and can cause big swings in your results. With a sticky bonus, you cannot use a conservative betting strategy to meet your wagering requirement, like betting $2 per hand for a 1,000 hands. That strategy will never extract the bonus value because you can't bet with the house's money until you first lose your whole $100 deposit. The house edge on those small bets will grind you down before you ever make any profit, and you'll never have a significant positive fluctuation. You must play sticky bonuses aggressively.

We'll get into bet-sizing and bankroll guidelines in the next chapter, but if you're starting this venture on a very tight bankroll, say $2,000 or less, you should concentrate most of your play on traditional, non-sticky, cashable bonuses, where you can play with smaller bets and build your bankroll with low variance. As your bankroll grows, you can add more sticky bonus plays to your repertoire.

WHAT THE LOOT & SCOOT PLAYER MUST KNOW

You do not have to memorize the mathematical methods described above, but what you absolutely must know before you ever deposit funds is whether a bonus is sticky or non-sticky. Read the definitions again carefully, and be sure you know the difference.

About 90% of all bonuses offered by online casinos are either sticky or non-sticky, so you must be able to recognize them immediately in order to figure out their value. Refer to this book after you identify the type, and just insert the bonus terms offered into the example above. After you do half a dozen bonuses or so, you won't have to look at the book any more.

But what about the other 10% of bonuses that are weird hybrids of the sticky and non-sticky varieties? I'm going to explain these here so that when you find one you'll know what to do.

THE SEMI-STICKY BONUS

There is another type of sticky bonus that we'll call the **semi-sticky** bonus. This type allows you to withdraw your full deposit and all winnings from your account after meeting the wagering requirement, without losing the sticky bonus. The sticky bonus itself will remain in your account *until you lose it*. This is a much better type of bonus than the standard sticky bonus, and allows players with smaller bankrolls to extract value from sticky bonuses with less variance.

Let's say you have already met the wagering requirement using the same sticky bonus offer as in the previous example. You have $190 remaining. With a semi-sticky bonus, you could withdraw your $90 and still have the house's $100 sticky bonus to wager with until you lose it. That's fantastic, since it means your total loss on this play, given these circumstances, cannot total more than $10. And, if you win just one all-in coin flip with the sticky bonus to win $100, you will already have extracted the full $90 expectation.

And here's the crazy thing: With this type of semi-sticky bonus, you can keep withdrawing your winnings again and again, and the bonus will remain in your account until you lose it. If you are on a short bank, you simply play this type of bonus conservatively until meeting your wagering requirement, then withdraw your funds and bang out the bonus.

If you win a few big bets with this strategy, you should stop playing and immediately withdraw your winnings, leaving the bonus money in your account to play with again the following day. You want to keep withdrawing your money and playing only with the house's money in order to extract the maximum value with minimum risk.

THE CASH BACK BONUS

Some online casinos offer cash back if you lose. This is a percentage rebate on your loss up to some specified amount. The math on a cash-back offer is nearly identical to the math on a sticky bonus, but with a slightly different approach if you must meet a wagering requirement before withdrawing the cash back amount.

Imagine that a casino offers you "25% cash back" on deposits up to $100 if you lose all of your money. Many players wonder how this could possibly be of value, since you get nothing extra if you win, and where's the value in trying to lose?

To simplify the logic, let's again imagine that you could bet on a coin flip. Say the casino offers you a deal whereby if heads comes up, you win $100; but if tails comes up, you only give the casino $75—which is precisely what happens if you lose $100 and the casino rebates $25 of your loss. Now it doesn't sound so bad, does it? You are essentially betting only $75 (since that's your total risk) to win $100. If we had this policy on every flip of the coin, where on average you'd win half the time and lose half the time, for every $150 of your action (two $75 bets), you'd come ahead $25. So, your dollar expectation per flip is $12.50 per $75 bet, which translates to a 16.67% advantage.

In an Internet casino, a rebate offer is not good on each and every separate bet you make, but *only on the amount of your deposit*. You must lose your deposit by the end of the play to collect the rebate. So, what if you decide in advance that if you win the first bet you will bang out a second bet of $200, and then walk with $400 if you win the second bet? On this second bet, you will either win $200 or lose $175, since you'd get the $25 cash back on your initial $100 deposit. Essentially, on this bet you are simply betting $175 (that's all your money now!) to win $200. For this second double-up attempt, and for convenience, let's again assume it's a coin flip that you'd win half the time and lose half the time (so one time you would lose $175, and one time you'd win $200), again you'd have a total profit of $25, or $12.50 on each $175 bet. This translates to a win percentage of about 7.1%.

If you win this double-up and go for a third double up, where you would be essentially betting $375 twice to win that $25 rebate, your win percentage for this bet drops to 3.33%.

With a loss rebate on your deposit amount, the dollar value of the rebate always remains the same (in the above examples: $25). As you bet a greater and greater percentage of your own money, however, your percentage advantage goes down. In addition, since you don't flip coins in casinos, you have to account for the house advantage on the wagering requirement. You do this in the same way that we have explained for bonus plays, totaling up the full amount of your own money that you wagered, and multiplying this amount by the house edge. I'm simply using coin-flip examples to simplify the explanation of the logic.

As with sticky bonuses, cash back bonuses only have value if you play aggressively enough to have a decent chance at losing your deposit. In other words, if you deposit $200 for a 10% loss rebate on your deposit, then you sit there betting $2 a hand, this cash back bonus has virtually no value to you, since you are so unlikely to lose a hundred $2 bets. If your bankroll is too small for you to risk a $200 negative swing, then you shouldn't be playing cash back bonuses. My advice to loot-and-scoot players is to think of any cash-back bonus as you would think of a sticky bonus. In the next two chapters, where we will discuss your bankroll requirements and optimal betting levels, you'll note that the non-sticky and sticky bonuses must be played differently. A cash-back bonus is more like a sticky bonus when it comes to betting and bankroll considerations. Aggressive betting is required to extract the value.

THE STICKY CASH-BACK DEAL

Some casinos offer cash back if you lose your deposit, but the cash they put in your account is "for wagering purposes only," like a sticky bonus. In other words, the sticky cash-back offer differs from the cash-able cash-back offer described above in that you cannot cash out the bonus money the casino puts into your account after you lose your deposit. Let's compare the value of the sticky cash-back offer to the cash-able cash-back offer described above, assuming otherwise identical terms. To keep it simple, we'll again wager on a coin flip.

You deposit $100 and bet it all. If you win, you leave with your $100 profit. If you lose, you get $25 put into your account that you can gamble with, *but not withdraw*. So, you bet it all. If you win, you take your $25 win and cash out. If you lose, you're out your full $100 deposit.

In this case, you win $100 two out of four times. One out of four times, you lose the $100 bet, but win the $25 bet, for a net $75 loss. And one out of four times, you lose both the $100 deposit and the $25 cash-back bet, for a total loss of $100 of your own money. So for every four times you play this strategy, you win $100 twice, lose $75 once, and lose $100 once. If you add up the results you get a profit of $25.

Note that you make this $25 profit on four plays, instead of on two plays, when the cash back is cashable. As with any type of sticky bonus, once you have the sticky bonus in your account to play with, you can continue to extract more value from the sticky cash back with each subsequent double-up attempt, but your overall percentage advantage keeps getting cut in half with each double-up. The important thing to note here is that a sticky cash-back offer has only about half to three-quarters the value of a cashable cash-back bonus. Therefore, you will need a bigger bankroll to take advantage of it. These types of bonuses are too weak for loot-and-scoot players on small bankrolls. If you have $4,000 or more, I'd suggest going after them when you get an advantage of 4% or more.

THE WIN-REQUIRED STICKY BONUS

Finally, there is a type of sticky bonus that requires you to win a specified amount—often the amount of the sticky bonus—in order to cash out any of the win.

For example, say you deposit $100 and get a $100 sticky bonus (non-cashable, for wagering purposes only). But the terms and conditions specify that after meeting the wagering requirement, you may not cash out any winnings *unless you have won at least the amount of the bonus*, or in this case, $100. That means that you must have at least $300 in your account ($100 deposit + $100 bonus + $100 win) before you can cash out any of the amount you won. If your account has only $275 in it, a $75 win, and you attempt to cash out, you will only get your $100 deposit back—none of your winnings.

For our purposes, this bonus is identical to any standard sticky bonus, since you are always going to attempt to make at least the amount of the bonus when you find one that meets your requirements for both dollar value and percentage value. The only thing you must keep in mind is that you must *never cash out before you hit at least the necessary win target*. Normally on a sticky bonus, once you've met your wagering requirement, you may cash out the full amount of your deposit and winnings. Not with this sticky bonus.

IMPORTANT: IDENTIFY THE TYPE OF BONUS BEFORE YOU PLAY

Again, you must identify exactly what type of bonus is being offered *before* you start playing it. As you can see from the analyses above, the various types of bonuses require you to use different betting strategies in order to extract their value. The sticky bonus is worth somewhat less than the cashable bonus, usually about 80 to 85% of the non-sticky value to a well-bankrolled pro, or only 50 to 70% for a non-pro playing on a smaller bankroll who can afford less risk. And the sticky cash-back bonus is the weakest of all.

THE DOLLAR VALUE OF SPEED

A $50 to $90 return on a $100 investment is excellent, but since you must play in order to get that return, let's take a look at it as a function of your time. The question is: how long will it take you to cycle through $2,000 in bets?

The answer depends on three factors:

1) The speed of your Internet connection.
2) The rate at which you play your hands.
3) The amount you bet per hand.

If you have a cable connection, DSL line, or fast satellite connection to the Internet, then the speed of play will primarily be dictated by the casino's software and your personal bankroll and skill. With a 56K modem connection, the games will definitely be slower. In a live casino game, a solo blackjack player heads-up with the dealer will play about two hundred hands per hour. An Internet player who really knows basic strategy inside out can easily play about four to five hundred hands per hour with a fast connection. A slower connection could cut this speed to that of a live game, about two hundred hands per hour, and a slow player with a slow connection might play only one hundred hands per hour.

Also, some casino software is faster than others. You would think that all of the major software companies would provide fast software to their clients, but this is not so. Microgaming Viper or Real Time Gaming software (RTG), both major brands, are very fast even on slow modem connections. Boss Media software, on the other hand, can be painfully slow even on a fast DSL connection.

But the factor that will most affect the amount of time it takes you to extract the value from the bonuses you play will be the amount of money you are betting per hand. If you have a $2,000 wagering requirement, and you can afford to bet $500 per hand, you will be finished with this bonus play—one way or another—within a few seconds. But many players just can't afford to bet the maximum allowed in order to get fast results. How much you should bet depends on the value of the bonus, the type of bonus, and the size of your bankroll. And that's the next chapter.

5. YOUR WIN RATE IN DOLLARS PER HOUR

There is one factor that you control completely and that influences the time it takes to collect a bonus more than any other. How much do you bet?

Consider the sample bonus situation described in the previous chapter, where you want to put $2,000 in action in order to meet your wagering requirement. If you bet $2 per hand, you need to play one thousand hands to meet the wagering requirement. With $20 bets, you'll meet the wagering requirement in only one hundred hands. Big difference. Let's compare various betting approaches to see how they affect your hourly expectation.

Betting $2 hands at a rate of four hundred hands per hour, it will take you two and a half hours to meet the wagering requirement. With a $90 expected value, your hourly rate of profit is $36 per hour.

With a slow modem connection, you may only be able to play one hundred hands per hour. It will take you ten hours to meet the wagering requirement, making your hourly expectation $9 per hour.

Not so great. In fact, considering that you have also invested time in reading the terms and conditions, downloading and installing the casino software, keeping your play log, and any communications with the casino, your actual return may be only $7 to $8 per hour. This bonus might not be worth the time and effort.

So, let's kick up the expected hourly return by raising your bet to $10 per hand, instead of $2. With only two hundred total hands now necessary to meet the $2,000 wagering requirement, if you play four hundred hands per hour, it will take you only thirty minutes to collect your bonus. With a $90 expected value, your hourly rate of profit would be $180.

Even if you are on a slow modem connection and you can only play one hundred hands per hour, it will take you only two hours to meet the wagering requirement, making your hourly expectation $45 per hour.

That $10 betting strategy looks a whole lot better than the $2 betting strategy in terms of return on your time investment. In both cases, your total expected profit from this bonus is $90. No matter what your bet size, that doesn't change. What changes is your ability to collect that bonus in thirty minutes to two hours of play, as opposed to two and a half to ten hours, and that's a huge difference if time is an important factor to you. In fact, following the same logic, if you bet $50 per hand, you can meet the wagering requirement in only forty hands, and collect your expected $90 in a matter of minutes. Even with a slow modem, you'll be working for an expectation of more than $200 per hour! At least, that's the math of it.

Unfortunately, it's not quite that simple. It may seem like a pretty easy decision. Why would anyone work for $9 per hour, or even $45 per hour, when they could simply adjust their bet size in order to work for $200 per hour? I'll tell you why: if you bet too much for your bankroll, you may go broke as a result of what mathematicians call "normal fluctuation" before you ever get to collect the potential profits from your bonus plays. The logic here is pretty simple, so let's look at it.

SURVIVING TO COLLECT YOUR PROFITS

Let's return to our example above, where we deposit $100 to get a $100 bonus. In this case, the total bankroll you'll have for this play is $200 (your $100 deposit plus the $100 bonus). If you place $50 bets, you have only four bets at your disposal. A double-down or pair-split would take half of your total bank. Whenever you are betting such a large proportion of the funds you have available to play with, there is a strong likelihood that you'll "tap out," gambler's jargon for going broke. A few bad hands early on in your attempt to collect this $90 bonus, and you will never get to play the forty hands required. A short losing streak of only a few hands could wipe you out. In fact, with a total balance of $200 and bets of $50, you would be far more likely to lose your $200 before you fulfill the $2,000 wagering requirement.

On the other hand, with bets of $2, you have to play 1,000 hands, but you have a lot of wiggle room. With 1,000 bets of $2, you can withstand quite a few losing streaks. Losing your whole $200 due to bad runs of cards is not likely to occur if you are playing 1,000 hands.

So your ideal strategy will be to bet somewhere between $2 per hand and $50 per hand in order to collect this bonus. Let's figure out the best approach. To do this, we need to look closely at the practical differences between conservative and aggressive betting strategies.

CONSERVATIVE VS. AGGRESSIVE

Here's a comparison of conservative versus aggressive playing strategies—assuming the same bonus offer described above:

The Conservative Player, betting $2 per hand will:
1) Earn, on average, $9 to $36 per hour.
2) Almost never lose his whole $100 deposit.
3) Almost always make a profit, usually between $30 and $150, but averaging $90.

The Aggressive Player, betting $10 per hand will:
1) Earn, on average, $45 to $180 per hour.
2) Often lose his whole $100 deposit.
3) Sometimes profit $200 to $400, but have an average result of $90 won per bonus played.

Both playing styles have their good points and bad points. And although that big hourly rate attainable with aggressive play may look attractive to you, definitely note the big difference between the two strategies on point number two. The conservative player will almost never lose his whole $100 deposit, while the aggressive player will often lose his $100 deposit. How many $100 deposits do you have available? If you have a small bankroll, and the prospect of losing $1,000 or more just due to negative fluctuations is of concern to you, then the aggressive betting approach would not be your ideal strategy, despite the fact that you may prefer the higher hourly return on your investment.

On the other hand, if you've got a $10,000 bankroll for Internet gambling, the more aggressive betting strategies will pay off. You will be going for fewer but bigger scores to make up for many relatively small losses. The bankroll flux will be greater, but the hourly returns will be higher.

THE PRO'S HIDDEN ADVANTAGE

There is another benefit to the aggressive betting strategy. Losses tend to generate more lucrative follow-up bonus offers from the casinos. Some casinos will even start sending special VIP offers that they do not send to the general public. These offers will often require bigger deposits, sometimes $1,000 or more, but the dollar value per bonus will be much higher than the $90 expected return of the initial sign-up bonus.

If you play 1,000 hands at $2 per hand, make your $90 in five to ten hours, then withdraw your funds, you probably won't get the kinds of bonus offers the more aggressive players get. You may receive additional bonus offers from this casino, but not with the same value.

But don't think I'm encouraging you to go blindly into this Internet gambling adventure with the aggressive approach. Aggressive play requires a professional-level understanding of risk versus return, and a large enough bankroll to finance a comeback after a long losing streak. For the average player, who considers a $5,000 to $10,000 loss to be significant, aggressive high-stakes play would be ill-advised.

THE WISDOM OF LOOT & SCOOT

For most players who want to make money in online casinos, a semi-conservative style of play—say, $5 to $10 bets on the non-sticky bonuses—will help them collect their profits without major fluctuations. You will have to accept an hourly rate of return that's well below the professional's standard, but you'll still have a decent win rate. If you don't receive valuable follow-up bonus offers, so be it. If you're on a very short bank, say $500 to $1,000, then go after your first bonuses with very small bets, say $2 to $5, until you've built up your bank to a healthier amount.

And avoid the sticky bonuses entirely if you're on a short bank. They have value, but they are the riskiest bonus offers since you cannot extract their value with small bets. Your bankroll should grow substantially in your first three to four weeks of play, after which you can afford to go after some of the better sticky bonus offers.

If you are an intelligent and careful player and use a semi-conservative betting style, you should be able to milk online casinos for $5,000 to $10,000 over a period of four to eight weeks, depending on how many hours per day you can devote to this project. After that you quit. The follow-up offers you'll get will generally be much less valuable than the initial sign-up bonuses, and Internet gambling may no longer be worth your time and effort.

You might occasionally get a good bonus offer from a new casino or simply find a good offer as you surf the Web, so you might want to keep a few hundred bucks in your Neteller account so you can take advantage of them. You'll probably pick up an extra few thousand per year for as long as the gravy train keeps rolling. But most people should view online casinos as a nice but limited little chunk of change that's just lying there in cyberspace, waiting to be picked up. After that initial go-round, the pickins get slimmer.

I'm not saying it's impossible to keep making significant amounts of money at this venture, especially if you've got a large bankroll behind you. But you will have to navigate a complex system in order to keep the welcome mat out.

Let's look at a few of the other important factors involved in bankrolling your play.

SLOW CASH-OUTS

When you finish playing blackjack in a casino in Las Vegas or Atlantic City, you present your chips to the cashier and exchange them for cash. Now you can take your money and play next door if you so desire. When you finish playing blackjack in an Internet casino, on the other hand, you go to the cashier page, request to have your funds withdrawn, and sometime between an hour and a month later, your funds will be credited back to your Neteller account and you can use them to play in another Internet casino if you so desire.

Needless to say, this is a pain in the ass, and it is also the main reason why your Internet gambling career will have an easier take-off if you've got a few thousand bucks to play with. You might think that since most sign-up bonuses require an initial deposit of only $20 to $200, you won't need very much capital to start playing. This is true, provided you're willing to wait around for days, and sometimes weeks, until the casino where you finished playing and requested a cash-out releases your funds.

In practice, you'll often have funds on deposit at up to a dozen online casinos at once—some that you are preparing to play in, some that you are in the midst of playing, and some that you have completed playing. Why do online casinos take so long to give your money back?

First of all, they don't all take this long. Some will have the funds back in your Neteller account within an hour. But the average amount of time is probably closer to two to four days after you cash out. Casinos that take a week or more —and sometimes over a month—to return your funds are the exceptions, but they do exist, and there's not much you can do but wait. You can send daily emails and make calls to their 800-number if they have one, but I'm not sure if this helps or not. I always do this after a week or so, figuring the squeaky wheel gets the grease.

But, back to our question: why do online casinos take so long to give your money back? There are lots of reasons.

Some simply have inefficient clerical policies. Some want to give you every possible chance to reverse your decision to withdraw, and gamble away your win. Some want the "float" on your money. Others are paranoid about bonus hustlers, and want time to do comprehensive checks on your identity and play. This is especially true if you are making a very large withdrawal of funds. Some may have already concluded that you are a bonus hustler, and want to discourage you from further play.

Other online casinos pay slowly because they are operating on shoestring budgets. Unlike casinos in Nevada, for example, which are required by law to have funds on hand to immediately cash out any player on any game, many online casinos are unable to do this.

In fact, there are no regulations that require Internet casinos to keep any amount of funds on hand. This is why some online casinos specify in their terms and conditions that a player may not withdraw more than $3,000 or $5,000 per week. If a player at one of these casinos hits a $25,000 jackpot on a slot machine, he'll wait a long time to get paid in full.

THE PONZI FACTOR

Some of the less financially stable Internet casinos seem to operate more like Ponzi schemes than legitimate businesses. With a real Ponzi scheme, failure is inevitable. Since there is no real profit from the phony business, the perpetrators of the scheme keep pulling money in from more and more suckers, continually paying off the earlier investors to prop up the illusion of the scheme, and then bail out when it appears that the number of new suckers investing in the scheme is no longer bringing in enough money to pay off the ever-growing horde of earlier investors. The perpetrators then skip town and leave the johnny-come-latelys high and dry.

Even if you are only trying to withdraw a few hundred dollars, some casinos will take their sweet time paying you. They may be using your deposit money to pay other players who cashed out days or weeks prior to you. In cases where I've waited a month or longer to get my money, I've had the distinct feeling I was in the middle of some kind of a scam operation. In some casinos, I do believe the casino was using bonus offers to bring in new suckers' money in order to pay off the suckers who came before them.

In most online casinos, the house edge on their games eventually works its magic and the casino keeps getting the operating funds it needs from the masses of losers. But if any Internet casino starts making bonus offers that seem too good to be true, it may be a sign that they are doing one last big money collection before disappearing. If you start seeing bonus offers of 400% or more on your deposit, watch out! There have been numerous online casinos that have disappeared suddenly after a month or so of incredible bonus offers. You definitely want to check with *blackjackforumonline.com* for any recent reports on these casinos. Check our "Online Burn Joints" list and search our discussion forums for reports on such casinos. You can also post any questions you may have about online casinos with complete anonymity.

In any case, the reason you need more funds to gamble in online casinos than you would need if betting at such relatively low levels in Vegas or Reno is that you can't just pull your money out of one casino and deposit it elsewhere.

THE MINIMUM BANKROLL REQUIREMENTS

Play smart and carefully follow my advice on analyzing bonus values and choosing games, and you can make $5,000 to $10,000 by milking the initial sign-up bonuses. With a starting bankroll of $2,000, it may take eight to twelve weeks to accomplish the task— primarily because your funds will sometimes be tied up in the casinos' snail-pace deposit/withdrawal process—but it can be done.

A starting bankroll of $4,000 to $6,000 is preferable, because it would allow you to play as many casinos as you can handle at one time, provided you neglect some of the bonus offers that require big deposits of $1,000 or more. You should be able to earn the majority of the best loot-and-scoot bonuses in four to eight weeks.

A player on a very short bankroll, say $500 to $1,000, will progress slowly at first as his funds will often be tied up. He will not be able to afford some of the more lucrative bonus offers that require deposits of more than $200, or any of the sticky bonuses that require aggressive high-variance play, until his bankroll has grown some.

Hustling bonuses on the Internet is the most lucrative profit opportunity for players with small bankrolls that I know of. Any blackjack card counter currently playing in live casinos on a small bankroll can increase the size of his playing bank by $5,000 to $10,000 fairly quickly. You cannot make $5,000 this quickly with such a small starting bankroll in any other legitimate advantage play that I know of—including card counting, poker, sports betting, or whatever—no matter how talented you are. Internet gambling is scary to get into, since it seems so easy to get ripped off. But if you follow a semi-conservative betting approach based on the limitations of your bankroll, apply the correct strategies for the games you play, and carefully select the casinos where you play, making money from Internet casino bonuses is like shooting fish in a barrel.

6. HOW MUCH SHOULD YOU BET?

Every casino game, whether it's a live game or a game you play online, has a built-in mathematical edge in favor of the house. But when an Internet casino offers a bonus to a player for making an initial deposit, the advantage can shift from the house to the player. The casinos hope that players will continue playing when the advantage from the bonus is gone. As winning players, we are only interested in the value of the bonus, period. We only want to play when we have an advantage.

In order to evaluate and compare bonuses, you want to know not just the dollar value of a bonus, but your percentage advantage over the house as well. There is a very good reason for knowing the percentage advantage. Two different bonuses may have identical dollar values but different percentage values, which can make one bonus too risky to play.

YOUR ADVANTAGE WITH A NON-STICKY BONUS

Let me illustrate this concept with an extreme example. Let's say that based on the deposit and bonus amounts and the wagering requirements, you have already calculated that two different non-sticky bonuses, which we'll call Bonus A and Bonus B, each have a dollar value of $75. In order to acquire Bonus A, however, you must wager $2,000 of your own money, while Bonus B requires that you wager $50,000. Despite their equivalent value in dollars, a few bells should go off in your head telling you that these bonuses are not in any way identical. The higher amount that you must wager for Bonus B will mean either more time spent playing or a whole lot more risk by placing much bigger bets. Even if you know nothing about the percentage edge over the house that these two bonuses provide, your intuition should tell you that these are entirely different situations.

In fact, you can figure out exactly how much more valuable Bonus A is than Bonus B by calculating the percentage advantages over the house that each of these bonuses provide. To calculate the percentage advantage from a bonus, divide the bonus value by the amount of your own money that must be risked.

Bonus A: $75 / 2000 = 0.0375 = 3.75\%$

Bonus B: $75 / 50,000 = 0.0015 = 0.15\%$

Bonus A looks pretty good. That 3.75% return on your very short-term investment is a decent percentage. But Bonus B, with that $50,000 you must wager, is only returning fifteen-hundredths of one percent. The wagering requirement is just too steep for the relatively small bonus to retain much percentage value.

If you have any intention of pursuing Internet casino bonuses for serious money, then you must always estimate the percentage advantage of a bonus, in addition to figuring out the dollar value.

There are two major reasons why you want a high percentage return on your investment. As already mentioned, the time investment in playing through $50,000 could make the $75 expected value less than enticing. Furthermore, with a percentage advantage as small as 0.15%, you can expect to have huge fluctuations in your results. It would take a millionaire's bankroll to be able to bet any significant amount of money with such a tiny advantage, and millionaires aren't interested in wasting much time to make a $75 profit.

SOME PRACTICAL EXAMPLES

The examples above are extreme ones. Let's look at a couple of non-sticky bonuses you might really find available and compare them. We'll call these Bonus C and Bonus D.

With Bonus C, if you deposit $150, you get a $150 bonus that is cashable after you meet the wagering requirement. The wagering requirement is 12 times the deposit plus the bonus.

With Bonus D, if you deposit $400, you get a $200 bonus that is cashable after meeting the wagering requirement. The wagering requirement for Bonus D is also 12 times the deposit plus bonus.

HOW MUCH SHOULD YOU BET?

Assuming you can play blackjack against a 0.5% house edge in order to meet the wagering requirement for each bonus, let's first figure out your expected dollar return for each bonus.

Bonus C:

First, the wagering requirement:

Deposit ($150) + Bonus ($150) = $300
Wagering Requirement = 12 x $300 (deposit + bonus)
Wagering Requirement = $3,600

Next, to calculate the expected average loss, multiply the wagering requirement times the house advantage:

$3,600 x -0.005 = -$18

Next, subtract your expected loss on the play from your starting total:
$300 - $18 = $282

Finally, to calculate your expected profit, subtract your initial deposit from this final total:

$282 - $150 = **$132 Expected Profit on Bonus C**

Bonus D:

First, the wagering requirement:

Deposit ($400) + Bonus ($200) = $600
Wagering Requirement = 12 x $600 (deposit + bonus)
Wagering Requirement = $7,200

Next, to calculate the expected average loss, we multiply the wagering requirement times the house advantage:

$7,200 x -0.005 = -36

Subtract this expected loss from our starting total:
$600 - $36 = $564

Subtract our initial deposit from this amount:

$564 - $400 = **$164 Expected Profit on Bonus D**

So, Bonus D is worth more in dollars than Bonus C. But let's look at the percentage returns you're getting with each bonus. To calculate your percentage return, divide the expected profit by the total amount of your own money that must be wagered to get it. It is very important that you divide your profit by the action you play on your own money only. For instance, with Bonus C, you wagered 12 times the deposit plus bonus, but only the deposit is your money. The amount of action on your money is simply 12 times the deposit ($150), or $1,800.

The profit divided by the action on your own money is:

$132/1,800 = .0733 = **7.33% Advantage on Bonus C**

With Bonus D, you wagered 12 times the deposit + bonus, but again only the deposit is your own money. The amount of action on your money is simply 12 times the deposit ($400) or $4,800.

The profit divided by your action is:

$164/4,800 = .0342 = **3.42% Advantage on Bonus D**

So, Bonus D has a dollar value higher than Bonus C, but Bonus C has more than twice the percentage value of Bonus D. For the professional gambler who understands the concepts of "Kelly Criterion" betting, this is an important difference.

The **Kelly Criterion** is a method professional gamblers use to size their bets for maximum return. Essentially, with a larger percentage advantage, a player would ideally bet more money. Professionals always look for a strong edge, as they can afford to bet a bigger percentage of their bank when they have a greater expected return. So, despite the fact that Bonus D has a higher dollar return than Bonus C, the percentage differences between them allow more aggressive betting on Bonus C than on Bonus D, especially for players on very limited bankrolls.

For loot-and-scoot players, I'm going to provide some simple rules for choosing the bonuses you play.

NON-STICKY BONUSES ON A SMALL BANKROLL

There are two rules for this:

1) Never play any non-sticky (cashable) bonus that does not have a percentage return of at least 3%.

2) Never place a bet that is bigger than 1% of your total playing bankroll. That means that if you have a total bankroll of $1,000, you should never place a bet greater than $10. Simply divide your total bankroll by 100 to get your max bet.

If you follow these two simple rules, you will keep yourself out of serious trouble and avoid extreme bankroll fluctuations. But remember that you must continually adjust your big bet to conform to these rules. If you start out with a $2,000 bankroll, place $20 bets, and have a negative fluctuation of $500 that takes your current bankroll down to only $1500, then you must lower your high bet to $15.

Professional players may follow Kelly Criterion betting guidelines more precisely and may find it worth their while to exploit bonuses that return as little as 1%. (If you are not a professional gambler, but this method appeals to you, then I advise you to get my book, *Blackbelt in Blackjack,* which describes the Kelly Criterion betting approach in detail.)

THE VALUE OF A STICKY BONUS

In our earlier discussion of sticky bonuses, I pointed out that the actual dollar value of a sticky bonus is nearly identical to the dollar value of a non-sticky bonus except that you must bet ever-increasing amounts of money to extract ever-decreasing increments of that bonus value.

As described in the previous chapter, if you bet your entire balance on a coin flip with a 100% sticky bonus, your advantage is 50%. That is a monstrous advantage. But if you bet it all on the very next flip, that advantage gets cut in half to 25%, then 12.5% and 6.25% on subsequent flips. A 6.25% advantage still sounds like a big advantage to most professional gamblers—blackjack card counters usually try to get an advantage of about 1% at live casino games— but look at how much you have to bet to get that 6.25% edge. The bet sizes go from $200 to $400 and then to $800 for that 6.25% advantage. The next bet up would be $1,600, and of that $1,500 is your own money. On this fourth attempt at doubling up, your advantage is only about 3.12%.

Some players have bankrolls that allow them to bet $1,500 with a 3% advantage, and many pros would consider this a fantastic profit opportunity. But many average players on smaller banks cannot afford the fluctuations that such bets would inevitably cause. In addition, blackjack, alas, is not a coin flip, so the fluctuations on that game are about 10% greater than in a coin flipping game, and there is also a house edge of a half-percent or so to consider. Professional players can use standard Kelly betting criteria to estimate the amount of risk they are comfortable with on sticky bonuses, based on the decreasing advantage and increasing amount of their own money that is at stake.

You do not have to play with the house's money on every bet to extract the value of a sticky bonus, but you must play aggressively enough that you are taking a real shot at losing enough of your own money to get into playing with the house's money. So, how should you bet a sticky bonus? Simply set a goal and go for it. Here are some guidelines for the loot-and-scoot player:

FOUR RULES FOR PLAYING STICKY BONUSES

1) If your total bankroll is less than $2,000, ignore the sticky bonuses until you have built up your bankroll some more by playing the non-sticky and semi-sticky bonuses. You do not need big fluctuations right now.

2) If your total bankroll is more than $2,000 but less than $4,000, never play any sticky bonus that is less than 100% of your deposit. If you deposit $100, then the bonus must be for at least $100. Set your win goal at twice the value of the bonus. If you are getting a $100 bonus for a $100 deposit, then set your win goal at doubling your total bank for that play, that is, turning the $200 total in your account into $400. Bet aggressively off the top, about 1/8 of your starting account total, until you hit your goal. With a deposit-plus-bonus total of $200 in your account, come right out with $25 bets. Do not lower your bets if you start losing. In fact, most pros would raise their bets as they got down into the house's money, as your advantage actually goes up at this time. If you lose everything, so be it. If you win your goal, making your total balance $400, then drop your bets to grind out the remainder of your play. Any time you go below your $400 target, raise your bet to $25 again until you either lose it all or come back up to your $400 goal.

In deciding whether or not to play the bonus, estimate the dollar value as one-half of the bonus total, in this case, one-half of $100, or $50. Over the long run, you'll lose your $100 deposit about half the time and win $200 the other half of the time. In the short run, you could lose your $100 quite a few times in succession, which is why you don't want to play stickies with a bankroll of less than $2,000. By the same token, you could also win quite a few stickies in succession. And that's never a problem.

3) If your total bankroll is more than $4,000 but less than $6,000, never play any sticky bonus of less than 100% of your deposit. But let your win goal be to double up twice. That is, if you are getting a $100 bonus for a $100 deposit, then set your goal at turning your $200 (D + B) into $800. Bet aggressively off the top, about 1/8 of your deposit plus bonus, until you hit your first double up. With a starting deposit plus bonus total of $200 in your account, come right out with $25 bets. And again, do not lower your bets if you start losing. If you lose everything, so be it. When you have doubled your starting bank once—so that your account totals $400—then raise your bets again to about 1/8 of your new account total—or $50 in this case—and shoot for that ultimate $800 total in your account.

If you hit this total, then grind out the remainder of your play with small bets. If you go below that $800 mark, just live with it and keep grinding. Do not raise your bets again. The closer you are to meeting your wagering requirement, the closer that money you've already won is to being yours to withdraw. You bet very aggressively at the start of this play when all you had to lose was $100. Don't take a chance now on giving it all back. If you hit a real bad streak of cards here, you'll sleep much better if you wind up with a profit of $400, or even $100, than if you lose it all. Only go back to aggressive $50 bets if your balance goes down to around your starting total, meaning you've lost virtually all of your profit. Now you've got to bang out some big bets again and hope the gods of flux are on your side.

In deciding whether or not to play the bonus with this strategy, estimate the dollar value as 75% of the bonus total, which would be $75 in this case. With this strategy, you can expect to lose your $100 deposit about three-quarters of the time, but you'll profit $600 about one out of four times. Don't be discouraged when you lose. You will lose more often than you'll win on the stickies—that's why you need a bigger bankroll—but when you win, it will usually be a good score.

4) If your total bankroll is more than $6,000, then either follow the advice directly above for players with bankrolls between $4,000 and $6,000, or read *Blackbelt in Blackjack* to learn the intricacies of Kelly betting principles and risk management that professional players use. With a substantial bank, you can often afford to go after sticky bonuses that add less than 100% to your deposit, provided you do the math and figure out both the dollar value and the percentage value for the play.

YOUR ADVANTAGE ON STICKY BONUSES

Knowing your percentage advantage on a few big bets will help you determine whether you should attempt to double, triple, or quadruple the bonus amount. But this is not the same thing as determining your **overall percentage advantage** from the whole play. This would be like a card counter figuring out his advantage on the few big bets he would make at high counts, but neglecting all of the small bets he must make when the house has the edge.

So, let's say you have a 100% sticky bonus of $100 for a $100 deposit, with a wagering requirement of 10DB. And let's assume that you have a $5,000 bankroll so you will be following the double-up twice strategy outlined above. The bonus value is therefore 75% of the $100 bonus, or $75.

You then have to estimate the house expectation on the $2,000 total action of your wagering requirement, which at blackjack is 0.5% or $10. This makes your overall profit from the play $75 (your expected bonus win) minus $10, or $65.And your overall percentage win is now figured out the same way as with traditional non-sticky bonuses. Divide the expected win by the amount of your own money that you must bet to get this win:

$65 / $1,000 = 0.065 = 6.5%

Now say you have a total bank of only $3,000, so that you can only afford one double up, giving the $100 sticky bonus a total value of $50. When you subtract the house expectation of $10, your expected profit is $50 minus $10, or $40, and your percentage advantage comes to:

$40 / $1,000 = 0.040 = 4%

WHAT MAKES A STICKY BONUS A GOOD VALUE?

As with traditional non-sticky bonuses, the percentage advantage with sticky bonuses is as important as the dollar expectation on any bonus play. With non-sticky bonuses, my advice to novice players is to never play any bonus with a percentage advantage of less than 3% over the house. With a sticky bonus, my advice is to never play any bonus with a percentage advantage of less than 4% over the house.

ADVANTAGE WITH A SEMI-STICKY BONUS

Professional players tend to play semi-sticky bonuses the same way they play sticky bonuses—with maximum aggression right from the start. If they lose it all in the process of attempting to make their wagering requirement, so be it. But once they make their wagering requirement, they take the same attitude toward semi-stickies that all amateurs should take: withdraw all of your own money, and play aggressively on the house's money.

As soon as you meet a win goal get your own money out of there so you can bang it out on the house's money.

If you are a loot-and-scoot player on a short bank, take a conservative approach to the semi-sticky bonus. But raise your bets if you start to lose. If you lose an amount equal to your initial deposit, meaning you are playing entirely on the house's money, then bang it out big time to either get back up to your starting amount or lose it all.

For example, let's say you're on a small $1,000 bankroll, and you find a semi-sticky bonus with otherwise the same terms as the sticky bonus described above: a 100% bonus of $100 on a $100 deposit, wagering requirement = 10DB. If this were a sticky bonus, you couldn't play it on such a short bank. Remember our rule that with any bank of less than $2,000, we do not play sticky bonuses. With a semi-sticky bonus, however, you can limit the losses on your own money by playing conservatively through the wagering requirement, then withdrawing your own money and banging out the house's money aggressively. If you've got the time to grind out your $2,000 wagering requirement with bets of $2 to $4, your actual expectation would be to lose $10, assuming you play blackjack with a house edge of 0.5%. You'd be highly unlikely to lose your whole $200 due to bad flux when betting at such a low level. And when you've made your wagering requirement, you can take a shot at making $50 or $75 with aggressive play on the house's money.

A player with a bigger bankroll may find this ultra-conservative strategy not worth the time, as the hourly rate would be poor. But if you're trying to build a bigger bank so that you can play at a higher level in the near future, then do what you have to do to get there.

Players on small banks can take advantage of semi-sticky bonuses even when the bonus is less than 100% of the deposit—provided they play conservatively on their own money, then pump up their action after they've met the wagering requirement and have withdrawn all but the bonus funds. Even on a small bank, however, you may elect to bang out the semi-sticky funds to a bigger win target than you would dare try with a sticky or non-sticky, since your aggressive betting with the semi-sticky bonus always starts after you've withdrawn your own money and only the house funds are in your account.

With a semi-sticky $100 in your account, doubling up means that you will be shooting for only a $200 target, as opposed to the $400 target you had with a sticky bonus when your own funds were also on the line. But my advice with the semi-sticky bonus is to bet even more aggressively than with the sticky, precisely because your own funds are not on the line. After you've gotten through the wagering requirement and withdrawn your own money, I recommend betting one-half of the

HOW MUCH SHOULD YOU BET?

amount in your account until you hit your target win. With $100 in your account after you've withdrawn your own money, bet $50. If you lose the $50 bet, bet the full remaining $50. You want to get a decision on this win as fast as you can, and you're hoping for early luck. Set a win target of at least $100 to $200, and go for it. If you lose it all, so be it.

In fact, the most conservative way to play a semi-sticky bonus and the method that I would recommend for any player on a really short bank, is to simply bet the whole bonus amount ($100 in this example) as soon as you withdraw your own funds. If you win, quit and take out the $100 (or $150 if you are dealt a blackjack) and play the bonus again the next day, the same way.

Blackjack players might disagree with this strategy since they lose the ability to double down or split pairs, but this is a minor issue when you are playing with a nearly 50% bonus advantage. Not being able to double down or split pairs raises the house advantage by less than 2%.

If you have to win two bets to make a $100 target, you'll only do this about one-quarter of the time. If you only have to win one bet to make your $100, you'll accomplish this almost half the time. So give up the extra 1.8% to the house that comes from giving up your ability to double down or split pairs, and go for the greater number of winning plays.

If you have a sizable bankroll, $5,000 or more, you can be even more aggressive with these semi-sticky betting opportunities. Shoot for $300 to $500. Players with larger bankrolls may aim at a target of thousands with a semi-sticky bonus. And remember to always withdraw all of your winnings when you hit your target, then return the next day to bang it out again with only the house's money.

If you are on a smaller bankroll remember that the biggest edge is in playing on the house's money, not your own, and that whenever you win even a single bet on a semi-sticky play, you will be betting with some of your own money (the win) on any subsequent bets. The greater the amount of your own money at risk the smaller your advantage over the house. Loot-and-scoot players should not go crazy trying to score monster wins.

For loot-and-scoot players, estimating the percentage advantage with a semi-sticky bonus is a bit different than with a sticky bonus, since you don't really know what your ultimate betting handle will be. You can easily figure out the amount you will bet to grind through the wagering requirement and what you will lose to the house expectation based on the game you are playing. But estimating the total bets you'll make after you start playing aggressively is not so cut and dried.

If you use the conservative strategy described above, you'll never have to bet with any of your own money on the bonus play. In the example given above, if you bet $100, then your expected win is approximately $47.50. (Note here that it is less than $50 only because I am including the extra house advantage for that aggressive bet-it-all strategy where I give up doubling down and pair splits. I'm giving the house about 2.5% just as a conservative estimate. I'm not doing any fancy math here. The precise expectation would depend on the number of decks and other rules but this is close enough for our purposes with these playing restrictions.)

Since we already met the wagering requirement, which was $2,000, of which $1,000 was our own money, we figure the percentage advantage on the play just as with other bonuses. We divide our expected win ($47.50), by the amount of our money we have to wager to get it ($1,000), and our advantage on the play as 47.50 / 1000, or 4.75%.

Aggressive players with big bankrolls may bet big from the start, rather than waiting until they can withdraw their own funds to start playing on the house's money, but as a loot-and-scoot player, you should wait until you have completed the wagering requirement in order to bet big with only the house's money, and estimate your percentage win rate the same as you would if the bonus was sticky.

However, you can play a semi-sticky bonus with an overall percentage advantage as low as 2%, provided you wait until the wagering requirement is complete, and you've withdrawn your own funds, to start betting aggressively with the house's money. If you have a bankroll of $6,000 or more and you want to play these bonuses more aggressively from the start, then analyze the bonus as you would a sticky bonus, but look for a percentage advantage of 3% or more.

SUMMARY

The problems you face when attempting to estimate the advantages associated with various types of bonuses can be complex. The guidelines I've provided here should steer amateur players to the most profitable and lowest-risk bonus opportunities. Here's a brief summary of what you need to know from this chapter. If you get this much, you should succeed in your online gambling adventure.

1) You must be able to identify the type of bonus. Is it sticky, non-sticky, or semi-sticky? Read the definitions carefully and make sure you understand them. If you are on a short bank this is the first thing you need to know when you read an Internet casino's terms and conditions. You won't even play the stickies if you have less than $2,000. And you cannot estimate your percentage advantage, or devise a betting strategy for any bonus, without knowing the bonus type.

2) You must estimate your percentage advantage according to the bonus type. Depending on your bankroll and the type of bonus, you will be looking for an advantage of at least 2%, 3%, or 4%. If the percentage advantage is below the standard required for your bankroll, pass it up. You might return to it later when your bank has grown. You do not have to memorize the formulas for figuring out your advantage on any of the bonuses. You simply have to recognize if the bonus is sticky, non-sticky, or semi-sticky. To figure your advantage, just open to the example I've provided and insert the numbers that apply to the bonus you're considering. It won't take you more than a minute or so with a pocket calculator to get the percentage.

3) If you are on a small bank—less than $2,000—then you should plan to start by making minimal bets, which means you will be working a lot of hours at a low hourly rate in order to increase your bankroll. As your bankroll increases, your hourly rate will increase dramatically. But whatever you do, *don't play with the rent money*. If you cannot take a loss in stride, then you are overbetting your bankroll.

7. CHOOSING WHERE TO PLAY

If you use any of the popular search engines, like Yahoo or Google, to find online casinos, you'll get hundreds of hits. But making a smart choice on where you will deposit your money requires careful research. Many online casinos list no physical address and some have no phone numbers. None are located in the U.S., and there are no laws regulating any of the games or the rights of customers.

Considering all of this, it's amazing that anyone in the U.S. gambles on the Internet, yet millions of people do. And among those are a handful of professional gamblers who make money gambling on the Internet, month after month and year after year. If you are going to gamble on the Web, you should use the same criteria as the pros to select the casinos where you play. There are four major factors to consider in picking a place to bet your money:

1) Watchdog Recommendations
2) Bonus Value
3) Property Group
4) Brand of Software

Let's look at each of these factors separately.

WATCHDOG RECOMMENDATIONS

Using a search engine to find an Internet casino is like using the Yellow pages to buy a car. I might use the Yellow Pages to locate a Honda dealership if my experience with owning a Honda has been favorable and the latest *Consumer Reports* praises the new models. The Yellow Pages can be useful when I already know what I want, but if I need guidance in making a decision, the Yellow Pages would be a poor place to start. Most of us prefer to go on recommendations from trusted friends and associates, reports in independent consumer publications, and our own personal experiences with similar products. Shopping for an Internet casino is like that. It's a big money purchase and getting a lemon can be a costly mistake.

AVOIDING THE LEMONS

So, where do we find anything similar to *Consumer Reports* for online casinos?

On the Internet, of course!

But there's a problem. There are dozens of Internet sites claiming to be Internet casino players' advocacy sites, but many of these sites that represent themselves as "independent" are in fact owned by the Internet casinos themselves. Their sole reason for existence is to steer customers to the site owner's casinos and away from the competition. In fact, most of the Internet casinos have a dozen or more phony websites that are set up solely for the purpose of steering gamblers to their casinos. Virtually every big property group has at least a couple dozen of these seemingly "independent" websites that praise all of the casinos in their property group as the best on the Web, with the best games and the biggest bonuses and the highest level of customer satisfaction. This is so common on the Web that it is not even considered a shady business practice. It's just standard advertising and promotion.

If you know which Web casinos are connected to the various property groups and management companies, it's not hard to spot these phony consumer advocates. All of their "objective" recommendations are for the same company's businesses.

But, just because you find a "watchdog" site that recommends casinos in different property groups, casinos that have different ownership, doesn't guarantee that this site is a real consumer advocacy site either. There are many Internet sites posing as player advocacy sites that are not officially connected to any individual casino or property group, but are simply portals for any and all online casinos that will pay them for "click-throughs." These casino "banner farms" spout whatever line the online casinos want them to in order to draw in customers. In fact, they have very little content at all, other than massive numbers of banners for casino websites. Most of their "editorial" content is on the line of "Hot Bonuses!" and "Win Here!"

So, when you start looking for an Internet watchdog, you need to sniff out the real watchdogs from the wolves in watchdogs' clothing. Look for websites that report on casinos in lots of different property groups, and that use different brands of software. Some banner farms are actually set up by software companies to promote just the casinos that use their software, since they get a commission from these casinos. Look for websites that have lists of casinos to avoid in addition to casinos they deem safe and reliable. Look for websites that have information on the games and the bonus offers, and other content that is not only informative but educational. And look for websites where online players can post their opinions, comments, and experiences—both good and bad—about the online casinos.

REAL INTERNET WATCHDOGS DO EXIST

I began Internet gambling only after a number of professional players I had known for years told me about some of the profitable opportunities they had found. They steered me to a couple of the authentic consumer advocacy sites they trusted, where online casinos were honestly reviewed and burn joints were blacklisted based on player reports.

These watchdog sites did earn money by providing marketing for the casinos they recommended, but they were also known to remove the banners of any casinos for which there were legitimate player reports indicating there were problems.

Despite the fact that these watchdogs were primarily funded by click-through revenues just like the phony watchdogs, they used their popularity with players to their advantage. Serious Internet gamblers recognized the credibility of these sites and used these sites to select the casinos where they played. The biggest and most reputable Internet casino operations, those that were not trying to rip off their customers, soon realized that these legitimate watchdogs were the best sites for attracting players.

In a sense, real watchdogs turned the tables on the industry. Big casinos needed acceptance from watchdogs in the same way that many businesses need membership in the Better Business Bureau or the Good Housekeeping Seal of Approval. What these reputable watchdogs did was tell the casinos that they would send them customers, but only if the casinos lived up to their standards.

As valuable as these watchdogs are, they lack necessary information for players who are actually trying to make money in online casinos. They provide little information on bonus terms, no information on bonus values, and often ignore other important factors, such as the property group affiliation of a casino or the brand of software being used. They also tend to hide other information on the casinos that advertise with them, if that information might discourage players, even casual gamblers, from clicking through. For instance, they fail to list the video poker pay tables or the casinos' slot payout percentages.

HOW I BECAME AN INTERNET WATCHDOG

After twenty three years of publishing *Blackjack Forum* magazine, a trade journal for professional gamblers, I folded the print version of the magazine in January of 2004. At the urging of some professional gamblers who were longtime associates and friends, I moved the magazine online.

Their idea was to set up a watchdog site for reviewing online casinos that would *include* the information that other watchdogs lacked. As players ourselves, our standards for listing sites would be tougher than other watchdogs'. Not only would we validate an online casino only if we had personally played in there, found their games to be fair, and verified that its management lived up to their terms and conditions, but, honest or not, we would not list any casinos that did not offer potentially profitable bonuses for players!

On December 26, 2004, we opened BlackjackForumOnline.com, the only site on the Web run by professional gamblers. The new issue of *Blackjack Forum* magazine was now online, and it was—for the first time in its history—free to the public. And, incidentally, there is nothing for sale on the BlackjackForumOnline website. We don't sell books, videos, software or gambling systems. All of the discussion forums and the gambling library articles are free. You don't have to give us your name or address, or even your email address. This is simply an information site for players who want to make money gambling.

My initial plan in writing this book was to publish a list of reputable online casinos that offer good bonuses, fair games, and reliable service, as well as a list of the casinos experienced gamblers consider untrustworthy. The problem is that these lists are continually changing.

In the year that our website has been up and running, we have added and subtracted dozens of casinos to and from both lists.

For our most up-to-date listings and reviews go to BlackjackForumOnline.com. You'll also get links to other watchdog sites we consider reliable, so that you can get a well-rounded perspective on what's out there and what players have to say about their Internet casino experiences. The single most reliable way to select an Internet casino is on the recommendation of trusted and knowledgeable sources— sources that are not Internet casino owners or management companies. You want recommendations based on knowledgeable players' recent experiences.

After you get a list of possible casinos to play in, look into the second most important factor...

THE BONUS VALUE

No matter what reliable sources say about any casino's great games and fair treatment, you must check out the precise terms of the casino's bonus offer. Bonus offers are constantly changing. To verify an offer you see on a casino's banner ad, you must go to the casino's website and click on the bonus offer or the promotions link. Some casinos post numerous different bonus offers, so look at all of them that seem like possibilities for you. Read the terms provided for the bonus itself, then go to the casino's general terms and conditions page and read everything through.

This can be one of the more tedious jobs you'll have as an Internet gambler, because these terms and conditions are often long, often redundant, and in many cases just plain poorly explained. But you've got to read them. Some specify that you must email a scan of your drivers license or passport in order to withdraw funds from your account. This is irritating, since you do not need to supply this documentation to deposit funds in the first place! Others state that withdrawals from your account are only processed on Mondays or that there is a maximum withdrawal amount per week. The main thing you are looking for is further information regarding the amount of the bonus, the type of bonus (sticky, non-sticky, semi-sticky, or loss rebate), the wagering requirement, and which games are excluded for meeting your wagering requirement.

But you also want to know any other important information on how the casino's bonus system works. After all, it's your money on the line. You may have to enter a special code to get the bonus or send an email with a special message in the subject line. There may be a waiting period after your deposit before the bonus is added to your account or some minimum amount of play required before the bonus appears in your account. Many online casinos will not allow bonuses for players in certain countries.

Until you have the experience to judge which online casinos are reliable, you should get screen shots of the terms and conditions for every casino where you put money on deposit. Casinos sometimes change their terms and conditions in the middle of your play, and you may need a copy of the precise terms that were in effect when you made your deposit. Many players have played through their wagering requirement only to find that the casino would not authorize their withdrawal of their winnings because the terms and conditions had changed and they had failed to meet the new ones.

With a shady casino, it does no good to insist that the terms and conditions used to say that blackjack was allowed if the current terms state that blackjack is not allowed. You must be able to prove your claim. If you have a copy of the terms that were posted when you made your deposit, however, you can email this file to them as proof that you complied with the terms in effect at that time. I have never heard of a casino that refused to pay based on changed terms and conditions if a player provided a copy of the terms and conditions in effect at the time he signed up.

THE PROPERTY GROUP

Many online casinos are not entirely independent. Often, several casinos will have a common ownership or management. Pros tend to lump these casinos together, as they tend to treat their customers the same. They tend to offer similar or identical terms and conditions, and use the same software, bonus system, and payout requirements. The casinos within these property groups often advertise for each other, and at BlackjackForumOnline.com, we categorize online casinos by ownership or management group.

If you have a positive experience in a certain casino, the other casinos in that group will probably treat you similarly. The same is true with bad experiences. But you have to be careful because some casino groups look out for players who sign up for deposit bonuses at every one of their casinos, and submit these players' names as suspected "bonus abusers" to an Internet casino blacklist. If you like a casino and have a good experience there, it's often worth it to wait until you are contacted by one of the casino's sister properties with a bonus offer before you play there.

SOFTWARE BRAND

There are half a dozen major software providers, a few more lesser brands, and many more software platforms that are unique to a single casino or property group. At BlackjackForumOnline, we list the software used by the casinos we review.

Professional players have built up a large body of data on their Internet casino results that tells them beyond a statistical doubt that a few of the major software brands are providing honest, randomly-dealt games. They also have a body of data that tells them that some of the lesser brands and the proprietary software are not. There are many reasons for you to be concerned with the software used by a casino beyond the fact that some software tends to run more smoothly than others. For one thing, casinos that use one of the large proven brands are generally unable to tamper with the program that runs the games and records the win/loss transactions. In fact, the software is often not even on the Internet casino's computer system. A major software provider simply leases the right to use its software to the Internet casino. When a customer of that casino plays a game, he is actually playing on the software provider's system, which might not even be in the same country as the casino offices.

Microgaming, a major Internet casino software provider, is located in South Africa. Yet most of the casinos that lease its software are located in island countries. When you play in a casino that uses Microgaming software, you are playing in South Africa, regardless of which country the Internet casino office is located in. The casino itself has no access to Microgaming's software program, so they cannot fix the software to deal you losing hands or to give the dealer more blackjacks than normal.

What's to keep Microgaming from leasing software that cheats to its Internet casino clients? Legally, probably nothing. There is no international governing body that oversees and regulates online casinos. But Microgaming is a multimillion-dollar corporation, audited by Price

Waterhouse Cooper. It leases its software to dozens of the biggest online casinos and many smaller ones. If it were to offer cheating software packages to its clients, this information would inevitably become public knowledge. Professional players and mathematicians would blow the whistle and bring down a lot of online casinos in addition to Microgaming itself.

We also have to consider that all casino games, whether on the Internet or on the Vegas Strip, are mathematically rigged against the players. That's what the house edge is—an accepted and legal way of rigging the games. In the long run, if you exclude the bonus values, the online casinos will win steadily with completely honest games, even against the best players. A small unlicensed Internet casino, using its own proprietary software, might attempt to rip off a bunch of naive players and disappear into the night with the money. But a Microgaming software lease is not inexpensive. Even casinos in the small Caribbean islands where many online casinos are located pay a six-digit annual licensing fee, so they tend to be companies that plan on staying in business. They don't want a scandal.

If a casino is using its own proprietary software, however, it could easily gaff the games to steal money from the players. It has, in fact, been shown by analysts at Blackjack Forum and elsewhere that some casinos have dealt non-random games. There are hundreds of ways games can be rigged. For a game like blackjack, for example, programming the computer to deal more tens and aces to the dealer than to the players is all that would be needed. Or the software could be rigged to give the dealer whatever hole card he needs to make him more likely to beat the players' hands.

In a game like roulette, a program could look at the numbers where bets were placed, then decide where the ball will land. You can probably imagine a hundred ways that a computer could be programmed to cheat you in casino games, and none of them would be difficult for a programmer to accomplish.

Frankly, after 30 years in gambling, I don't much trust humans. Many people will do whatever they think they can get away with, especially in a business as unregulated as online gambling. I will discuss the possibilities of being cheated in online casinos—and the signs of it—in a separate chapter, but avoiding this possibility should be a concern for every Internet gambler. Playing in casinos that use well-known and reputable software is your prime protection.

8. BLACKJACK, INTERNET STYLE

This is not a book on how to play blackjack, so I'm not going to explain all of the rules and procedures of the game. If you do not know how to play, you'll find a complete explanation of the game, and correct strategy, free of charge at BlackjackForumOnline.com. The Internet casino games are essentially the same as in live casinos, with these few differences:

1) The blackjack games offered in online casinos are generally heads up, meaning, it's just you against the dealer, with no other players at the table. Some online casinos allow you to play in games with other players at the table, but this doesn't interest most serious online players. We're going for speed of play with minimum distractions.

2) The cards are shuffled after each round so there is no possibility of card counting. There are a few online casinos where the dealers deal out more than one round, but these games are rare. If you are a card counter, you may be interested in games like these when you can find them, but as bonus hustlers, we're not all that interested. We're looking for much bigger advantages than card counting can provide.

3) Some online casinos use the European "no hole card" rule, which means that if you double down or split a pair when the dealer has an ace or ten upcard, you will lose all double and split bets if the dealer makes a blackjack. This rule is not that costly, but you must be aware of it when it is in effect, as you will want to make a few strategy changes against dealer aces and tens.

PLAYING YOUR HANDS

The on-screen interface differs from casino to casino. Until you become accustomed to the common variations, you may want to learn new software by first playing in the casinos' free games.

After a few free hands, you will understand the software's interface. Most have hit and stand buttons, but betting methods vary. Some software programs have graphic representations of chips that you click on to place your bet. Some have +/- buttons for raising and lowering bets. Most have a button that allows you to repeat the previous bet without re-entering it, and some allow you to click on extra betting spots to play more than one hand.

Most game play screens have a help button that takes you to an explanation of all the rules, payouts, and procedures. When you first play on any unfamiliar software, it's a good idea to read this information. Some casinos place a time limit on your decisions. If you are not a skillful basic strategy player and you have to look up the correct plays in charts, it's important that you know the time limit.

SELECTING THE RIGHT GAME

Many online casinos offer blackjack games with a variety of table limits, rule variations, and sometimes different numbers of decks in play. These are important considerations, as they will affect the house advantage. In the blackjack examples we've been using so far, we've assumed the house advantage to be 0.5% (one-half of one percent), but it's a bit more complicated than that.

The actual house advantage over you could be anywhere from zero to a full 1%, though it's usually closer to one-half of a percent. When estimating any bonus value, it's generally no problem to use the 0.5% value, as you may not be able to read the rules of the game until you download the casino's software. Once you have access to the complete game rules, recalculate using the precise value.

To do this, use the following chart.

THE EFFECT OF THE NUMBER OF DECKS AND RULE VARIATIONS

Number of Decks:	1 D	2 D	4 D	6 D	8 D
Deck Effect:	+.02	-.31	-.48	-.54	-.57

RULES VARIATIONS

Stands Soft 17:	.00	.00	.00	.00	.00
Hits Soft 17:	-.19	-.20	-.21	-.21	-.22
Double Any 2 Cards:	.00	.00	.00	.00	.00
Double 8-11 Only:	-.13	-.11	-.10	-.11	-.11
Double 9-11 Only:	-.13	-.11	-.10	-.11	-.11
Double 10-11 Only:	-.26	-.21	-.20	-.19	-.18
Double 11 Only:	-.78	-.69	-.67	-.65	-.64
Double After Splits:	+.14	+.14	+.14	+.14	+.14
Double on 3+ Cards:	+.24	+.23	+.23	+.23	+.23
No Resplits:	-.02	-.03	-.04	-.04	-.04
Resplit Aces:	+.03	+.05	+.06	+.07	+.07
Late Surrender:	+.02	+.05	+.07	+.08	+.08
Early Surrender:	+.62	+.62	+.63	+.63	+.63
Eur. No Hole Card:	-.10	-.11	-.11 *	-.11	-.11
No Insurance:	.00	.00	.00	.00	.00

Let's look at an example. The game is six decks, dealer stands on soft 17, double down on any two cards, double after splits, no resplits, and the European no-hole-card rule. We go to the 6 D column to get the cost of a six-deck game, then add them all up. Here's how it looks (all rule effects are expressed in percentages).

Deck Effect:	-.54
Stands Soft 17:	.00
Double Any 2 Cards:	.00
Double After Splits:	+.14
No Resplits:	-.04
Eur. No Hole Card:	-.11
Total:	**-.55**

So, this particular game has a cost of slightly greater than the 0.5% we've been using for all of our examples. If you find payouts for unusual hands, like a player hand of three sevens pays 3 to 2, or anything similar, just ignore the effect. Most of these special payouts have little value due to the rarity of their occurrence.

If you happen to find a game with three, five, or seven decks, estimate the cost by averaging the values of the adjacent number of decks. For example, for a five-deck game, calculate the average of the values for the four-deck game and the six-deck game. In the above example, the cost of the four-deck game with the same set of rules as above comes to -.49%, and the six-deck game costs us -.55%. For five decks, we could use the average of the two games, which is -.52%.

THE BASIC STRATEGY

Contrary to what many gamblers may think, blackjack is not just a guessing game. Correct blackjack basic strategy is based on mathematical odds, and will maximize your wins and minimize your losses on each hand over time.

Blackjack typically has a cost of only about 0.5% for players using basic strategy. If you are guessing at how to play your hands or just playing the way you always felt was right based on your experience at the casino blackjack tables, you are probably giving up quite a bit more than 0.5%.

Here is a complete basic strategy chart.

BASIC STRATEGY FOR ANY NUMBER OF DECKS

HIT / STAND

	2	3	4	5	6	7	8	9	X	A
17	S	S	S	S	S	S	S	S	S	S
16	S	S	S	S	S	H	H	H	H	H
15	S	S	S	S	S	H	H	H	H	H
14	S	S	S	S	S	H	H	H	H	H
13	S	S	S	S	S	H	H	H	H	H
12	H	H	S	S	S	H	H	H	H	H
A7	S	S	S	S	S	S	S	H	H	H

DOUBLE DOWN

	2	3	4	5	6	7	8	9	X	A
11	D	D	D	D	D	D	D	D	D*	D*
10	D	D	D	D	D	D	D	D		
9			D	D	D	D				
A7			D	D	D	D				
A6			D	D	D	D				
A5				D	D	D				
A4				D	D	D				
A3					D	D				
A2					D	D				

PAIR SPLITS
NO DOUBLE AFTER SPLITS

	2	3	4	5	6	7	8	9	X	A
AA	$	$	$	$	$	$	$	$	$	$*
99	$	$	$	$	$		$	$		
88	$	$	$	$	$	$	$	$	$*	$*
77	$	$	$	$	$	$				
66		$	$	$	$					
33			$	$	$	$				
22			$	$	$	$				

S = Stand H = Hit D = Double Down $ = Split ¢ = Surrender
* = *If European no-hole-card rule, hit instead of double or split.*

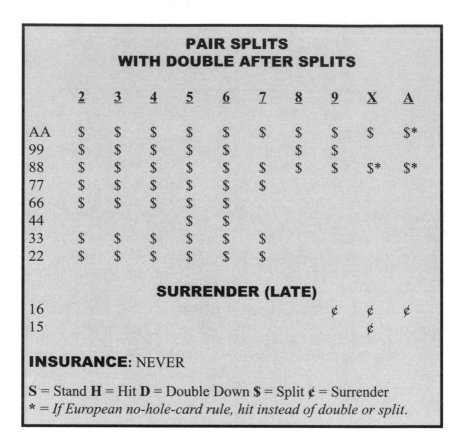

PAIR SPLITS WITH DOUBLE AFTER SPLITS

	2	3	4	5	6	7	8	9	X	A
AA	$	$	$	$	$	$	$	$	$	$*
99	$	$	$	$	$		$	$		
88	$	$	$	$	$	$	$	$	$*	$*
77	$	$	$	$	$	$				
66	$	$	$	$	$					
44				$	$					
33	$	$	$	$	$	$				
22	$	$	$	$	$	$				

SURRENDER (LATE)

	2	3	4	5	6	7	8	9	X	A
16								¢	¢	¢
15									¢	

INSURANCE: NEVER

S = Stand **H** = Hit **D** = Double Down **$** = Split **¢** = Surrender
* = *If European no-hole-card rule, hit instead of double or split.*

USING THE BASIC STRATEGY CHART

This generic chart may be used for any game. The player's hands are listed vertically down the left side. The dealer's upcards are listed horizontally along the top. Thus, if you hold a hand totaling 14 vs. a dealer 6, you can see the correct basic strategy decision is to stand. With a total of 14 vs. a dealer 7, you would hit. Note: If your total of 14 is made up of a pair of sevens, you must consult the pair splitting chart first. You can see that with a pair of sevens vs. a dealer 6 or 7, you would split your sevens.

Most card counters know basic strategy perfectly. As an Internet gambler, you have the luxury of being able to look at a chart while you play, even though it might slow you down a bit. It is more important for you to play slowly and correctly than quickly and incorrectly. The average casino blackjack player gives up about 2% to the house, which is about four times greater than a perfect basic strategy player. That's a lot to give up when you consider that you have to multiply the cost of the house advantage over you by the wagering requirement.

As conditions change, some of the basic strategy decisions also change. Usually, these changes are for borderline decisions, and do not significantly alter the amount of money you will win or lose over time. Also, there are a few borderline basic strategy changes that occur only when you are playing on a wagering requirement. You can find very comprehensive strategy charts at Blackjack Forum Online. However, I know a number of high stakes pros who know only one basic strategy and ignore the minute changes caused by rule variations, wagering requirements, and the number of decks in play. The above chart will work very well for any traditional blackjack game with most any rule set.

Two pair-splitting tables are presented here. I use the symbol "$" to indicate a split. The first pair-split table assumes that you are not allowed to double down after splitting a pair.

THE ORDER OF DECISIONS

Use the basic strategy chart in this order:

1. If surrender is allowed, this takes priority over any other decisions. If basic strategy calls for surrender, throw in the hand.

2. If you have a pair, determine whether or not basic strategy calls for a split.

3. If you have a possible double down hand, this play takes priority over hitting or standing. For example, if you may double down on any two cards, then with a hand of A-7 (soft 18) vs. a dealer 5, the correct basic strategy play is to double down. If you may only double down on 10 or 11, your correct play with A-7 versus 5 would be to stand.

4. After determining that you do not want to surrender, split a pair, or double down, consult the Hit/Stand chart. Always hit a hard total of 11 or below. Always stand on a hard total of 17 or higher. For all stiff hands, hard 12 through 16, consult the basic strategy chart. Always hit soft 17 **(A-6)** or below. Always stand on soft 19 **(A-8)** or higher. With a soft 18 **(A-7)**, consult the chart.

You may have noticed that basic strategy calls for never taking insurance. Unless you are counting cards, insurance is always a bad bet. And there is no use counting cards in online casinos because they shuffle after every round of play. Don't take insurance, even when you have a blackjack.

As I've said, blackjack is the game of choice for taking advantage of bonus offers. Unfortunately, some online casinos disallow blackjack play from qualifying toward a bonus's wagering requirement. If this is the case, then you must look for a game that is not restricted and has a low house advantage. In the next couple of chapters we'll look at some of the other games online casinos tend to allow for meeting your wagering requirement, so that you're not out of luck when blackjack is prohibited.

9. BLACKJACK SWITCH

Many online casinos use Playtech software that offers a unique game called Blackjack Switch. It is similar to regular casino blackjack in many ways, but different enough that you must use a different strategy.

Blackjack Switch is an excellent game for bonus qualifying when allowed. In fact, most pros choose Blackjack Switch over standard blackjack if both are available. When you apply the correct basic strategy at blackjack switch, the house advantage against you is even lower than at regular blackjack, only about 0.10%, compared to traditional blackjack's typical 0.5%.

In addition to a lower house edge, Blackjack Switch has milder fluctuations than regular blackjack.

Still, I would advise most players to play traditional blackjack if allowed, as it will take some time to learn the Blackjack Switch strategy, which is more complex than the strategy for regular blackjack. If you intend to stick with bonus hustling longer than most loot-and-scoot players might be inclined to, you should take the time to learn this game.

The unusual feature of Blackjack Switch is that you play two simultaneous hands, and you are allowed to switch the *second* cards dealt to each hand if you so desire. That is, if one of your hands has a 6 and a 10, and the other hand has an ace and a 5, you may exchange the 10 for the 5 to make hands of an 11 and a blackjack!

The rules compensate for this advantage by paying player blackjacks only even money. In addition, a dealer total of 22 is an automatic push on any hand other than a player blackjack. In other words, if you double down on that 11 and catch a ten for a total of 21, and the dealer proceeds to hit his hand to 22, your 21 hand just pushes. If you are holding a blackjack against the dealer's 22, your blackjack wins—but only even money.

THE RULES OF THE GAME

The game is dealt face-up from six decks. You must play two hands, and both hands must have equal bets. Only the second card (or top card) dealt to each hand can be switched. You cannot switch a first card from one hand with a second card from the other.

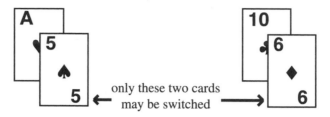

only these two cards ← may be switched →

In the two hands shown above, we cannot switch cards to make a blackjack and an 11, much as we'd like to.

Other rules: the dealer hits soft 17. You may double down on any two cards and double down after pair splits. No resplits are allowed. The European no-hole-card rule is used—that is, if you double or split against a dealer 10 or ace, you will lose all bets if the dealer gets a blackjack. On the positive side, you may make a switch before the dealer plays his hand, so that if you make one hand into a blackjack by switching top cards, that hand will push the dealer's blackjack—that is, it will be a tie. A player blackjack pays even money and is the only hand that will beat a dealer total of 22. Otherwise, a dealer total of 22 will push all other player hands, including 21. A dealer blackjack will push a player blackjack.

The difficulty for most players in this game is knowing when to switch. Some hands—such as the first hand described above, where a player could switch to make a blackjack and an eleven out of a hard 16 and a soft 16—are obvious switches. Anyone with a basic understanding of the game would know that this switch will create two strong hands out of two weak hands. But it's not always so obvious whether to switch or not. For instance, what do you do with the A-5 and 10-6 above? Is it better to have A-6 and 10-5? If so, why?

The switch strategy provided below will get the house edge down to about 0.10%, a smaller house edge than a traditional blackjack shoe game. After you have made your switch decision, basic strategy is very similar to that of a regular blackjack game, with slightly more hitting on stiffs and slightly less doubling. The hard part is the switch, and it's not really that hard—just different from any decision you're accustomed to making in a blackjack game. It's not just a question of which hand is better against the dealer upcard, but which *two-hand set* is better against the dealer upcard. So, let's learn to switch!

THE SWITCH

Before you can play your hands, you must decide if you would be better off with the two different hands you can get by switching your top cards. The first step in making this decision is defining the dealer's upcard as strong, weak, or deuce.

DEFINING THE DEALER'S UPCARD

We have three types of dealer's upcards in Blackjack Switch:

1. Strong: Any upcard from 7 to ace.

2. Weak: Any upcard from 3 to 6.

3. Deuce: Any 2. We have separated this upcard from the Weak upcards because the deuce is less likely to bust in Blackjack Switch. That's because a dealer total of 22 is an automatic push against all player hands except blackjack.

DEFINING THE PLAYER'S HANDS WITH THE WLPC SYSTEM

After you categorize the dealer's upcard, you must consider each of the two hands you have been dealt. There are four different types of player hands: **Winner, Loser, Push**, and **Chance.** I call this the **WLPC** classification. In defining the player hands, we always assume that the dealer has a 10 in the hole, and that any player hand that requires a hit will catch a 10 for a hit card. Here are the WLPC player hand definitions:

WINNER

Any player blackjack and any hard or soft total from 18 to 20 *that beats the dealer's total* (assuming 10 in the hole) is a Winner. So is any player total of 8 to 11 that beats the dealer upcard. Examples: Player 18 vs. Dealer 7 is classified as a Winner. Player 9 vs. Dealer 8 is a Winner. Note that although we classify a dealer upcard of 7 as Strong, we *never* classify a player total of 7 or 17 as a Winner.

A pair that we would split is a Winner only if each of the split cards would qualify as Winners vs. the dealer upcard. Examples: 8-8 vs. 7 is a Winner. 7-7 vs. 6 is not, because although we would split 7-7 vs. 6, a player 7 is never classified as a Winner.

Finally, the only player hands that qualify as Winners vs. a dealer 2 are: 10, 11, 19, 20, and 21. That's because the dealer's deuce will just not bust as often in Blackjack Switch as it does in regular blackjack.

LOSER

Any player hand, pat or stiff, that is beaten by a dealer's Strong upcard (7 through ace) is a Loser. Examples: A5 vs. 7 is a Loser. 19 vs. 10 is a Loser. 8-8 vs. 9 is a Loser.

PUSH

Any player hand from 18 to 20 or 8 to 11 that would push the dealer's Strong upcard is a Push. Examples: 19 vs. 9, 20 vs. ten, 8-8 vs. 8, and A7 vs. 8. Note that 16 vs. 6 is *not* a Push because it fails to meet the definition in two ways:

1. 16 is not a total from 18 to 20 or 8 to 11
2. 6 is not a Strong upcard for the dealer.

Likewise, 17 vs. 7 is not a Push, because 17 is not a total from 18 to 20 or 8 to 11.

CHANCE

Any player soft or hard hand totaling 3 to 7 or 12 to 17 against any dealer upcard from 2 to 6 is a Chance hand. 2-2, 3-3, and 6-6 that you would split vs. a Weak dealer card are Chance hands. All hard and soft totals other than 10, 11, 19, 20, and 21 vs. a dealer deuce are Chance hands. A Player 7 or 17 vs. a dealer 7 is also a Chance hand. In other words, a Chance hand is a hand where your cards are weak, but so is the dealer's total. A player 17 vs. a dealer 6 is a Chance hand.

Despite all of the precise definitions above, there is a pretty easy and logical method for quickly classifying the player hands. Assuming the dealer has a 10 in the hole, and if the player needs to hit he'll draw a 10, does that player hand win, lose, or push? If both the player and dealer totals look weak, with no clear winner or loser, then it's simply a Chance. The only weird exceptions to this 10-in-the-hole/10-hit rule are that the dealer deuce is assumed stronger than the other low upcards, and a player's 7 or 17 is never considered a Winner, or even a Push. The WLPC classification system allows you to quickly make a judgment as to whether your hand is more likely to win, lose, or push. If both your hand and the dealer's upcard look weak, then you simply have a Chance.

SOME SAMPLE HANDS

A few sample hands will show you how quick and easy this WLPC system actually is. Look at the sample player hands below versus various dealer upcards and be sure you understand why each one is categorized as Winner, Loser, Push, or Chance.

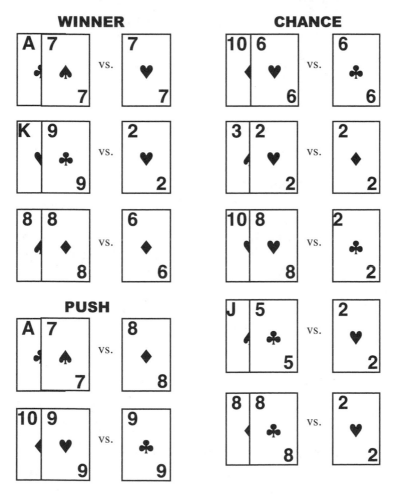

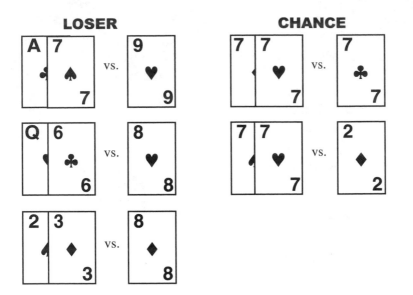

I purposely threw lots of sevens and twos into the sample hands because those are the hard ones. Once you get those down pat, the rest are a piece of cake. It shouldn't take a lot of studying for you to remember that 18 vs. 6 is a Winner. But you will have to make an effort to remember that 18 vs. 2 is just a Chance. When you can quickly classify any two-card player hand v. any dealer upcard as a Winner, Loser, Push, or Chance, you must learn how the different types of hands should be ranked according to your win potential. These rankings are pretty logical. From best to worst, the hands we'd like to hold are:

          1) Winner
          2) Push
          3) Chance
          4) Loser

The Winner and Loser classifications as first and last choice are obvious. Note that a Push is better than a Chance. That's the only hard part of this chart.

THE TWO-HAND SET RATINGS

Now the game starts to get interesting. Since you will always have two hands in play, you must be able to quickly classify both of your hands versus the dealer upcard. Then you must be able to mentally switch the top cards of each hand, and classify the two other hands you could potentially hold if you choose to switch. Here's an example:

Both hands (17 and 15 versus 8) are Losers. Consider the possible switch:

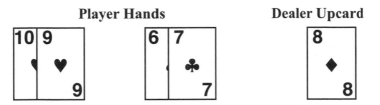

Now the hands have changed from Loser/Loser to Winner/Loser, so we make the switch. It's pretty obvious that it's better to have one Winner and one Loser than two Losers. That one was easy.

There are only nine possible two-hand combinations that we can be dealt. Based on our overall win potential, this is how we rank our two-hand totals, from best to worst:

Two-Hand Set Power Ratings

1) Winner/Winner
2) Winner/Push
3) Winner/Chance
4) Winner/Loser
5) Push/Push
6) Push/Loser
7) Chance/Chance
8) Chance/Loser
9) Loser/Loser

It may not be obvious to you that a Winner/Loser is better than a Push/Push, but mathematically a single winner in your hand is always better than no winner. Again, before you can make your switch decision, you must know what you are switching from and to, and which two-hand set is stronger.

Also note that there is no listing for a Push/Chance set. Based on our hand definitions, this combination is impossible. A push hand requires a dealer upcard from 8 to ace, while a chance hand requires a dealer upcard of 2 to 7. Those two classifications are mutually exclusive.

The best way to practice the switch decisions is to download Playtech software from any casino you are considering playing, and play the Blackjack Switch game for free until you get the hang of it.

SAMPLE HANDS

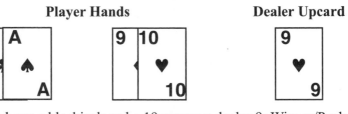

Player Hands	Dealer Upcard

You have a blackjack and a 19 versus a dealer 9: Winner/Push. If you switch, you have 10-10 and 9-A versus dealer 9: Winner/Winner. Contrary to what your intuition might tell you, you will sometimes be better off switching from a blackjack if it means turning a non-Winner—in this case a Push—into a Winner. (If blackjack paid 3 to 2, we would not switch. But with blackjacks paying even money, a blackjack is just another winner.)

Player Hands   **Dealer Upcard**

Same two hands, blackjack and 19, this time versus a dealer 10: Winner/Loser. If you switch, you have 10-10 and 9-A versus dealer 10:

Push/Push. Because Winner/Loser beats Push/Push in our power ratings, you do not switch.

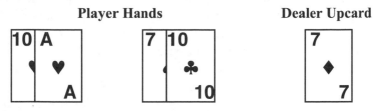

You have a blackjack and a 17 versus a dealer 7: Winner/Chance. If you switch, you have 10-10 and 7-A versus dealer 7: Winner/Winner. Again, it is better to switch from the blackjack to turn a Chance into a Winner.

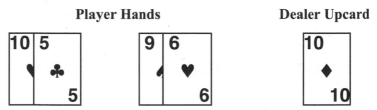

You have a 15 and a 15 versus a dealer 10: Loser/Loser. If you switch, you have 10-6 and 9-5 versus dealer 10: Loser/Loser. Same power rating. Abysmal situation. It doesn't make any difference what you do. Pray! Sometimes, even though switching might change your hand totals, it doesn't change the power rating, so we do nothing. But let's look at some exceptions to this rule.

WHEN SWITCHING DOES NOT CHANGE THE POWER RATING

The above hand brings up a good question. If our two sets of hands have the same power rating, is it always just a coin flip? No. In certain situations, one set of hands is notably better than another, even if they have identical power ratings. If you have the two losers we described above—say, two 15's versus a dealer ten—turning them into a 16 and 14 versus a dealer 10 is a waste of time. Both sets are equally bad. It makes little difference whether you switch or not. But let's look at some hand combos where we would switch despite the fact that the power ratings of both two-hand sets are identical.

SWITCHING A CHANCE/CHANCE FOR ANOTHER CHANCE/CHANCE

THE RULE: Switch if it means you can take action on a hand.

A stiff hand that you can take action on is better than a stiff that you will just stand on, all other factors being equal. This is an important concept because when you study the basic strategy for Blackjack Switch, you will see that it is different from traditional blackjack in that there are more stiffs that we hit versus dealer low cards.

Let's say you have two 13's versus a dealer 3 (Chance/Chance), and you could turn them into a 12 and 14 versus a dealer 3 (Chance/Chance). In this case, you would be better off switching. Why? Because your basic strategy with the two 13's is to stand on both hands. With a 12 and 14, your Blackjack Switch basic strategy is to stand on the 14 but *hit the 12*. Because you are turning a stiff that you would stand on into a hand that you can take action on, this 12 has a chance of becoming a strong hand. The idea is to grab that opportunity to try to improve.

WHEN TO SWITCH A LOSER/LOSER FOR ANOTHER LOSER/LOSER

THE RULE: Switch if you can turn a stiff loser into a pat loser.

If you have two stiff Losers (hands totaling 12 to 16 or 2 to 6), but you can make one stiff Loser a pat or potential pat hand (17 to 20 or 7 to 11) by switching, even though it would still be classified as a Loser, switch. Here's an example:

Player Hands	Dealer Upcard

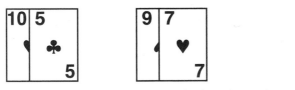

With a 15 and a 16 versus a dealer 10, we have two Losers. By switching, we'll get a 17 and a 14, still two Losers but with one hand now a pat 17. So we switch. (In actuality, a pat Loser is not always a better hand than a stiff Loser. For instance, a pat 17 vs. a dealer ace is a worse hand than a 12, 13, or 14. But whenever you switch to make a stiff Loser into a pat Loser, your switch will lower the total of the other stiff hand, and increase its chances of making a stronger total when you hit it. Plus, a total of 17 is *always* better than a 15 or 16, so the easy rule to remember when you are considering any Loser/Loser switch is that you should make the switch if it makes a stiff Loser into a pat Loser.)

WHEN TO SWITCH A WINNER/WINNER FOR ANOTHER WINNER/WINNER

THE RULE: If you can make one Winner stronger versus any Strong dealer upcard, switch.

If you have two winners of different value versus a strong dealer upcard (say a player 20 and 18 versus a dealer 7), always switch to improve the weaker winner, even if the stronger winner will get weaker.

Player Hands   Dealer Upcard

With a 20 and an 18 versus a dealer 7, you have two winners. With a switch, you'd have 19 and 19 versus 7, still two winners. Do the switch because you are improving the weaker winner versus a strong dealer upcard, even though you are weakening the stronger winner.

WHEN TO SWITCH A WINNER/CHANCE FOR ANOTHER WINNER/CHANCE

THE RULE: If you can make one Winner stronger versus any Weak dealer upcard or deuce, switch.

Let's say you have an 18 and a 14 versus a dealer 6. This set is classified as Winner/Chance. By switching, you can make yourself a 19 and 13 versus that dealer 6, still a Winner/Chance set. Do the switch in order to make that winner a stronger winner. Remember that a chance hand only wins if the dealer busts, so a 13 and 14 versus a 6 are virtually identical hands. Totals of 18 and 19, on the other hand, are not identical. Your 19 will beat more dealer hands.

SWITCHING TO OR FROM A BLACKJACK

There are also two exceptions to the rules on switching that only apply when you have a blackjack or can make one.

1. Versus any dealer upcard from 2 to 6, always keep a blackjack, or switch to make one, if possible.
2. Versus any Strong dealer upcard (7 to ace), never switch from a blackjack unless it raises the power rating of the two-hand set. Specifically, ignore the rule about making a weaker winner into a stronger winner if you must give up a blackjack to do so.

CONCLUSION

You will be surprised at how fast you'll pick up the WLPC strategy. The logic will sink in pretty quickly if you're an experienced blackjack player. There will be many hands where switching does not raise the two-hand power rating, and there is nothing you can do but pray. For example: you have a 20 and an 18 versus a dealer ace: Loser/Loser. You can make two 19's if you switch, but you'll still have two pat Losers. It really doesn't matter if you switch or not. Or, you have a 14 and a 16 versus a Dealer 5, Chance/Chance. If you switch, you can make two 15's, still Chance/Chance, with no possible action on either set of hands. All you can do is hope the dealer busts. Don't fret over hands like these. They make no significant difference in your overall result.

You will make most of your money by following the WLPC strategy to raise the power ratings of hands. When switching does not change the power rating of a two-hand set, you'll gain a small amount more by paying attention to such factors as stiff hands you can take action on versus stiff hands you cannot take action on, and the few other refinements based on the logic of the game described above. These refinements will squeeze a small percentage more from the house edge on this game.

One thing you will discover as you practice on any Internet casino's free game is that the switching decision quickly becomes automatic. Most hand sets play themselves as you will primarily be turning losers and pushes into winners.

BASIC STRATEGY FOR BLACKJACK SWITCH

The basic strategy for Blackjack Switch is the strategy you follow *after you make your switch decision.* I've boiled it down to sixteen rules. If you want to learn perfect basic strategy for Blackjack Switch, you'll find it in the Appendix. Other than a few minor pair-split decisions, it is identical to the strategy below.

HARD HIT/STAND RULES

1. Stand on all hard totals of 17 or higher.
2. Hit hard 12 to 16 vs. 7 to ace.
3. Hit hard 12 vs. 2, 3, and 4; and hit hard 13 and 14 vs. 2.
4. Stand on all other stiffs vs. 2 to 5.

SOFT HIT/STAND RULES

5. Always stand on soft 19 and 20.
6. Stand on soft 18 vs. 2 to 8, but hit vs. 9, 10, or ace.
7. Always hit soft 17 and below unless doubling.
(See soft doubling strategy below.)

HARD DOUBLING RULES

8. Double down on 10 and 11 vs. 2 through 8.
9. Double down on 9 vs. 6.

SOFT DOUBLING RULES

10. Double down on A-6 and A-7 vs. 5 and 6.
11. Double down on A-5 vs. 6 only.

PAIR-SPLIT RULES

12. Split aces vs. 2 to 10.
13. Split eights vs. 2 to 9.
14. Never split fours, fives or tens.
15. Split all other pairs—twos, threes, sixes, sevens, and nines— vs. 4, 5, or 6.
16. Also split nines vs. 8 and 9.

10. PONTOON

Pontoon is an interesting and fun eight-deck blackjack variation you'll find on the Internet. At some casinos where traditional blackjack play does not count toward meeting your wagering requirement for a bonus, pontoon is allowed. In this case, it is an excellent choice for three reasons.

1. With the standard rules, the house edge on this game when you employ correct basic strategy is very low, only 0.17%, which is significantly lower than most traditional eight-deck blackjack games. (But make sure the casino is employing the standard rules. The pontoon game available in Playtech and some RTG casinos—as of this writing—employs a non-standard set of rules which raises the house edge. The standard rules for pontoon are described below.)

2. The game software is fast.

3. The strategy is easy to learn.

On the downside (for players with small bankrolls), much of your advantage comes from very liberal double down options and 2 to 1 payoffs on special hands, so the fluctuations on the game are much higher than with traditional blackjack. If you're playing on a tight bankroll, then you may prefer a traditional blackjack game if available, even with a typical house edge of 0.5%. The fluctuations on pontoon are much less drastic, however, than the fluctuations on any form of video poker.

The name pontoon was once the common name for blackjack in Australia, but this Internet version of blackjack is not the way blackjack is played in Australia.

Pontoon is downright weird. There are lots of strange rules. The game is dealt from eight standard fifty-two-card decks, and both the player and dealer get two cards—but the dealer has no upcard. Also, the dealer wins on ties. That sounds bad, and it is, but there are lots of great rules that compensate for this.

PONTOON PAYS 2 TO 1

An ace and any 10-valued card is called a pontoon, and is an automatic win (unless the dealer also has a pontoon), paid off at 2 to 1 even after splitting. So if you split a pair of aces and catch a 10 on one or both hands, those hands pay 2 to 1. The only time player pontoon doesn't win is when the dealer also is dealt a pontoon, as a dealer pontoon beats a player pontoon because the dealer wins all ties. If the dealer is dealt a pontoon, he will immediately turn it up and collect your bet.

FIVE-CARD CHARLIE PAYS 2 TO 1

A five-card Charlie is defined as any hand that contains five cards and has not busted. The hand total does not matter. A five-card Charlie pays 2 to 1 unless the dealer gets one too, in which case you lose. But if you have a five-card 18, and the dealer has a two-card 20, you win, and you will be paid 2 to 1 on your bet. A five-card Charlie can only be beaten by an unbusted dealer hand that also contains five cards. If the dealer makes a five-card hand, he will stop taking hits regardless of his hand total, and his five-card Charlie will beat any player hand. The good thing is that the dealer only wins even money on his five-card Charlies (or on his pontoons), while you get 2 to 1.

ALL OTHER WINNING HANDS PAY EVEN MONEY

Other totals are valued just as in traditional blackjack, and if they beat the dealer hand, they are paid 1 to 1 on the bet. But again, the dealer wins all ties.

THE HIT/STAND RULES

The player *must* hit any total of 14 or less. In other words, if your hand totals 14, you must act on it—either hit, double down, or split (if two sevens). With totals of 15 or more, you may hit or stand as you please. This is another real difference from traditional blackjack, where you are allowed to stand on any total.

The dealer must hit on any total of hard 16 or soft 17 or less, and stand on totals of hard 17 or soft 18 or more.

PAIR SPLIT RULES

You may split any pair, and resplit once to three hands total. After splitting a pair, as with any other hand, you may not stand on any total under 15. But split hands are paid 2 to 1 on pontoons or five-card Charlies, just like non-split hands. (Note: This is where the pontoon game on some software differs from the standard game. With some software, if you are dealt a pontoon after splitting a pair, you will not be paid 2 to 1, but only even money if your total of 21 beats the dealer's total. This type of software pays two-card 21's after a pair split the way that traditional blackjack pays these hands—just another total of 21. If pontoons are not paid 2 to 1 after you split a pair, the house edge on the game goes up from 0.17% to 0.62%. So, before you elect to play pontoon for a bonus play, read the house rules.)

DOUBLE DOWN RULES

You may double down once on any hand, with any number of cards, including after a pair split. Note that if you double down on any four-card hand, and you do not bust, your five-card Charlie will pay 2 to 1 on your total doubled bet. Example: you have a $10 bet with a four-card total of soft 19. Since you cannot bust a soft hand, you double your bet to $20 and unless the dealer also makes a five-card Charlie, you will win $40.

Players are also allowed to hit after doubling down. If you double down on a soft 14 (A-3), and you catch a deuce for a total of soft 16, you may hit this hand, and you may hit again as many times as you like. In fact, since players may not stand on any total under 15, you will automatically hit after a double down if your total is under 15. Let's say you double down on a total of 10 and catch a 4. The dealer will automatically hit this hand again, since it is the only option allowed. Because pontoon is a fast game, this automatic hitting is sometimes disconcerting. You might double down, then immediately see multiple hits, and your hand busts. If you look at the series of cards that came down, however, you'll see that any hit cards were dealt because your hand total was under 15, and you had to take a hit.

PONTOON BASIC STRATEGY

# of Cards				# of Cards		
2	3	4		2	3	4
Player Hand				Player Hand		
18	S	S	S	A / T	S	D	D
17	S	S	H	A / 9	S	D	D
16	S	S	D	A / 8	S	D	D
15	S	S	D	A / 7	H	H	D
14	H	H	D	A / 6	H	H	D
13	H	H	D	A / 5	H	H	D
12	H	H	D	A / 4	H	H	D
11	D	D	D	A / 3	H	H	D
10	D	D	D	A / 2	H	H	
9	H	D	D				
8	H	H	D	A / A	$		
7	H	H		8-8	$		

S = Stand   H = Hit   D = Double Down $ = Split

Note: Always hit a hard total of 7 or less. Always stand on a hard total of 18 or more. A/10, A/9, etc., means any soft 21, 20, etc.

Since the dealer's cards are dealt face down, basic strategy is based entirely on your hand and the number of cards you hold. Note that with a four-card hand, you double down on all soft hands and any hard hand that does not total 17 or more. And, yes, that *is* the correct strategy.

When doubling a soft four-card hand, you cannot bust, so you are assured of making a five-card Charlie. Provided the dealer does not make a five-card Charlie, that's an automatic 4 to 1 payout on your original bet. It doesn't get any better than that.

A couple of fine points: if you double down on a three-card soft 19, and you catch an ace or a deuce to give yourself a four-card soft 20 or 21, you should definitely hit this hand, as you still cannot bust and you will make a five-card Charlie. Note that the only four-card hands that you ever stand with are hard totals of 18 or more. You even hit a four-card hard 17 and double down on a four-card hard 16! So, if after doubling on any three-card hand, your four-card hand does not yet total hard 18 or more, hit that hand again. The payoff on the five-card Charlie is worth the risk of busting.

11. VARIANCE: OUR FRIEND AND FOE

As loot-and-scoot players, you prefer to get as big an advantage as possible with the minimum variance. Professional players have the bankrolls to withstand a lot of variance and may use the variance on a game to their advantage. Variance not only provides built-in camouflage for an advantage player, but is also the reason why the high-variance sticky bonuses have value.

Variance, as the word itself implies, is coming up with any result that *varies* from your actual mathematical expectation. Let's say you're in a typical fairly low variance game, like blackjack, in a live casino (not online) with a 1% advantage from card counting. If you play a hundred sessions, you're likely to win about half the time and lose about half the time, but your wins will be slightly bigger than your losses. You might, in fact, have losing streaks that last for quite a few sessions, and you may even finish the whole hundred sessions well under or well over your expected result of 1%. In the long run, however, you'll get pretty close to a 1% profit on your action.

In a high variance game, like video poker, you might lose on 80% or more of your 100 sessions even with a 1% advantage over the house based on perfect play with a cash-back bonus. You will have winning sessions only when you hit the bigger payout hands, like straight flushes and four of a kind. And unless you hit a royal flush once every 40,000 hands or so, you may be well below our 1% expectation on this game for quite some time.

WHAT CAUSES VARIANCE?

Generally, if a game has mostly even-money payouts, like blackjack, the variance is low. The more your result is based on big payouts that occur on very few hands—as in video poker—the higher the variance. Blackjack Switch has an even lower variance than regular blackjack because there are more even money payouts. In Blackjack Switch, blackjacks pay even money, and there are fewer double downs and pair-split plays. Also, you'll often win one hand and lose one, because you so often switch your top cards to make one strong hand, while weakening the other hand.

Pontoon, on the other hand, has higher variance than blackjack, though the variance on pontoon is still much lower than the variance on video poker. The casino games with the lowest variance of all are baccarat and craps, because all of the payouts are even money payouts, assuming that you never place the tie bet at baccarat or any of the field bets at craps. (Note: taking the odds at craps lowers the overall house edge on the game because the odds bets themselves have no house advantage. But at the same time, taking the odds raises the variance on the game, because the odds bets do not have even money payouts.) Very few online casinos, however, allow baccarat or craps play for bonuses.

As a loot-and-scoot player, that's about all you need to know about variance. You're going for big percentage advantages, with high dollar returns for the amount of action you'll put in on any given bonus. On the non-sticky (cashable) plays, you should profit on 75% to 85% of your plays, because even when you lose, you will often collect more from the bonus than you lost.

But you've got to watch out for the high-variance games, even when the house edge is small for the wagering requirement and you're getting a good return in both dollars and percentage from the bonus play. Variance is a killer for a small bankroll. Professional players may spend as much time figuring out risk-averse betting strategies as they will figuring out ways to beat the games. As an amateur, protect yourself by sticking to the low variance games at all times.

12. VIDEO POKER AND OTHER GAMES

If a Web casino disallows blackjack, pontoon, and Blackjack Switch for meeting your wagering requirement, my advice to most loot-and-scoot players is to skip the offer and find another casino. The only other online casino game that is typically allowed for meeting the wagering requirement and that has a house advantage low enough to interest most new players on a tight bankroll is video poker. If you have a bankroll of $5,000 or more—and especially if you are already a knowledgeable video poker player—you may be interested in going after some of the better bonus offers that restrict blackjack play but allow video poker.

THE BASICS OF VIDEO POKER

If you are familiar with video poker as offered in live casinos, you'll find the Internet casino versions of the game just about identical—the main difference being that you'll use your mouse to press the buttons for betting, dealing, holding, and drawing cards. If you are not familiar with casino video poker, here's a quick and dirty primer on the game.

HOW TO PLAY VIDEO POKER

Technically, video poker is not a traditional poker game in any sense. You do not play your hand against any other player's hand, so it is a form of poker without an opponent. You win at video poker simply by making five-card hands that pay roughly according to the traditional ranking of poker hands. The amount you are paid on your wins is based on the size of your bet and the ranking of the hand you make.

Video poker is a highly simplified draw poker game. You are dealt five cards, with an option to discard any number of them from one card to all, in order to draw new cards in an attempt to make a poker hand that pays.

The typical poker hand rankings are used, but it is unlike a normal poker game because the rankings are very broad. In one common form of video poker, called jacks or better, the minimum paying hand is a pair of jacks. A pair of tens pays nothing. But unlike traditional poker, a pair of aces is worth the same as a pair of jacks. Likewise, if you make two pair, it does not matter which two pair you make. Twos and threes pay the same as kings and aces. This same broad payout structure is used for all paying hands. Three of a kinds all pay alike. Any straight pays the same as any other straight, etc.

So, don't confuse video poker with any traditional form of poker. It's simply an electronic card game where the hand rankings are loosely based on traditional poker rankings.

All forms of video poker accept one to five "coins" for the bet on each hand. If you do not play five coins, the royal flush payout is usually substantially underpaid, so the only intelligent way to play is with maximum coins. Internet games typically accept 5-cent, 10-cent, 25-cent, 50-cent, $1, and $5 coins. After you select your coin value, you hit the "Bet Max" button, and five cards appear face up. You may then use your mouse to point and click on the cards you want to keep, hit the "Draw" button, and the cards not held will be replaced with new cards. If your five-card hand is a winner, your account will be credited with the amount won.

That's the entire game in a nutshell.

For loot-and-scoot players, I'm going to cover only the most common and popular form of video poker, jacks or better. The house advantage on this game, assuming a full-pay payout schedule, is similar to the house advantage on a blackjack shoe game, about 0.5%. There are many other forms of video poker that you'll find on the Internet and in live casinos, some of which even offer a tiny player advantage (a few hundredths of a percent) with perfect play. Unfortunately, these games are not common online, and when they are available, they often have less than standard payouts that increase the house advantage significantly. More importantly from the loot-and-scoot player's perspective, they are even more volatile than jacks or better. Players with limited funds should avoid these games even when the full-pay versions are available.

So, if you are a video poker nut, and you already know all of this stuff—including the strategies for playing the various games—then make your decision on whether to play based on the bonus value and your bankroll.

With video poker you can usually play for very low stakes, 5 cents or 10 cents, and you can often find software that will play multiple hands, even as many as 50 hands simultaneously. With these programs you are dealt multiple hands with identical cards. You then make your hold decisions, and all hands will hold those cards. Each of the hands is then dealt new cards, with each hand dealt from a separate deck.

On a short bank, you will have much less variance on a multiple-line game than you would with a single-line game. Your speed of play on a ten-line 5-cent game will be similar to a single-line 50-cent game, but you will smooth out the fluctuations dramatically with the ten-line game—because you will have many more chances to hit some of the higher paying hands.

THE HOUSE ADVANTAGE AT JACKS OR BETTER

Just about every Internet casino that offers video poker games offers jacks or better, so if you can't play a blackjack variation for the wagering requirement, see if the casino offers a jacks or better video poker game with a full-pay pay table. For video poker games, we estimate the house advantage by looking at the pay table for the game. Each game has a pay table that is considered full pay, and any variations from the standard full-pay chart make the game a **short pay** game. We have no interest in a short pay game, as the house advantage is generally much higher on these games.

The pay table is a chart that displays the payouts for the various hands. Again, in most cases, you must play five coins in order to get the full payout on a royal flush. So, on a 5-cent machine, you will bet 25 cents per hand, and on a 25-cent machine, you will bet $1.25 per hand. This is the jacks or better pay table you are looking for:

FULL-PAY JACKS OR BETTER PAY TABLE

	One Coin	Five Coins
Royal Flush	800	4000
Straight Flush	50	250
Four of a Kind	25	125
Full House	9	45
Flush	6	30
Straight	4	20
Three of a Kind	3	15
Two Pair	2	10
One Pair, Jacks or Better	1	5

Do not play jacks or better with any other pay table. If the one-coin pay table is not full pay (the one above is), but the five-coin pay table is full pay, then only play the game with five coins per bet.

Be especially careful to read all of the payouts before you play. A typical short-pay jacks or better game will pay only eight coins for a full house, and five coins for a flush, instead of nine coins and six coins for each of these hands respectively. This short-pay pay table gives the house almost a 3% advantage, which is unacceptable for most loot-and-scoot players.

A common trick online casinos use to confuse players about a pay table's value is to increase the payouts on one or more rare hands, while decreasing the payouts on more common hands. Don't be fooled. If a jacks or better pay table is not identical to the pay table above, forget about it. I've never seen an altered pay table that doesn't screw the player and increase the house advantage.

DOUBLE OR NOTHING

Many Internet casino video poker games give the player the option to play double or nothing on any win. That is, if you hit, say, three of a kind with five coins in for a fifteen-coin payout, you have the option to try to double your win to thirty coins by picking a card—one out of four—against the dealer's card. If your card beats the dealer's card, you may continue to play double or nothing on the thirty-coin win, and again on the sixty-coin win, etc., until you are satisfied, you lose it all, or you run into the house's doubling maximum.

This feature is available on video poker games at most online casinos (though not on all games at these casinos). These bets may or may not count toward the wagering requirement—depending on the software and the casino. The terms and conditions rarely state this. There is no house advantage on a double bet. It's like flipping a coin, but it increases the variance on the game.

THE JACKS OR BETTER STRATEGY

The strategies for playing video poker are more complicated than the strategies for blackjack. A comprehensive jacks or better strategy covering every possible five-card combination of cards you might be dealt is complex, difficult to use, and even more difficult to memorize. Luckily, you can get almost all of the value simply from playing correctly on the most important hands. If you use the comprehensive jacks or better strategy, the house advantage over you is just slightly less than 0.5%. With the simplified strategy below, the house advantage over you is just slightly more than 0.5%. This simplified strategy works well and makes playing fast and easy. Fast, highly-accurate play is more important to your overall profits on bonus plays than perfect strategy to the last hundredth of a percent. The hands in this chart are in order of value, from the most valuable to the least valuable.

THE LOOT & SCOOT JACKS OR BETTER STRATEGY

Hand	Draw
1. Royal Flush, Straight Flush, or 4-of-a-Kind	0
2. Four Cards to a Royal Flush	1
3. Full House, Flush, or Straight	0
4. Three of a Kind	2
5. Four Cards to a Straight Flush (Open-ended)	1
6. Two Pair	1
7. Four Cards to a Straight Flush (Inside)	1
8. Pair Jacks or Better	3
9. Three Cards to a Royal Flush	2
10. Four Cards to a Flush	1
11. 10-J-Q-K	1
12. Pair Tens or Lower	3
13. Four Cards to a Straight (Open-ended)	1
14. Two Suited High Cards	3
15. A-K-Q-J	1
16. Three Cards to a Straight Flush	2
17. J-Q-K	2
18. Two Unsuited High Cards	3
19. Suited 10-J, 10-Q, or 10-K	3
20. One High Card	4
21. Any Other Hand (All Low Cards)	5

HOW TO USE THE CHART

In using the chart, you always want to keep the most valuable hand, so if you have two possibilities, look at how the hands are ranked and keep the hand with the higher ranking.

For example, let's say the initial five-card hand that is dealt consists of a pair of jacks, a pair of queens, and a king. And let's say that one of the jacks, one of the queens, and the king are all spades. Do you throw away the non-spade jack and queen and draw to the three-card royal flush, which has an 800 for 1 payout, or do you keep the two pair, which pays out only 2 for 1? You find the answer by looking in the chart. We see that two pair (ranked at #6) is higher on the chart than three cards to a royal flush (ranked at #9), so we keep the two pair and only draw one card, hoping to hit a full house.

Note that "High Card" always means a jack or higher, and "Low Card" always means a ten or lower. One immediate thing you should note in this chart is that if you have a paying hand already made (a pair of jacks or better), the only non-paying hands that would ever cause you to throw away the paying hand are four cards to a royal flush or four cards to a straight flush. So, if you have a paying hand, unless you have four cards to a royal or straight flush, you don't even have to bother looking at the chart. Keep the paying hand.

One other thing you might notice is that you never keep a **kicker**, a side card to a pair or three of a kind. In a regular live draw poker game, you might sometimes be correct to keep an ace kicker if you have a pair. This is *never* correct in video poker. If you have a pair, you should hold the pair and draw three cards to it trying for a three of a kind or better. There are various strategic reasons why holding an ace kicker is correct in a live poker game. One big reason is that if you draw another ace that pairs your kicker, having two pair with the top pair being aces is a very powerful hand. In video poker, as already noted, any two pair hand pays the same. You may as well keep a deuce as an ace, since the probability of pairing any card is identical and has the same payout. Holding a kicker is a common error that poker players make when they first start playing video poker.

Note that there is no entry for three unsuited high cards, other than J-Q-K (ranked at #17), yet there is an entry for two unsuited high cards (ranked at #18). That's because you should never hold three unsuited high cards if they are not J-Q-K. Any other three would contain an ace, in which case you should throw away the ace, and keep the other two. That's because the other high cards are not only more likely to make a straight, but also have more chances to turn into a pair.

In addition to the above, here are a few other quick tips to remember so that you do not need to consult the chart so often:.

1) If you have one or two high cards (J, Q, K, or A) in your hand, and no other made or potential hand of value (no pair, and no three cards to a possible straight or flush), just keep the high cards and throw away the others.

2) If you have three high cards and no pair, and two of the high cards are suited, throw away the non-suited high card and draw to the two suited cards. Obviously, that's because they have a slim possibility of turning into a royal flush, but you also keep the flush possibility alive.

3) Always draw to a small pair unless you have four cards to a flush or three cards to a royal flush, in which cases you would draw to the flush or royal. Even with four cards to an open-end straight, keep the small pair.

4) Always draw to a high pair, even when you have four cards to a straight or flush. A high pair means a payout, and in video poker, a bird in the hand is almost always worth more than two in the bush.

5) If you have no high cards, no open-end straight draw, and no four to a flush, don't grasp at straws. Bite the bullet and throw all five of your cards away so that you can draw a completely new hand.

6) If you have four to a royal flush, always draw to the royal, unless it means breaking a straight flush. That is, if you have a 9-10-J-Q-K suited, keep it. But if you have 8-10-J-Q-K suited, throw away the 8, even though you are throwing away a made flush hand. It's hard to throw away a made flush, but if you're this close to a royal, you've got to go for it. (In this case, you've got 6 birds in the hand, but 800 in the bush!)

Finally, if you are playing bonuses at a high level, and you have the bankroll to take on the games with more variance than jacks or better—like deuces wild, joker poker, double bonus poker, and many other variations—you will find strong, simple strategies for them at BlackjackForumOnline.com.

GAMES OTHER THAN VIDEO POKER

As loot-and-scoot players, no games other than blackjack, blackjack switch, pontoon, or jacks or better video poker interest us. The house advantage and/or variance on most other games is too high for consideration for any but professional players. If craps, baccarat, or single-0 roulette are allowed for the wagering requirement, we might find opportunities for exploiting bonuses on these games, but they are rarely allowed.

All casinos allow slot play for meeting your wagering requirement, but all slots have even higher variance than video poker. Even if a casino claims that a certain machine returns 99.5% to the players, which would translate to a 0.5% house advantage—the same as blackjack or jacks or better video poker—the variance on slots is through the roof, making slots unplayable for most loot-and-scoot plays.

Other games typically allowed toward the wagering requirement are games professionals call the **carny games**, because of the high house edge. Some of the more popular carny games, with their house advantages, are:

Three-Card Poker (pair plus bet only)	2.32%
Let It Ride (with best strategy)	3.51%
Caribbean Stud Poker (with best strategy)	5.22%
Red Dog (single-deck, with best strategy)	3.20%

You might note that I quote the house advantage for three-card poker as the house advantage on the pair plus bet only. That's because the ante/play option has a 3.37% house edge, so we would never place that bet if we were to play three-card poker. But compared to the games with house advantages of under 1%, all of these games are unacceptable for loot-and-scoot players.

In the Appendix of this book, you will find a chart with the house advantage for just about all of the games available in any online casinos. You can find strategies and other information on these and other online games at BlackjackForumOnline.com.

13. CAMOUFLAGE

Card counters in live casino games must constantly employ camouflage techniques to appear to be regular gamblers to the casino personnel. They may act drunk or disinterested in the game, or they may misplay hands or make bad bets. The sole purpose of camouflage is to convince the casino personnel that they are not counters, just gamblers, and therefore should be allowed to continue playing.

Camouflage, however, often has a cost. Misplaying hands and making bad bets takes a chunk out of a card counter's win expectation. The smartest counters understand the cost of their poor plays, and they make these plays only when they deem it absolutely necessary.

You can't count cards in online casinos, but as bonus players you still must employ some camouflage if you want to keep the welcome mat out. Online casinos are well aware that there are players who are making money by exploiting bonuses, and—just like casinos in Las Vegas—they will bar such players from further play if they detect them. Some disreputable online casinos have even confiscated winnings from players they believe to be bonus hustlers.

In many ways, online casinos are similar to those in Vegas in that they cannot worry too much about a handful of players that may be trying to squeeze $50 or even a couple of hundred out of them when they have thousands of regular customers every day losing hundreds and even thousands of dollars. But just like live casinos, they are afraid of any players that reduce their overall profits, so they are always on the lookout for the signs of the bonus hustler.

In order to understand how to camouflage bonus plays, you need to know what a bonus hustler looks like to online casinos. The bonus hustler tends to do things that distinguish him from most recreational and compulsive gamblers that the casinos want as customers.

The bonus hustler typically buys in for the exact amount necessary to collect the bonus offered, immediately plays the exact amount of the wagering requirement, then immediately cashes out. He often goes through this entire process on the same day, and often within the same one-hour or two-hour time period.

To the casino, this type of player looks less like a regular gambler than like a wise guy trying to pick up free money. Some players who are in fact recreational gamblers do this in order to test a casino. They want to be sure that if they deposit money and win, they will be paid with no glitches. So the casino can't really be sure right away, even if they are suspicious that a player may be taking them for a ride. The player played by the rules, wagered the amount they stated was required, and did nothing unethical or fraudulent.

But if that player returns only when another bonus is offered, and proceeds to follow the same pattern as on his first play, he may find himself cut off from future bonus offers from this casino or property group. The casinos will take only so much of what they believe may be intelligence before they throw in the towel.

As a bonus hustler you would like to keep the welcome mat out so that you can take advantage of follow-up bonuses when they come along. Therefore you should go out of your way to look different from the standard bonus hustler. So far, in this book, I have been describing the strategies you use to extract the maximum dollar amount from any bonus offer that we can afford to play. Now, I'm going to advise you to give a small amount back. It can be more profitable over the long run to appear more like a regular customer, not the hit-and-run profiteer that you are!

CAMO TIPS FOR THE LOOT-AND-SCOOT PROFITEER

1) In meeting your wagering requirement, it's better to extend your play over a number of play sessions over the course of several days. You want to look like a customer who deposited his money, then came in to play several times.

2) If you have the bankroll, it is better to go for bigger wins than the bonus value itself. Bill Haywood suggested that a player who attempts to either double his deposit or lose half of it with aggressive betting would be pretty indistinguishable from a regular gambler. That is still true.

3) Continue playing a small amount even after you have met your wagering requirement and earned your bonus. If you play only the required number of hands, then immediately make a request to withdraw all of your funds, you may get tagged as a bonus hustler. A good rule of thumb is to give a small percentage of action over the wagering requirement— ten to fifteen percent, maybe more if you've had a really big win, just as you would leave a tip for a waiter after good service in a restaurant.

4) Vary your bet size. Instead of flat-betting $5, spread your bets from $2 to $10 using a progressive betting scheme. That is, increase your bet after a win, and decrease after a loss. These types of betting schemes will slightly increase the variance on a game, but will have no effect on the house advantage or your expectation in dollars or percent from your bonus plays. This is a common way gamblers bet.

5) Mix up your game play. If both blackjack and video poker are eligible for meeting your wagering requirement, play some of each. If slots are allowed, play a small amount in the casino's slot machines occasionally as well. You want to look like a gambler. Concentrate most of your play on blackjack, but put some time and money into a few of the other allowed games.

6) After earning your bonus and giving them a little extra action, wait another day or two before requesting a withdrawal.

7) When you make this first withdrawal, leave a small amount of money in your account and come back to play on it a day or two later. After all, you want to appear to be one of their "regular" players now.

8) Watch your email for a follow-up bonus offer.

A few things you must be careful about:
1) Never play sign-up bonuses in two casinos that belong to the same property group in the same month. Give the first casino at least a follow-up play or two before you move to a second in the group.

2) If you are mixing up the games you play, be absolutely certain that you do not play any game that is not eligible for the wagering requirement. Many casinos will completely void your bonus and all winnings if you play an unauthorized game while you are on a bonus play.

3) If you are extending a bonus play over a number of days or weeks, make certain that you don't go beyond any time limit or deadline by which you must finish the bonus play. Any time limitations will be stated in the casino's terms and conditions.

4) As with card counting in live casinos, losing is the best camouflage. You do not have to give anything extra when you lose. Take what's left of your money and get out. You will likely get a follow-up bonus offer.

5) When you get a follow-up offer, don't necessarily take it immediately. Often, if you wait a week or two, the offer will get better.

14. DO ONLINE CASINOS CHEAT?

Technically, no.

It's impossible for a casino, or a player for that matter, to cheat at a game unless there is a law defining exactly what constitutes cheating. This is true in live casino games as well as on the Internet.

In 1997, for example, the state of Arizona legalized "social gambling" in bars and nightclubs. This made it legal for customers of these establishments to play poker, blackjack, craps, and other gambling games, provided the house did not bank the games, and the players used their own cards and dice and agreed to the rules among themselves.

The night spots in Phoenix and Tucson were soon overrun with cheaters of every stripe. Marked cards, loaded dice, and every other type of scam was being employed. It didn't take long for the local cops to figure out what was going on, but they couldn't stop it. Arizona had no laws regarding gaming regulations or equipment, so technically everything was legal. The scams continued until the state legislature passed another law revoking the first law.

In 1994, a customer of an Indian reservation casino in California suspected that he was being cheated via marked cards. He got hold of one of the tribe's decks and had an expert ascertain that the cards were indeed marked. A later investigation conducted by the tribe itself discovered that all of the decks of cards in their stockroom were similarly marked. These were their house cards, with their logo, used on all of their card games, still in sealed boxes.

Unfortunately, the player was unable to recover any of the money he had lost in the scam because California had no laws regulating casino games at that time, and the Indian tribe had no regulation requiring them to return money to a player who was cheated.

Both Arizona and California now have state gaming control agencies that oversee the casino games in their respective states. The point is that such regulations do not exist for most online casinos. There is no international governing body that defines the games, oversees the games, or has any authority to take legal action against cheaters.

There is some local regulation, in that online casinos usually must be licensed in the countries where they are physically located. Online casinos located in Australia, for example, are probably among the safest anywhere, as they are regulated by the same gaming control agency that regulates Australia's land casinos. In fact, many of the Australian online casinos are run by the same companies that own the casinos on land. I trust the Australian online casinos to be using honest software and to be among the least likely to try and disappear with any customer's deposit or winnings.

But most online casinos are located in small countries, often on islands—Antigua, Belize, Cyprus, Costa Rica, Gibraltar, Curaçao, etc.—and these countries are eager for online casinos that will pay taxes and license fees. Do these little island countries have regulations defining the electronic card games to be honestly and randomly dealt? And if so, do they have a viable method of testing the casinos' software to verify that it performs as required?

Another problem is that some online casinos have claimed to be licensed in various jurisdictions, even when no such license ever existed! They operate in cyberspace like pirates, collecting money, then disappearing just as fast as they appeared.

Is there any way we can know for sure that any particular online casino is honest?

Cheating can be proven by statistical evidence. By simply recording and analyzing the data on all hands played and all results—including percentage of wins and losses, percentage of player blackjacks versus dealer blackjacks, and percentage of video poker hands resulting in jacks or better, three of a kind, etc.—players can determine whether the results lie within the realm of probability. Unfortunately, this is a tedious chore.

And, unfortunately, if you are cheated in an Internet casino, you will never get your money back. That is the simple reality you must accept. There is no practical way for you to sue a company located in Bali or Costa Rica for $400, especially when this country may not even have laws defining the casino's unethical practices as illegal.

Some online casinos post notices that they are audited by Price Waterhouse. This may be true, but that in itself guarantees nothing about the fairness of the games. Often, all that Price Waterhouse certifies is that the payout percentages are what the casino claims. Other casinos post guarantees that their games are dealt randomly, but the guarantees do not usually specify that the games use standard 52-card decks!

Lots of Internet casino associations, commissions and councils put their stamp of approval on certain online casinos' games. The certifications of these dorky organizations mean even less to me than the certification by Price Waterhouse. If you look at the requirements for certification by these agencies —and you can look up this stuff on the Internet—they typically specify that the casinos that earn their approval must be adequately funded to pay winning customers promptly. They may also require their approved casinos to live up to any claims in their advertisements or any offers they make. But I have yet to see one of these agencies require their approved casinos to deal games randomly from complete decks.

The best protection against being cheated, as explained earlier, is to follow the advice of the reputable watchdog sites that report on which casino software is regarded as fair, and which is not, as well as which casinos are paying and which are not—based on actual player reports. At BlackjackForumOnline, we monitor play and hand data collected by a large number of professional gamblers who have put millions of dollars in action through just about every casino on the Internet. These players make a living by making sure they know which casinos are honest, and which are not.

And yes, our site monitors have been cheated at some online casinos. I have been cheated myself in two online casinos. They were new casinos with great bonus offers, and I convinced myself that the fantastic bonuses were being offered simply because the casinos were new and were trying to attract customers through aggressive marketing. The watchdog sites had no information on these casinos yet. I took a chance and regretted it. Lesson learned. You will find detailed reports on cheating incidents at Internet casinos in the online library at BlackjackForumOnline. We take this stuff very seriously.

15. ODDS & ENDS

Let's cover a few odd items I haven't mentioned yet...

1) One thing that will anger an Internet casino more than anything else is if you try to play under more than one name. Generally, a player might attempt this in order to get another sign-up bonus. Not a good idea. It's much easier to play anonymously or with a fake ID in Las Vegas than it is on the Internet. You must provide Neteller with a real bank account and a real name and address in order to set up an account with them. You can't fake this. Don't try.

2) You might want to contact the casino for help to ask about a withdrawal, find out how a game is played, get help with the software, or find out what the terms and conditions are if they are not clear to you. Most casinos have toll-free phone numbers you can call to talk to customer service—a real plus. I also really like casinos that have an online chat feature. There is also the email option. You can access this contact info at their website. Don't be shy about asking if you are confused about anything. I have generally found the Internet casino support personnel to be helpful.

3) I have mostly avoided discussing specific online casinos, watchdog sites and even software brands in much detail because the Internet changes so fast. With that in mind, below are a few comments on some of the most common software options. Check with Blackjack Forum Online for the most current information on these and other online casino software options.

MICROGAMING SOFTWARE

Microgaming has upgraded to new software called Viper, which is very fast and has a great selection of games. One special feature of Viper is that it will tell you the correct basic strategy play when you are on a video poker game, which really speeds up play. They have a variety of video poker games, and on most of them they offer multi-hand play. All the games have the double-up feature.

For blackjack players they offer many choices, from Atlantic City eight-deck rules to Downtown Vegas double-deck, to classic single-deck. They also offer a feature called **Playcheck**, which allows you to view every transaction, including each hand or play, in detail. This feature goes a long way toward convincing knowledgeable players that the software is dealing fair games. Some Microgaming casinos offer **auto-play** and **auto-hold**.

Auto-play lets you tell the machine to play 100 hands, or 50, or 27—whatever you want—automatically, with either the preprogrammed basic strategy or any strategy you input. Be sure to check the preprogrammed strategy before you set the game on auto-play, as in the past it has had minor mistakes. You can also use the feature on video poker and it will play the hands for you, and play them perfectly.

Auto-hold means the video poker games will tell you the correct cards to hold.

PLAYTECH SOFTWARE

Playtech is another excellent type of software, with good graphics and good games. The software is slow on some 56K modems, especially the Blackjack Switch game. For blackjack players they offer multi-player blackjack, which means you can chat with other players at your table or play with friends at the same table. Of course, you can also play alone, if you prefer that, which I do. They also offer live dealer games, with an Internet cam showing a dealer chained to a table somewhere actually dealing cards out of a shoe. You can chat with the dealer while playing. Playtech casinos tend to be generous with bonuses. As of this writing, Europa has a $2,400 sign-up bonus, divided into twelve $200 chunks available monthly. Golden Palace has a sign-up offer of a $300 bonus for a $100 deposit, and follows up with excellent bonus offers every month.

Unfortunately, most Playtech casinos use sticky bonuses. These casinos also take slightly longer to cash you out. The first time you withdraw, expect them to ask you to send copies of documents like a driver's license and utility bill. And once they have received those documents, cash outs may take another four or five days.

CRYPTOLOGIC SOFTWARE

Cryptologic has been on the Internet since 1996. They were the first to offer multi-player games where you can play with friends. They offer a variety of blackjack games, including VIP single deck and many full-pay video poker variations from single hand play to ten-play. Cryptologic software is starting to show its age. Some people have problems with it if they are not using Windows XP, and sometimes there are problems with Windows XP. The software company is aware of this and is upgrading, so you may well never have any problems. A more annoying drawback with Cryptologic is their personal identification number (PIN) system. When you register an account they send you a PIN via snail mail. You need that number in order to make a cashout. They also nick you for a buck every time you make a withdrawal.

RTG (REAL TIME GAMING) SOFTWARE

RTG casinos had a bad reputation for non-payment for some time, but the software itself is excellent. The company has more recently been requiring its casinos to clean up their acts. Still, it pays to be extra careful when selecting which RTG casinos to play.

RTG software is very fast and easy to use, and it offers a large selection of blackjack games. In addition to regular blackjack they may offer Double Exposure, Spanish 21, pontoon, and Super Fun 21. For video poker players, there are over a dozen games to choose from.

There is an important fact to be aware of at all RTG casinos. Each owner can set the payouts on every slot machine and video poker game. They have three settings: tight, medium, and loose. For example, the tight setting for jacks or better is payouts of 6 for 1 and 5 for 1 on full houses and flushes respectively, the medium is 8 for 1 and 5 for 1 on these hands, and the loose is the traditional full-pay 9 for 1 and 6 for 1.

At some RTG casinos you may find that the 5-cent jacks or better is a tight 6/5 game, the 25-cent is a medium 8/5 game, and only the $1 is the loose 9/6 game. Not only that, but you may be used to playing the loose $1 game (9/6) at a given casino, only to log in one day and find that it has changed to a medium 8/5 game. RTG is the only software I know of where the video poker payoffs can change on your machine at home from one day to the next. There is a tip-off to this. If you log in and you get a pop-up that says, "Downloading New Lobby," it may mean they have changed the payoffs on video poker. So, always be sure to check the pay tables before you play any video poker at an RTG casino.

BROWSER-BASED SOFTWARE

Some of you may use a Mac or have a dial-up account that makes downloading big files of casino software a pain. With browser-based casinos you don't have to download any software. You just play online. These games will tend to play more slowly than games you download. Because these browser-based software programs are often proprietary to the Internet casino or property group, many smart players avoid these types of games. But they're not all dangerous.

OTHER PROPRIETARY SOFTWARE

Experienced players have encountered cheating at a number of casinos that use proprietary software, or lesser-known brands. But some of this software is reputable. For example, Lasseters and Aus Vegas both use proprietary software, but they are licensed and regulated by the government of Australia, and they are as reputable as you can get. They have frequent bonuses and a sterling reputation. Follow-up bonuses for regular customers have included a 100% match bonus of up to $1,000 for high-stakes players, or 100% up to $150 for those who play at lower stakes. Aus Vegas is currently offering a welcome bonus of 100% up to $100.

Unfortunately, the first time you cash out from either of these casinos, they must mail you a check. It then takes thirty or forty days for them to verify that you deposited the check in a bank account. Once that is done you can withdraw via Neteller. In my opinion, the account is worth the initial set-up hassle.

ONLINE CASINOS BY PROPERTY GROUP

Finally, here are some of the current property group affiliations and available bonuses. This is to give you an idea of how many good places we've found.

FORTUNE LOUNGE GROUP

7 Sultans Casino
Microgaming Viper
$100 bonus

Desert Dollar
150% plus $10

Fortune Lounge
Microgaming Viper
Up to $2120 Free!

Fortune Room
Microgaming Viper
Up to $750 free!

Vegas Palms
Microgaming Viper
$250 bonus

Vegas Towers
Microgaming Viper
$50 bonus
No wagering requirement

Vegas Villa
Microgaming Viper
$310 free

WAGERSHARE GROUP

Ruby Fortune Casino
Microgaming Viper
125% to $100 bonus

Spin Palace Casino
Microgaming Viper
100% to $75 bonus

VEGAS PARTNERS LOUNGE GROUP

777 Dragon
Microgaming Viper
Play online blackjack at 777 Dragon Casino

Arthurian Casino
15% to $1500 monthly

Casino US
Choose your bonus

Cinema Casino
250% sign-up bonus
Or 15% to $3000

Crazy Vegas
Microgaming Viper

Maple Casino
Microgaming Viper
150% sign-up bonus
+ $3000 every month

Sun Vegas Casino
Microgaming Viper

CASINO PROFIT SHARE GROUP
Music Hall Casino
100% to $150
Up to $500 total

Challenge Casino
Microgaming Viper
100% to $100
To $1,000 total

Golden Reef
100% to $100

Aztec Riches
100% to $100
Up to $850 total

UK Casino Club
100% to $125
Microgaming Viper

ADRICHES GROUP

Phoenician Casino
Microgaming Viper
50% match up to $100!

Nostalgia Casino
Microgaming Viper
50% match up to $100!
Instant Payments on your winnings

VEGAS AFFILIATES GROUP

Coliseum Casino
Microgaming Viper
$135 welcome bonus
(No BJ/VP on bonus)

Grand Hotel
Microgaming Viper
$132 welcome bonus
(No BJ/VP on bonus)

Vegas 7 Casino
Microgaming Viper
150% to $75
(No BJ/VP on bonus)

Vegas Joker Casino
Microgaming Viper
$100 welcome bonus
(No BJ/VP on bonus)

Vegas Country
Microgaming Viper
100% to $75
(No BJ/VP on bonus)

Royal Plaza
Loyalty bonuses

Vegas Slot Casino
Microgaming Viper
100% to $100
(No BJ/VP on bonus)

32RED GROUP
32Red Casino
32% to $320
+ $32/month match
Fast unlimited payouts

GOLDEN PALACE GROUP
Golden Palace
200% to $200

Flamingo Casino
200% to $200

Aspinalls Casino
200% to $200
Grand online
$200 to $200

24kt Gold Casino
200% to $200

TROPEZ GROUP
Casino Tropez
$300 welcome bonus

Casino Del Rio
$600 welcome bonus

VegasRed Casino
$888 welcome bonus

Casino Europa
Up to $2400

LAS VEGAS USA GROUP
Las Vegas USA
100% to $100
Or 25% to $500

PEAK ENTERTAINMENT GROUP
Sands of the Caribbean
100% to $50

Omni Casino
$100 welcome bonus

49er online Casino
10% back on losses

PARTNERLOGIC GROUP
VIP Casino
100% up to $90

Intercasino
100% to $90 every month

OTHER SOFTWARE
Casino-On-Net
100% bonus to $200
Proprietary Software

Inetbet Casino
30% bonus up to $150
RTG Software

Bodog Casino
RTG Software
Sportsbook/Poker too

Lasseters Casino
100% to $100
Up to $480 total
Australia License
Proprietary Software

Aus Vegas Casino
100% to $100
Australia License
Proprietary Software

AFFILIATE LOUNGE GROUP
Cherry Casino
Dep. $100 get $30
Proprietary Software
No Download

Casino Domain
Dep. $100 get $30
Proprietary Software
No Download

Speedbet Casino
Dep. $100 get $30
Proprietary Software
No Download

PART II

Making Money in Internet Poker Rooms

1. INTRODUCTION

The perspective on poker provided in this book is different from the perspectives of most books. None of the books I've read discuss online poker room bonus money opportunities in any detail. None describe how you should evaluate or choose an online tournament when you have virtually thousands of buy-in and blind structures to choose from. The Internet has created a world of poker opportunities that never existed before. So I'm going to focus on how you can exploit values and opportunities that exist in online poker rooms that never existed in traditional live casino poker rooms.

Making money in the Internet poker rooms is not as cut and dried as making money in the Internet casino games. There is a lot of psychological strategy in poker, even in an Internet poker room where you cannot actually see your opponents to look for "tells." A **tell** is any mannerism, posture, movement, facial expression, or even a sound that a player involved in a hand might make that could indicate to an opponent whether his hand is strong or weak. In live poker games, the ability to "get a read" on an opponent by observing him is a big part of the game.

This entire facet of the game—making judgments about players based on physical signs they exhibit during hands—does not exist in the online game where you cannot see or hear your opponents. But this does not mean that the psychology of the game is removed, or that the game becomes nothing more than an exercise in math. Even without physical tells, there are still complex psychological and strategic factors based on things like seat position, chip position, your knowledge of a player's prior history of bluffing, overbetting, aggression and/or passivity, your own table image, and so on.

I will teach you how to think about the low-limit Internet games and small buy-in Internet tournaments that you are more likely to be playing. I want to show you how to beat a lot of the truly bad players that are playing online, and how to recognize and be cautious of the good players. But don't expect this book to make you into a poker pro. Poker is a complex game and my coverage will be limited to some of the idiosyncrasies of online play, as opposed to play in live casino poker rooms. Much of what I will cover applies just as well to live games. But I will focus on the online games, and I will ignore factors that would apply to live games only. I will make no attempt in this book to teach you how to play poker at any advanced level.

Also, I do not recommend that any player attempt to get into the Internet poker rooms simply to exploit the sign-up bonuses. Most online poker rooms do offer various types of sign-up and deposit bonuses but the value of these bonuses is much less than the value of bonuses in the casino games.

If, however, you are already an online poker player, you should definitely take advantage of deposit bonuses. If you are just learning to play poker, these sign-up bonuses can substantially reduce the cost of your education. It is conceivable that you may lose money in poker games, but still come out ahead on bonuses. And if all the bonuses do is cut your losses while you are learning the game, that in itself is valuable.

An aggressive player with many hours to devote to online poker can realistically get $10,000 to $15,000 per year in online poker room bonus money. For a professional player, this is money in the bank. It makes no sense to leave this free money out in cyberspace. So I will not ignore the poker room bonuses. In fact, I will describe the different types of bonuses in detail and explain how you can figure out their dollar values. For a player who is just learning the game, this money could mean the difference between continuing to learn the game or quitting in frustration. Poker can be a very expensive game to learn.

In fact, this is one of the major attractions of online poker. Compared to live poker, Internet poker can be an inexpensive training ground. There are four main reasons for this:

1) In Internet poker rooms, just as in live poker rooms, the house makes its money by taking a rake, a percentage of money from the pot. But the cost of the house rake online is generally only 50% to 60% of the rake in live games. That means that more of the money the players bet goes to the winner of the pot.

INTRODUCTION

2) The smallest limit hold'em games I've seen in Las Vegas have blinds of $1/$2. On the Internet, many poker rooms offer hold'em with 5¢/10¢ blinds, and some Internet poker rooms have hold'em with 1¢/2¢ blinds. Most online poker rooms also offer free games, but these games are mostly useful for learning how the software works. Players in free games do not play anything like players who have money on the line, so you can't really learn poker skills in the free games.

3) You don't have to tip the dealer in an online game. Tipping can be a considerable "tax" on your winnings in live games.

4) Finally, online poker rooms offer bonus money on your deposits—traditional, cashable bonuses that are yours to keep once you've met your play requirement.

The convenience of playing poker online not only attracts many players, but makes the game much easier to learn. The selection of games available is astounding, especially when compared to live poker rooms. Any time, day or night, you can find all of the common and popular games and many less common games. And you can find these games at just about any limits, including free games. Further, that game selection includes tournaments of every buy-in level and every size, from single table to mega-tournaments with monstrous prize pools.

Online, you can get into and out of cash games very quickly. Let's say you sit down at a $10-$20 hold'em game in an online poker room, and for some reason you don't like the players, your position, the overall aggressiveness, the tightness, or whatever. You can usually be off that table and seated at another table within seconds. In a live casino poker room, this is not as easy to do. The poker room may have only one table available with those limits, or there may be a sign-up sheet with a long wait for the only other table. The big online poker rooms usually have dozens of tables at each limit level. You can join and quit games quickly and easily with a few clicks of your mouse.

In this book, when I talk about poker, I'm always talking about hold'em, and when I talk about tournaments, I'm always talking about no-limit hold'em tournaments. My own poker education included reading and studying just about every book written by every major poker author on Texas hold'em and tournament play, and I purposely limited my focus. Since I didn't come from a poker background, I did not want to overwhelm myself with the theoretical differences between the strategies of hold'em, 7-card stud, Omaha, and razz. I wanted a very strong background in the literature of one game. That's just the way I do things. And, frankly, I would advise anyone who is truly serious about any one game to do likewise.

You can get a whole library of poker books for a few hundred bucks, and that's nothing compared to the cost of ignorance in a game with even modest limits. Reading will not in and of itself teach you to beat the game, but it will teach you how some of the world's smartest analysts and most successful players think about the game. The only way you will learn to beat the game is by gaining experience at the tables. But knowing how the different experts think can save you years of trial and error in figuring out how to play your hands.

Unfortunately for new players, many of the authors who have written about poker, and especially about hold'em, have provided us with insight into how they play hands against the tough opponents they face in the biggest high-limit games. Much of what is written has little application to the opponents you will be facing in $1/$2, $2/$4 or even smaller limit games online. Also, much of what has been written on no-limit tournament strategy is based on analysis of and experiences in the big money live tournaments.

In the no-limit Internet tournaments where you are most likely to begin your education, the buy-ins are $100 or less, sometimes only $5 or $10. You will often be short on chips from the get-go, and if not, you will be short-stacked within the first hour if you do not increase your chip position quickly. Blind levels in these fast tournaments often increase every ten, fifteen, or twenty minutes, not every 60 to 90 minutes as in the big buy-in tournaments. You don't have the luxury of playing the first day of the tournament for "survival," since the entire tournament will be over in a matter of hours. You must often approach these types of tournaments from a more aggressive do-or-die strategy from the start.

Before we get into poker strategy, however, let's discuss the basics of playing poker online. How do you buy chips, watch games in progress, enter and exit games, bet, raise, fold, and cash out? How do you choose a poker room based on their bonus offers? In the next two chapter, we cover the basics.

Then we'll get to the strategies.

2. GETTING STARTED

THE GENERAL PLAN OF ATTACK

The general plan is to play in games where you earn a deposit bonus. In the next chapter, I'm going to describe how to read the online poker rooms' terms and conditions in order to locate the bonuses of most value to you. But before we start analyzing bonus values, I want to cover a few basic facts of online play.

DEPOSITING MONEY IN AN ONLINE POKER ROOM

In order to gamble for real money in Internet poker rooms, you have to deposit money with the online poker room cashier. If you live in the U.S., you cannot deposit funds into any Internet poker room or casino via a bank credit card, nor can you use PayPal. As we discussed earlier, Neteller is the most convenient and widely accepted banking service welcomed by the most popular poker rooms, though there are other similar online services that will also work well.

(If you have not read my discussion of depositing money in Internet casinos for playing online casino games, go to the Internet Casino section of this book, the Business End chapter, and read the text under the heading "Deposit Methods.")

DOWNLOADING POKER ROOM SOFTWARE

The next thing you need to do is download poker room software from one of the reputable Internet poker rooms. In fact, I suggest that you take time while you are waiting for your Neteller funds to clear to evaluate bonuses and download software from several online poker sites. You may already have a specific poker room in mind, based on television or magazine ad enticements. Or you may already be playing online in one or more online poker rooms. If not, you'll find links to reputable online poker rooms at Blackjack Forum Online.

THE FREE GAMES

Free or "play money" games are available in most Internet poker rooms and are excellent for learning how any online poker room's software works, including the mechanics of signing up for tables, buying in, betting, calling, raising, folding, and chatting with other players at the table. Sites use slightly different methods for all of these, so the last thing you want to do is buy in at a table, then sit there wondering how to make a raise.

The method for carrying out most of the common poker actions— bet, call, fold, raise—will be obvious simply by looking at the options on your monitor. But most online poker rooms have options that you will not find in live games. It's a good idea to look through the poker room's help screens for features that you may not be familiar with. For example, you need to know how to sit out a hand without giving up your seat. You should fully understand how the automatic check/call or check/fold features work. Do you want your blinds to be automatically put into the pot, or do you want to manually take these actions?

Learn how to watch tables in action without joining in. Learn how to look at your play history, and the play histories of others if that's allowed. Learn how to take notes on your opponents, how to play at multiple tables simultaneously, and any other special features of the site. Many online poker rooms also offer various types of **freeroll** tournaments, especially for new players, where you can win money with no buy-in.

CAN YOU LEARN TO WIN IN THE FREE GAMES?

Many online poker sites advertise their free games as excellent ways to learn how to win at poker. The idea of learning for free is enticing. If you could play in free games until you acquired the skills needed to start beating players in the real money games, you'd have it made.

Unfortunately, it's not going to happen. The only value of the free games is in helping you learn the mechanics of how the games are structured and how the software features work.

Free games are nothing like real money games. Since nobody in a play-money game has anything invested in the outcome of any hand, players will often play recklessly just to see what happens, to experiment, or to find out if someone else is bluffing. You will be tempted to play this way yourself, once you see how wild some of these games are. If you are in a play-money no-limit hold'em game, and a player moves all in on you for $500, and all you've got is top pair, it's easy to call him down. If he busts you, no problem. It's play money. Besides, aren't you going to be curious about whether or not he was trying to steal the pot?

Poker is a different game when a player's actions have real consequences. What if this were a real money game and it was going to cost you $500 to find out if your top pair is good? Now you've got a real decision. Even 5-cent/10-cent games are more realistic than free games, though even these games can be pretty unrealistic, especially if they're limit games and the biggest bet or raise allowed is a dime.

WATCH THE TOURNAMENT PROS

Assuming you understand the basics of poker well enough to get through some hands, and you've fooled around with an online poker room's features enough to know how they work, you should focus on learning who the professional players are on the sites where you will play before you start playing for real money. This is not difficult to do. If you are planning to play primarily in tournaments, many sites list their biggest tournament winners. You can find data on how many tournaments each of them has won, sometimes how much they've won, and how many times they've placed in the money.

And here's the good part: you can watch these players actually play in tournaments. You can camp out at their tables, follow them around, and take notes on exactly what they are doing. When there's a showdown, you can see the hands they were playing and keep records of how they played them. Even if there's no showdown, and no complete hand history available for the tournament, you can gain a lot of insight into how often they play a hand, what positions they play from, and how often they bet, raise, limp in, call, or fold.

This is an education you cannot get in live casino games.

While you're taking notes on winners, look for weak players who play too many pots and who call too often on draws without sufficient pot odds. (Note: If you are a beginner, I will cover the topic of pot odds and other strategic poker concepts later in this section. For now, just take note of the fact that you can watch and study players in online tournaments in a way that is impossible to do in live poker room tournaments.)

WATCH THE CASH GAME PROS

One of the best ways to find the pros in the non-tournament cash games is to view the lists of all of the players in the games that interest you. Players who are active at three or more online tables simultaneously are often skilled players. If the same players play at these tables day after day, and they seem to be doing well, they may even be professional online players.

So, take notes on their play and the players they choose to play against. See if you can figure out who will win the pot prior to the decision. Try to predict who has the stronger hand, who is bluffing, or who is making a mistake if they call, raise, or fold. When you get to the point where you are consistently correct in your opinions, you will have come a long way toward playing a winning game yourself. Use these online games as a poker school that allows you to watch real players, including many successful professional players, in real money games.

TAKING NOTES

Most major online poker sites allow you to take notes on the players at your table. By right-clicking with your cursor over a player's name, you will see an option to take notes. Always check the poker room's features to see exactly how their note-taking feature works. This feature opens a notepad page for this player, and you can type comments that will be saved. These notes are saved on the poker room's software, not on your computer. But any time you are in a game with this player in the future—even many months or years later—you can access the notes you made on him. This player will not know you are taking notes on him, nor can you tell when another player is taking notes on you. But this is a highly useful feature for recalling information about your opponents, as you may go through hundreds of different opponents in a single week of play. Some of the major sites have more than 10,000 players.

One thing you must keep in mind about note-taking is that you can only recall your notes on a player when you see him at a table. You have no access to your whole notebook on players. You can always use your own computer's notepad to take notes on your opponents, but you won't have the convenient recall feature you have by using the poker room's notepad.

Also, you do not need to be in a game with a player to take notes on him. If you are watching a game in progress, you can take notes on any and all players at the table. You can collect notes on hundreds of players before you ever join a game!

TYPES OF NOTES YOU SHOULD RECORD

You definitely want to make an assessment of the player's skill if you feel you have seen enough to make such a judgment. If a player is particularly loose in calling raises with marginal hands, this is good to know. Likewise if a player is very tight, and only enters pre-flop with premium hands. You want to note if a player is very aggressive, or very passive, or always calls rather than raising. Or that he plays too many pots, or always raises on the button. Or limps in with pocket aces or kings. You can even develop abbreviations to record the details of plays on specific hands. All of this could prove useful if you find yourself facing a player whose handle you recall from a game weeks earlier.

HAND HISTORIES

You should also familiarize yourself with the "Hand History" feature of the sites where you play. This feature allows you to look at the complete history of the hands that occurred at your table. If a player calls a bet on the river, for instance, and loses the pot, you will most likely not get to see the hand he called with. Most players will use the "Muck Losing Hand" option so that opponents will not see the cards they lost with. The hand histories, however, *show these hands,* and this information provides insight into your opponents that you cannot get from watching live games.

POKER CHAT

All poker rooms provide a small chat section of the screen where players at the table may talk among themselves. This is a feature that may be turned on or off as each player desires. Most rooms also offer an option of disabling the remarks of specific players only. If the chat function is completely turned off, then the screen displays only comments from the dealer, such as remarks that, "A new player is entering in seat eight."

Some players find the chat distracting and always leave it turned off. Others use it as a source of information about their opponents, or as a social function. Some poker room chat abbreviations are identical to generic Internet chat room lingo, such as j/k = just kidding, lol (laughing out loud) or rofl (rolling on the floor laughing), etc. Other common lingo is poker-room specific.

Here are some common abbreviations:

Common Poker Chat Abbreviations

bb = big blind
bl = better luck
brb = be right back
gc = good call
gl = good luck
n = no or nice,
   (as a compliment to a winner)
n1 = nice one
nc = nice catch
ne1 = anyone
nh = nice hand
ott = over the top
pls = please
ru = are you
sb = small blind
tx = thanks
ty = thank you
u2 = you too
y = yes
yw = you're welcome

3. EXPLOITING THE BONUSES

I want to emphasize that you should always try to play a bonus offer that will pay a good portion of your blinds. This is not a strategy I've seen discussed in other books, but I believe it is a huge factor for new players who are learning the game. Playing poker online, even at low stakes, can cost a new player a lot of money just due to common beginners' mistakes. That's just the cost of learning the game. When you are not yet a winning player and you are on a tight budget, this makes the game very tough.

There has been quite a bit of discussion about the value of poker room bonuses in the various online poker forums. In fact, there are entire Internet sites dedicated to exploiting these bonuses, but unfortunately, I have seen no decent analysis of the bonus values, comparable to the types of analyses presented in the first part of this book for the Internet casino game bonuses.

If you are already a winning online poker player, simply look at the total dollar value of the bonus and estimate the amount of time it will take you to meet the play requirements. If you are new to poker, or still learning the fine points of play and using the low-limit games to hone your skills, then you have to look at the bonuses from a different perspective. You have to be much more concerned with how long it will take you to extract the bonus value because the longer it takes, the more you stand to lose while getting there.

Online poker rooms offer sign-up bonuses for the same reasons that online casinos do—to entice new players into their games or to bring former players back. Poker rooms do not want you flitting from one bonus offer to another. They want to keep you as a loyal customer. In most cases, their bonus offers accomplish this purpose. Poker players get comfortable with a poker room's software and crowd, and they end up staying there.

Because of this, poker rooms are not as concerned with bonus hustlers as online casinos are. Nobody can extract enough of a profit from poker room bonuses to make bonus hustling a viable way of earning a lot of fast money. So most online poker rooms, and all of the major ones, offer sign-up bonuses for new players. You deposit a certain amount, you then play a certain amount, and bonus money gets added to your account.

Unlike the Internet casino bonuses, online poker room bonuses are always *cashable* bonuses. Some online poker rooms add the full bonus amount to a separate account, which you have no access to for playing or withdrawal until you have met the play requirement. Then the funds are added to your account as fully cashable funds. Other poker rooms add bonus funds to your account in small increments as you earn them. For example, a $100 bonus may be added $10 at a time as you fulfill the play requirement.

The "sticky" type of Internet casino bonus that allows a player to gamble with the bonus money, but not cash it out, does not exist in the online poker rooms. There is a good reason for this. In a poker game, you are playing and betting against other players, not against the house. If you lose bonus money to another player, the poker room cannot tell that player that the money he won from you was "sticky" money and not cashable. Any online poker room that tried a stunt like that would not have many players for long.

So we will not be using the terms sticky, non-sticky, or semi-sticky when we discuss online poker room bonuses. Cash is cash in an online poker room, and when you get bonus money added to your account, you may cash it in immediately or use it to buy into games. Either way it is always considered your money.

COMMON TYPES OF ONLINE POKER ROOM BONUSES

Although we do not have to consider whether or not a poker room bonus is "sticky," there are other types of differences between bonuses that are unique to the online poker rooms, and that greatly affect their value, especially to beginners.

Here are the five most common types of bonus offers:

1) Number of Hands Dealt in Raked Pots
2) Total Dollars Raked for Dealt Hands
3) Number of Hands Bet in Raked Pots
4) Total Dollar Amount Bet in Hands Played
5) Tournament Bonus Structures

Most of these types of bonuses are available as both initial deposit bonuses and as reload bonuses. A **reload** bonus is the common term the poker rooms use for what the Internet casinos call a "follow-up" bonus. The poker room reload bonus terms are often similar or identical to those of the initial sign-up bonus—unlike the follow-up bonuses for Internet casino games, which are usually for less.

Also, unlike bonuses offered for the Internet casino games, poker room bonuses are often **stackable**. This means that you may take advantage of a second bonus offer for a poker room even if you have not completed the play requirement of a current bonus offer. You simply deposit more funds in your account, and the new bonus is stacked on top of the first one. You definitely want to make sure of this prior to making a new deposit because not all of the poker rooms allow bonuses to be stacked. In fact, just like Internet casinos, some poker rooms require your account be empty of funds prior to depositing funds for any bonus.

Let's look at each of the different types of bonuses to see how they work and how we can estimate their value.

1. NUMBER OF HANDS DEALT IN RAKED POTS

This type of bonus gives you credit for having cards dealt to you in any raked pot, even if you do not play the hand or contribute to that pot.

A bonus currently available at one of the most popular online poker rooms offers a bonus of 20% up to $100 (with a $500 deposit required to get the maximum bonus). You must be dealt cards for seven raked hands for every $1 in bonus money, and you must earn your bonus within seven days of your deposit.

Let's analyze the value of this bonus for a limit game. The first thing we need to know is: what are the minimum blind levels available for the limit hold'em games where the pot is raked? Let's say they offer $1/$2 limit hold'em games with blinds of 50 cents and $1.

What would happen to your bankroll if you simply sat through all hands, never played, and forfeited your blinds when the blinds came around to you? At a ten-player table, you would lose $1.50 (the total of the small and the big blind) every ten hands. This means that the cost of sitting at this table is about 15 cents per hand. However, every seven hands, you'll earn $1 of bonus money, and $1 per seven hands is worth 14.3 cents per hand.

So, while you are earning the bonus, the actual cost of sitting at the table in this game is only 15 cents minus 14.3 cents, or 0.7 cents per hand, as opposed to 15 cents per hand without the bonus. That makes a difference to a new player who is just learning the game. If you consider that it takes 700 hands to collect your $100 bonus, and if you were paying the full 15 cents per hand cost of the going through the blinds for these 700 hands, the cost of the blinds alone comes to $105. So with this bonus, the cost of playing these hands has gone from $105 to only $5.

This is the best type of bonus for beginning players. To extract the maximum value of the bonus, you should always join full ten-player ring games at the minimum blind level allowed. The reason I specify that you should join full ten-player games is that you will go through the blinds more rapidly in short-handed play. At full tables, you will pay the least to complete your bonus requirement the fastest. Note that you will not actually make money from this bonus. If you make money, it will have to be from actually playing your poker hands profitably.

The other nice feature of this type of bonus is that you do not have to be a great poker player to make some money while you are learning. You can use an extremely conservative strategy as you learn the game, knowing very little other than that certain strong starting hands are likely to win. For instance, over the course of 700 hands, you can expect to be dealt either pocket aces, pocket kings, or pocket queens about ten times. If these were the only ten hands you played, and you played them aggressively, you would expect to win more than the $5 cost of the blinds not covered by the bonus money.

In fact, my advice to those learning poker is that you should begin by playing extremely conservatively—or "tight," as such players are commonly described by other poker players—playing only the strongest hands with maximum aggression. This is not an optimal poker strategy, bonus or no bonus, but is meant to illustrate a highly simplified approach that a new player might employ to come out ahead a few bucks as opposed to behind a few bucks during a bonus play. (I'll discuss more practical strategies later.)

Another nice thing about this particular bonus program is that the online casino that offers it repeats the offer with what's called a reload bonus about once every four or five weeks. You can get a lot of real money experience at a discount at this one online poker room. Again, this is the type of bonus that I recommend most highly for beginning players. If you seek out only this type of bonus and play only when you are on a bonus, you will essentially be playing in games where the house is paying your blind costs. That is a good deal for a beginner.

2. TOTAL DOLLARS RAKED FOR DEALT HANDS

This type of bonus credits you for having cards dealt to you in any raked pot, even if you do not play the hand or contribute to that pot. The only difference between this type of bonus and the one above is that the amount of bonus earned is based on the actual dollar amount raked from that pot. Here is a description of this type of bonus from the actual terms and conditions of a popular online poker room:

> *XXX Poker Room is pleased to continue offering deposit bonuses to new players. New sign-ups will receive a 100% matching bonus up to $600 on your initial deposit to XXX Poker Room.*
>
> *For each dollar raked from a pot, every player who was dealt cards for that hand will earn one point. You can earn partial points if less than one dollar is raked, and you can earn up to three points per hand.*
>
> *Each point is worth $.06, so you can earn up to $18 per hundred hands.*
>
> *The bonus amount will be automatically credited to your Bonus Account where it will be held and released to your cash account in increments of 10% of your initial deposit, or $20, whichever you earn first. So if you do a one-time deposit of $100, each $10 (10%) earned will be instantly*

released into your account. Deposit the full $600 and your account will get credited for each $20 of bonus earned. At three points per hand, each $20 increment can be earned in fewer than two hours of play at only one table.

You can see your cash total and bonus cash amounts in the Cashier window. You will continue to collect cash until you have received 100% of your bonus money. You have 120 days to earn your deposit bonus.

This offer is available to players making their FIRST deposit at XXX Poker Room.

In order to estimate the value of this bonus, you need to know one more piece of information. Since essentially you receive 6 cents for every dollar raked from the pot, you need to know what the rake is. In order to find this out, you have to click around on the various site information buttons—and it's never easy to find this technical information, but it's always there if you look—until you find a link to their **rake structure** page. What you'll find for this poker room is that for limit games, the lowest blind level available for earning our bonus points is $1/$2, but the max rake on these games is only $1, no matter how big the pot. The rake is taken out at the rate of 25 cents for every $5 in the pot, so there must be $20 in the pot to earn the maximum 6 cents per hand.

Although the wording of this bonus is similar to the prior one, it doesn't even begin to compete with the prior bonus offer. Consider that if you go through the $1/$2 blinds once every ten hands, you pay $3 every ten hands, or an average of 30 cents per hand. But the maximum bonus you can earn in ten hands is only 60 cents, or 10 cents per hand, and that's only if all ten hands played on that round have a pot of $20 or greater. This is not as good of a bonus for beginners trying to learn the game. Experienced players, however, who are playing in bigger games where the rake will frequently be $3 on a $60 pot, will likely find this bonus more attractive than the prior one. These players will like having that total $600 of bonus money available.

The reason I chose this bonus as an example is precisely because of the contrast to the previous bonus. Many online players who look for valuable bonuses are more attracted to the total dollar amounts available than any other bonus feature. This is fine if you're already playing a winning game, but those who are still learning to play should use other criteria.

No-limit players may find this site's no-limit bonus structure attractive. You can play no-limit hold'em here with blinds as low as 5 cents/10 cents, and the pot is raked at the rate of 5 cents for every $1 in the pot. This is the same percentage rate as at the limit games. Even in a 5 cent/10 cent no-limit game, you could theoretically earn up to the full 18 cents on a $3 rake for a pot size of $60 or more, though it's unlikely for a 5 cent/10 cent game to have many $60 pots. This size pot would not be so unusual in higher-limit no-limit games. With 50 cent/$1 blinds, and the cost of going through the blinds 15 cents per hand, we'd need an average pot size of $50 to fully pay our blind costs. The actual average pot size in a no-limit game with these blinds is generally in the $10 to $15 neighborhood. So with this bonus in a no-limit game, you could get about a third of your blinds costs paid. Note that most poker rooms do provide the average pot size at all of the tables they have in action.

In any case, the first type of bonus described, in which you earn the bonus simply by being dealt a hand, is clearly superior for beginning players than a bonus based on the amount of rake, which will favor players in higher limit games.

3. NUMBER OF HANDS BET IN RAKED POTS

This type of bonus credits you for having a hand in any raked pot, but only if you have contributed money to that pot. If you fold preflop without calling the blind, your hand does not count toward the bonus.

It is very important to note when the bonus terms specify the number of hands *bet* in a raked pot, as opposed to the number of hands *dealt,* as in the prior two types of bonuses. This type of bonus has very little real dollar value for beginners. Plus, one popular poker room that uses this bonus structure does not allow bonus points to be converted to cash. Bonus points can only be used for tournament entries.

Basically, you will earn one bonus point for each rake of $1 or more, if you have contributed to that pot, with smaller bonus point increments for smaller rake amounts. But consider the difficulty of actually estimating the dollar value. First, you are only awarded bonus points if you have contributed to the pot on any given hand. So you must first figure out approximately what percentage of pots you will play. Then, you have to figure out the approximate average size of the pot you will play, so you can estimate what the rake will be and how many bonus points you will earn for playing.

Finally, the points can only be used to buy into special tournaments. For example, the site offers one tournament that you can enter if you have earned 200 bonus points, and the prize pool for this tournament totals $1,000. Unfortunately, the site does not specify what the total number of tournament entries will be, so how do we estimate our chances of winning or the dollar value of this free-roll buy-in?

The most amusing thing about this bonus program is that the terms and conditions warn players that: "Professional players or players considered to be abusing the bonus system by any means may have bonuses revoked and be subject to further sanctions... " In fact, there's no way to "abuse" this bonus program. It's just not worth much, and it's impossible to figure out the actual dollar value. This inexplicable attitude toward potential bonus "abusers" is reflected in many of the poker rooms that are sponsored by online casinos that have bonus programs for their casino games. Bonuses for casino games can be legally hustled for a good chunk of change by smart players, as described in the first section of this book. But I have not found any poker room bonuses that offer much in the way of dollar profits to anyone who's not actually a pretty decent poker player.

A lot of players like this poker room, however, which also has one of the biggest and most reputable sports books on the Internet. Many serious and professional poker players like the games here, and I'm sure many appreciate getting into free-roll tournaments when they earn the bonus points to qualify. But this site would not be a good poker room choice for a beginner trying to reduce his costs of learning the game.

Any time your bonus is based only on the hands where you put money into the pot, assume the value is pretty low until you are an expert player.

4. TOTAL DOLLAR AMOUNT BET IN HANDS PLAYED

This type of bonus credits you for having a hand in any raked pot, but you must contribute money to that pot, and the amount of the bonus points earned depends on the actual dollar amount that you personally bet in your played hands.

This type of bonus is offered in another Internet casino-sponsored poker room, and like most of the bonus programs I've found at online casinos that also have poker rooms, this bonus program is less than generous. Casino game sites all seem to be afraid of bonus "abusers," so they offer pretty stingy poker bonuses that couldn't possibly be abused. This site announces in their bonus offer that you will get a "deposit bonus of 25% up to $100 max." Okay, so for a $400 deposit, I can get a $100 bonus. How do I collect it? They continue: "125 points must be accumulated for every $1 in bonus money." Understood, so how do I accumulate these 125 points? "You get 100 action points for each dollar you contribute to the rake."

Now, try and figure that one out. Let's say the rake here is 25 cents for every $5. If the pot has $20 in it, the rake is $1. My bonus is based on how much I contributed to that $1 rake. So if $4 in that pot is mine, then I contributed 20% of the $1 rake, and I will be awarded 20% of 100 points, which is 20 points. Since 125 points is worth $1, then 20 points is worth 16 cents.

Now we're cookin'! I can actually figure out the percentage value of my bonus. With this bonus, I'm basically getting back 4 cents for every dollar I bet. Not bad, assuming I am a good poker player and can make money on the games. But again, this is not a bonus that should be sought out by beginners. In order to extract the full $100 value of this bonus, I'd have to wager $2,500 in pots as described above. That could take a beginner a hell of a long time in a $1/$2 game, and unless you have a lot of past data on your play, it's impossible to figure out the blind costs on this one.

Another problem with many of the Internet casino game sites that have poker rooms is that they may take forever to let you cash out. With the dedicated poker rooms, there's never any run-around. Your Neteller transactions go in and out in a matter of hours, if not minutes. With poker rooms that also do business as online casinos, you will often have to fax them your driver's license, bank statement, utility bill, etc.—the same hassle you get with the Internet casino withdrawals. Because of the bonus values of Internet casino games, these hassles are sometimes worth it. But with most dedicated poker rooms doing fast and efficient Neteller transactions, I wouldn't go through this myself for a wagering requirement bonus in an Internet poker room.

There are almost as many variations on bonus programs as there are online poker rooms. You may have noticed in the above descriptions that action that would earn you a single bonus point in one poker room is worth 3 points in another, 6 points in another, and more than 100 in another. And "points" themselves have different values in every bonus program. There is no standard.

Here is one of the more ridiculous bonus programs I found. What evil genius could have dreamed up this nonsense?

To enter the *** VIP Club, first you have to be a real money player on ***. Then, you need to accumulate points and reach a minimum of 5,000 points by playing for real as often as possible. As soon as you reach 5,000 points, we'll notify you via e-mail that you're in the Club...

Points will be calculated on a daily basis, and accumulated according to the following set of rules:
RAKED HANDS: Square Root of the number of raked hands.

For Example:
Number of raked hands: 121
Points for player: 11

What? My bonus is based on *the square root of the number of raked hands?* Now that's downright devious!

This is one of those bonus programs where you know that anyone who signs up for it has no concept of the way square roots work. Essentially, the bigger a number gets, the smaller (as a percentage of that number) the square root is. According to the explanation in the poker room's terms and conditions, in order to accumulate 11 points per day, the player must play 121 raked hands. The square root of 121 is 11. The average person who knows little about math might think that by playing twice as many hands—242 hands per day—he can earn 22 points toward his 5,000 point requirement in order to get into the VIP club. Not so. The square root of 242 provides the player with only 15.5 points. If he wants to earn 22 points per day, he will have to play 484 hands per day. He earned his first 11 points with only 121 hands, but the second 11 points takes three times as many hands to accumulate—363 more hands!

An aggressive multi-table player might think that at the rate of 11 points for every 121 hands played, he could earn 100 points per day by playing nine times 121 hands, or 1,089 hands per day. Actually, 1,089 hands per day will not earn you 99 points, but only 33 points. In fact, the more hands you play per day, the less valuable the bonus is and the more you are penalized! This bonus program is the opposite of a "customer loyalty" reward. It actually penalizes the most loyal customers. And even if you play 484 raked hands per day here, five days per week, to earn 22 points per day, it will take you about 45 weeks to earn 5,000 points to become a VIP! All of this before you get a single buck of actual bonus value! Anyway, you can also earn bonus points here by participating in tournaments, but that 5,000-point qualification for the VIP program will probably not be worth many beginners' time or money.

As I say, always read the terms and conditions. Pull out a calculator if necessary and figure out what the offer amounts to.

Many of the online casinos that offer casino game bonus programs in addition to poker room bonuses use standard wagering requirement type bonuses. That is, you must wager the total bonus amount a certain number of times before the bonus is applied to your account. My advice to beginners is to avoid online poker bonus programs like these. In the casino games, where we can figure out the cost of our wagers based on the house advantage, we can easily judge when a bonus has enough dollar value to make it worth our time. But beginners cannot do this in poker.

If you are a winning player, and you find a low wagering requirement for acquiring a bonus, go for it. Definitely shop around for the best deals, however. Some online poker room wagering requirements are as low as two times the bonus amount, and some are as high as forty times. Big difference.

5. TOURNAMENT BONUS STRUCTURES

Online poker rooms apply bonus points for tournament play based on the amount you contribute to the tournament in entry fees. So free roll tournaments do not generally qualify for earning bonus points. Some online poker sites ignore tournaments completely for bonus awards. So if you intend to play tournaments, you should always read what the terms and conditions state about tournament play eligibility for bonus qualifying before you deposit funds.

Typically, an online poker room that awards bonus points will state something like this in their terms and conditions:

> *For every dollar paid in tournament fees, you will receive 7 Poker Room Points. There is no cap on the number of points you can receive. Each point is worth $.06.*

The value of this bonus is fairly easy to calculate. Since "for every dollar paid in tournament fees," you will receive 7 points, and each point is worth exactly 6 cents, then during the bonus period, the house is covering 42% of your tournament entry fees. Note: If you are unfamiliar with tournament buy-in structures, every tournament, whether online or in live casino poker rooms, has a **buy-in**—that goes toward the players' prize pool—and an **entry fee**—that is the house take on the tournament and does not go into the players' prize pool. In other words, if the buy-in is $20, and you must pay a $2 entry fee, with the above bonus program you'll get 14 bonus points worth 84 cents. That makes your actual entry fee only $1.16.

So if it is primarily tournaments that interest you, don't expect the bonus dollars to ever do anything but lower your entry fee costs. To compare the various poker rooms' tournament bonus values to each other, simply use the method illustrated above to compare what proportion of your entry fees each poker room will pay.

SUMMARY

Accept the fact that you cannot make a living exploiting online poker room bonuses. The poker room deposit bonuses simply lower the cost of playing. To make money in the online poker rooms, you've got to be able to win at the game of poker. Can you do this?

What makes Texas hold'em such an interesting (and difficult) game—whether limit, no-limit, or tournament—is that the logic of winning is based on continually changing factors. A player's actual cards are only one of many considerations. An expert player will play the same hand at the same table entirely differently based on his seating position, his chip position, the number of players already in the pot, who the players in the pot are, the prior betting action, and whether the current action is preflop, on the flop, on the turn, or on the river.

You cannot make a basic strategy chart for hold'em based solely on hands. This is how poker differs most dramatically from blackjack, the strategies for which are based almost entirely on math.

So, let's look at the structure of the game before we go on to the strategies for making money online.

4. HOW TO PLAY TEXAS HOLD'EM

If you are already an experienced hold'em player, you may skip this chapter. The typical hold'em game has nine or ten players, and these games are considered **full ring games**. I will focus on full ring games, which are the most popular games, and the most assessable to new players learning the game. Internet poker rooms offer many games with fewer players, with 6-player games being very popular. You can also find heads-up games, where only two players are at the table. Short-handed games require a greater understanding of hand values, position, bluffing, and other advanced skills.

THE COMMON POKER BETTING ACTIONS

CALL: To "call" a bet is to place the minimum amount of money into the pot that will keep your hand alive. To call the minimum bet on the first betting round is called "limping" into the pot.

CHECK: To "check" is to place no money into the pot when no bet is necessary to keep your hand alive.

RAISE: To "raise" is to place a bet into the pot larger than the minimum necessary bet, a bet that other players must call if they want to keep their hands alive.

RERAISE: To "reraise" is to place a bet into a pot larger than the bet of a player who has already raised. Reraising is also called "going over the top" of a prior raiser.

FOLD: To "fold" is to throw your hand away (also called "mucking" your cards) rather than placing any required money into the pot to keep your hand alive.

THE BLINDS

Texas hold'em requires only two players to put money in the pot prior to the dealing of the first cards. These bets are called **blind** bets, and they are posted by players in adjacent seats. The requirement to post the blinds rotates clockwise around the table. The **small blind** is typically half the **big blind**, and is posted by the player on the right. (The small blind may also be some other fraction of the big blind.) A disk, called the "button," that is rotated around the table clockwise, denotes the dealer position—which is to say the last player to receive cards, and the last player to bet, after the initial betting round. This button is always the player hand to the right of the small blind. The big blind represents the minimum bet any player must call to enter the pot on the first betting round.

THE DEAL

After the blinds are posted, the dealer deals one card to each player clockwise, starting with the small blind, and continues dealing around the table until each player has two cards. These cards are dealt face down and are known as **hole cards.**

THE PREFLOP

After receiving these cards, each player must decide if he wants to enter the pot with a bet that either matches the big blind, or matches the bet of any player who has already entered the pot with a raise, or if he wants to raise, or reraise, himself. The player to the left of the big blind—a position called **under the gun**—is the first to act, and all players either bet, call, raise, or fold, clockwise in turn. The big blind is the last player to act on this first betting round. If no player has raised the big blind, then he is automatically in the hand. Since his money is already in the pot, he has the option to either "check" or raise the bet himself. If there has been a raise, he must decide if he wants to call the raise, reraise, or fold.

Ultimately, each player in the pot will use his hole cards to make the best five-card poker hand possible utilizing the "community cards" that will be dealt face-up on the table. So, each player's decision to enter the pot on this first betting round is often determined by his assessment of the strength of his hole cards, either as they stand, or according to their potential to make a strong poker hand when the community cards come down.

Let's look at the hand values.

HAND RANKINGS

Texas hold'em uses the same hand rankings as any traditional poker game. From best possible hand to worst, these are the rankings:

Royal Flush: A-K-Q-J-10 of the same suit.

Straight Flush: Five consecutive cards, such as Q-J-10-9-8, of the same suit.

Four of a Kind or Quads: Four cards of identical value, such as 9-9-9-9.

Full House: Three cards of one value, and two of another. Example: K-K-K-8-8.

Flush: Five cards of the same suit. Example: A-K-8-4-3 of hearts.

Straight: Five consecutive cards, such as Q-J-10-9-8 of differing suits.

Three of a Kind or Trips: Three cards of identical value, such as 9-9-9.

Two Pair: Two cards of one value, and two of another. Example: J-J and 6-6.

One Pair: Two cards of one value, such as 10-10.

High Card: If no player has any of the above hands, then the player with the highest card wins. Ace is highest and deuce is lowest. If two players have an identical high card, then the second highest card determines the winner, then the third, etc.

Note: Any time two or more players have identical best hands, then the pot is split equally between them.

THE FLOP

After the initial betting round is completed, and all players have decided whether or not to enter the pot with their two hole cards, three cards are dealt face up in the center of the table. This is called the **flop**. Each player must now decide on his betting action.

This betting round starts with the small blind, or if he has folded, the first active player to his left, and rotates to the button, who is last to act. If the button has folded, then the first active player who sits to his right will be last to act.

Basically, each player must look at the three cards on the table to determine how well they combine with his two hole cards to make a good poker hand. There are still two more cards to come, so each player's current five-card hand may improve to a better hand, and a big part of skillful hold'em play is evaluating this potential. For example, a player may have four cards to a straight or flush, but otherwise no ranked hand. He must decide if he wants to continue playing in an attempt to draw to one of these high ranking hands.

THE TURN

When the betting on the flop has been completed, the fourth community card is dealt face up onto the table. This card is called the **turn**. Each player must now decide on his betting action.

This betting round again starts with the small blind or the first active player to his left, and rotates to the button or the last active player clockwise, who is last to act.

THE RIVER

After the betting on the turn has been completed, the fifth community card is dealt face up onto the table. This card is called the **river**. After the river card is dealt, there is another betting round. When this betting round is completed, any players still in the pot show down their hands, and the highest ranking hand wins. This is called the **showdown**.

If at any point before the showdown, all other players fold in response to a player's bet, then the last remaining player wins the pot.

THE BETTING STRUCTURE

Limit games follow strict betting structures. The size of the big blind is normally the minimum bet size for entering a pot on the preflop betting round and after the flop. A raise on the first two betting rounds is always the amount of the big blind. On the turn and river, bets and raises are always by double the big blind amount, no more, no less.

For example, a $10-$20 hold'em game requires the big blind to post a $10 bet and the small blind to post a $5 bet. The minimum bet to enter the pot preflop is $10. If a player wants to raise, it will be $10 more for a total bet of $20 to any player who has not yet called the original bet—and $10 to any player who has. Any player who doesn't wish to call the big blind or any raises must fold his hand and is out of the pot.

This same betting format is followed after the flop, with a $10 minimum bet and raises of $10 more. If no players with active hands bet on this round—that is, all players check—then all player hands remain live and see the next card for free.

After the turn card is dealt, the minimum bet doubles to $20, and all raises and reraises will be in $20 increments. This betting format is followed again after the river card is dealt.

Most limit games also have a limit to the number of raises that can be made in any round, usually three or four. This limitation is often waived if only two players are involved in the pot.

In **no-limit** games, the maximum amount that can be bet or raised is limited only by the total number of chips a player has in front of him. Raises must usually be at least the size of the prior bet, if any, but can be any amount greater than this. There are no restrictions on the number of raises on any betting round in no-limit games.

Hold'em tournaments have these same betting and blind structures, except that in tournaments the blinds continually increase at predetermined time intervals.

5. TEXAS HOLD'EM STRATEGY

If you have never read a book on Texas hold'em, and you are not an experienced winning player, then this chapter is for you. Whether you are playing in limit games, no-limit games, or tournaments, the soundest approach to hold'em for beginners is to play few hands—only the strongest—preferably in late position (we'll discuss position in depth later in this chapter), and to play those hands aggressively—betting and raising to maximize your wins.

Over the past few years, there have been dozens of books written on Texas hold'em. Some major poker authors have written two to three books apiece on hold'em. Some books cover limit games only, some cover no-limit games only, some cover tournament play, some cover low-limit games. Simple as the game appears to be, the strategic complexity of the game makes for never-ending discussion and argument among the experts.

So I won't try to convince you that I'm going to turn you into a professional hold'em player with a couple of chapters in this book. You could read ten books on the subject and still not have what it takes. What I want to give you are the fundamental strategies and concepts of hold'em, especially as they will relate to the Internet games. This is a crash course in Texas hold'em.

If you are already a successful hold'em player in live casino games, then the strategic concepts I present here will seem elementary. But you may find some of the online-specific information I provide to be helpful. Online $10/$20 limit game players who are top players at this level, and who can manage four or more simultaneous online tables, can often earn $50,000 to $80,000 annually with full-time play, four times what they could earn in live games with these limits. This is not because they play better online, or because online opponents are notably inferior at this level. The increased profit comes from the simple fact that the online game plays about twice as many hands per hour, and if you can play four tables, that's eight times the play in the same time frame. Your $12,000 to $20,000 annual live game income takes a huge leap because of technology.

POSITION

In limit hold'em games, all of your decisions to bet, call a bet, raise, reraise or fold, are based on your seating position in relation to the button. Early positions are weak. Late positions are strong. Let's define the positions at a full 10-player hold'em table more precisely.

First, the **button** is the strongest position. Preflop, the only players who have more information before betting are the blinds, and they immediately go to the earliest (weakest) position after the flop. After the flop, and through the turn and river, the button, or if he has folded, the first active player to his right, always bets last.

The two seats to the right of the button are **late position** seats. At a 10-player table, with all hands in action, these players will be betting 8th and 9th after the flop and through the river.

The three seats to the right of them—the players who would bet 5th, 6th, and 7th after the flop—are in **middle position**.

The two blind positions, as well as the two seats to the left of the big blind—that is, the players who will bet 1st and 2nd preflop, then 3rd and 4th post-flop—are all **early position** seats.

In determining whether or not you should enter a pot, and then whether or not you should continue in a pot, and whether you should do so with bets, raises, or calls, it's important that you play based on your position.

THE IMPORTANCE OF POSITION

Coming to poker from a blackjack background, I had little difficulty comprehending the mathematics of poker. Blackjack is all math. Card counting systems are based entirely on statistical probabilities. The math of poker is not a whole lot different from the math of blackjack. The language is different, but essentially probability is probability, and figuring out the probabilities for a deck of cards is not rocket science.

The poker concept I truly had difficulty understanding at first, however, was position, and this is one of the most fundamental concepts to winning at hold'em. You'll often make more money with pocket nines in late position than you'll make with pocket aces in early position. It is, in fact, difficult to make money at all if you're playing your hand from early position. Position, in and of itself, has a huge value in hold'em.

In Texas hold'em, *position is information.* When you are in early position, you have no information about what the other players may be holding preflop, yet you must make a decision about whether or not to bet, raise or fold. In late position, after other players have already acted, you know a lot.

As an example, let's say you're holding an A-10 under the gun, that is, the first position to bet before the flop. How do you play this hand? If you raise with it, then get reraised, should you call? You'll be worried that the reraiser already has you beaten with a high pair, or an ace with a better kicker. And what exactly would you be hoping for on the flop? If an ace comes down, and you bet, and you get raised again, there's a good possibility your kicker is already beaten by the raiser. If instead a 10 comes down, and you bet, and get raised, does the raiser already have your tens beat? Did his preflop raise mean he already had a bigger pocket pair than tens? And what if the flop comes down K-10-5? Are you comfortable betting at all with that king on board?

Under the gun, this hand is a throwaway.

But, what if you're in late position? First, if no one raises the pot, you can pretty well assume that there are no high pocket pairs at the table, and any aces being played probably have poor kickers. If the flop comes down with an ace, and a player in front of you bets, you'll bet your kicker is better than his and you'll feel comfortable calling that raise, and perhaps even reraising, playing the hand for value. If the flop comes down K-10-5, and no one bets, then you can assume no player has that king, and that your tens are the best hand. You'll bet, and probably take the pot. Any caller is probably on a draw.

Position provides information, and information spells money.

BEGINNERS PREFLOP BETTING STRATEGY

Based on position, these are the hands to enter the pot with, and how to enter the pot:

Early Position

Raise with A-A, K-K, Q-Q, and A-K. Call (one bet but not two) with J-J, 10-10, A-Q, A-Js. (Small "s" means "suited.")

Middle Position

Raise or reraise with A-A—J-J, A-K, A-Qs. Call (one bet but not two) with 10-10, 9-9, A-Q, A-J.

Late Position

Raise or reraise with A-A through 10-10, A-K, A-Qs, A-Js. Call (one bet but not two) with 9-9 through 6-6, A-Q, A-J, A-10, K-Qs, Q-Js.

On the Button

Use the late position strategy above, and in addition, also call in any *unraised* pot with: 5-5 through 2-2, A-9, J-10s, 10-9s, 8-7s.

As you can see, you will rarely play a hand in early position. As you gain experience, you may enter the pot more often, but this strategy is designed to keep you out of major trouble before the flop. Ideally, you would adjust these guidelines by the number of players already in the pot, and the number of players to act behind you. The more players in an unraised pot, and the later your position, the more marginal hands you may play. Marginal hands don't win very often, so you need a much bigger payoff potential to invest any money in them at all.

The single biggest mistake amateurs make is playing too many hands. It's much less costly a mistake to play too few hands than it is to play too many. Also, the preflop raising strategy here is conservative. In the higher limit games, where you'll find better players, it is often correct to raise with a much greater variety of pocket pairs and even suited connectors, especially as your position gets better. But in the loose low-limit games, especially at a 10-player table, you can often expect to have every **bad ace** (that is, any ace with a poor kicker) and many marginal kings in play. Raising with medium and small pairs just isn't cost effective in these loose low-limit games, as you will almost always have to abandon these hands after the flop.

In the low-limit games, you should save most of your aggressive play for after the flop, when you have more of a handle on the actual value of your hand and possible dangers presented by the cards on board.

Before you can apply any actual strategy, however, you first need to choose a table to play at. I'll assume you have set up your Neteller account, that you have checked out various bonus offers, selected the best values available, and downloaded the poker room software.

CHOOSING A TABLE

The best type of table for a beginner to make money at in online limit games is a loose, passive table. By **loose**, I mean a lot of players are playing a lot of hands, with five or more players often seeing the flop. By **passive**, I mean there is very little raising, mostly checking and calling, and players usually show down their hands, often with three or more players in the pot till the showdown. Let's look at these factors more closely

LOOSE TABLES

It's not uncommon in low-limit hold'em games for five or more players to see the flop. As betting limits go up, play gets tighter. At lower limits, inexperienced players tend to play too many hands because they do not understand which hands actually have preflop value and because they have no concept of position. For example, it would not be a mistake to play pocket fours from the button in an unraised pot with a lot of callers, but a loose player will often call with any pocket pair from any position.

Loose players will also play many hands that have little value from *any* position at a ten-player table, just hoping to hit something on the flop. These players have often learned poker by watching tournaments on television, usually final tables, which are short-handed. With six or fewer players, the values of hands are very different than they are when ten players are at the table. The likelihood of premium starting hands being dealt to one or more players at your table is much higher when more hands are being dealt. That means you need a stronger hand to enter a pot when there are more players.

Here are some of the common types of players you will run into again and again in the low-limit games:

TYPES OF PLAYERS

ACE MASTERS

An **ace master** will play any ace and will even call preflop raises no matter how bad his **kicker** is. A kicker is the other card in his hand. Kickers are often important in breaking ties, if, say, two players make top pair. This type of player will contribute greatly to your overall profits. An ace master will often call to the river if an ace has not appeared on the board, no matter how scary the board may look to a more skillful player who will see not only the potential straights and flushes, but the betting action of his opponents that might indicate that they could already have two pair or three of a kind.

And if that ace lands, the ace master will call any bets and raises, hoping that his pair of aces will hold up. You will identify these players quickly by noticing the hands they show down, such as ace-6 offsuit, and realizing that they actually entered the pot in early position, or called a raise from a middle position, with that hand.

FLUSH MASTERS

Another common loose player is the **flush master.** A flush master will enter a pot with any two suited cards from any position, no matter how bad those cards are. You will identify these players when they win (or lose) pots with very weird flushes that they show down at the river. They will sometimes show down a suited 8-3 or a suited 10-2, for example, having entered the pot from early position. They live for flushes. They don't realize that the odds of making a winning flush don't justify their overall investments in these otherwise low-profit-potential hands.

A less valuable flush master, though still a great contributor to your profits, is one who plays suited cards only when one of them is a high card—J, Q, K, or A. These **big flush masters** often make top pair, then get beaten by a player with a better kicker. In some sessions, you will see these types of showdowns over and over again, but the losers never learn.

Flush masters and ace masters will sometimes win pots with very unusual two-pair hands. For example, a flush master may enter a pot with a suited J-4, and win the pot by making jacks and fours. This will drive you crazy when you are in there with A-J, but you will have to put up with it. You'll make a lot more money from these players than you'll lose to them.

Most ace masters and flush masters never bluff. This is why you want to identify these players at your tables. If an ace master bets when an ace hits the board, just throw away your kings. Game over. It will be frustrating when this ace hits on the river, since you were the one building the pot with your aggressive raises, but again, you'll get a lot more from these players in the long run than they'll get from you, and if they didn't draw out occasionally, they wouldn't keep playing.

This is why you want to bet aggressively into these players. Make them pay to draw out on you. Despite the fact that you can rarely drive them out of a pot and they will occasionally hit the card they need, you will profit from them by making them pay to draw, because they will not draw out often enough to cover their losses. Both ace masters and flush masters hate aggressive players, and you will sometimes drive one away from the table if you keep hammering at them when they want to see the next card for free. You will always be sad to see one go.

BLUFF MASTERS

A **bluff master** is another type of player who has learned to play poker by watching TV. Gus Hansen is his hero. Bluff masters occasionally have short runs of success against ace masters and flush masters. The bluff master likes to play position (he's not totally ignorant) and he will *always* bet when everyone else checks. If he bets after an ace hits the board, or after the third card to any suit falls, any ace masters or flush masters who checked will fold. Bluff masters are great to have in the game (preferably on your right side), because you can count on them to build the pot when you have a strong hand.

CALLING STATIONS

Both ace masters and flush masters tend to be calling stations. They rarely bet aggressively, even if they hit their ace or flush, because they usually have a bad kicker with their ace, or a poor flush, far from the nuts. (The **nuts** is the best possible hand, given the cards on the board.) So, they know they don't have the nuts, but neither can they lay their hand down. They simply call.

Many flush masters are also ace masters. And, because these players play so many poor starting hands, when they are actually dealt a premium hand, they will typically overplay it. An ace/flush master who is dealt an A-K suited will fall deeply in love with this hand. This is one hand where he will raise before the flop, and will often call any bet on the flop, no matter what cards hit the board. He will also often call to the river no matter what cards are on the table. There can be four cards to an open-end straight on board, with no connection to his A-K, and he will play his hand to the death.

Likewise, a loose player who is dealt, say, pocket jacks, will often be unable to lay it down. Even if a king comes down on the flop, and two other players are betting and raising, he will play those jacks to the bitter end.

In any case, these are the types of weak players you tend to find in the loose, passive, low-limit games where you can make money. These tables will definitely have a number of smarter players also, and you need to identify which players are which. When a loose passive player bets or raises, you must get out of the way if you have any marginal hand.

At higher limit tables, you will find many more tight aggressive players. Rarely will more than three players see the flop at the higher-limit games, and there is often a preflop raise. At the higher-limit tables, aggressive betting and raising after the flop will also more often win the pot for a player prior to the showdown. These tables are not for beginners. You want to play at a loose, passive table, where your strategy will simply be to play a tighter and more aggressive game than your opponents.

SLOWPLAYING PREFLOP

I am not opposed to slowplaying any hand, from any position, preflop. Even with aces, slowplaying will often pay off as your hand will be disguised. The argument for raising with strong hands preflop is that it "limits the field," getting rid of many small pairs and marginal connectors (adjoining cards like 6-7 or 8-9) that may not call a raise. Unless you're *reraising* in a low-limit game, however, and reraising early enough that most players would have to call two bets to enter the hand, your raise will be unlikely to eliminate many players in a loose low-limit game. Lots of players want to see lots of flops in most low-limit hold'em games—entering the pot is like buying a lottery ticket for many players—and a single raise will not deter them. I think it makes a lot of sense to call with a raising hand like A-K, because you not only disguise your hand, but you will likely continue to get action from all of the bad aces that entered the unraised pot if an ace comes down on the flop. If you eliminate the bad aces preflop with a raise or reraise, then you'll get no action when the ace comes down.

Slowplaying K-K before the flop also pays off well in these loose games. If the flop comes with no ace and a bunch of rags, most of the overcard hands, and especially the players with aces, will continue to call. In fact, many players in these games with hands like A-Q and A-J will not only call a bet, but will often reraise you, thinking you're trying to steal it. And if the flop comes down with a queen or jack as the high card, you will likely get reraised by any A-Q or A-J player who believes his top pair to be good. If an ace comes down on the flop, you will have to abandon your kings in the face of any betting, but you will have gotten out cheaply. And there is no guarantee that a raise before the flop would have eliminated the ace masters anyway. There is a chance that one of these ace holders had an A-Q, A-J, or A-10, or any suited ace, and these hands will rarely fold to one preflop raise in low-limit games.

Whenever you are in a loose game, where you expect five or more players to see a flop, and often seven to eight players, it makes sense to slowplay almost any hand before the flop, then either bet aggressively or get out of the way when you see how well your cards hold up. If you never raise before the flop with any hand, you will find that although it reduces the size of some pots you win, and allows some players into pots who might have been eliminated preflop because of their marginal hands, but who instead made winning hands, you'll also often make much more money on the pots you take down because your starting hand is disguised.

This flies in the face of some traditional hold'em thinking, but these low-limit games are often far from traditional. So, don't take my standard raising hand chart above to be a strict guideline. Every poker book will tell you to "mix up" your play so that players can't figure you out so easily. If you find that your table is so loose that your pre-flop raises rarely limit the field of players, one of the best places to start mixing up your play in these low-limit games is by limping in with strong hands before the flop.

PUT EACH PLAYER ON A HAND

In a low-limit game, with so many players in to see each flop, it is not always easy to make assumptions about what each player might have before the flop. But this is an exercise you should always do. Put each player on a hand. I do this by using whatever stereotype I have for each player. I'll assume the ace masters are in on their typical bad aces. The flush masters have two suited cards, the tighter players have high cards, the raiser has an A-K or A-Q, etc. As the cards come down and the play continues, I adjust my reads to correspond with their actions. You do this for every pot, whether you are involved in the pot or not.

You will get better at this with experience. You will know you are becoming a dangerous player when you virtually always know which player will win the pot before the showdown. You will also learn to read some of the more difficult-to-read hands, like sets. A **set** is three-of-a-kind where two of the cards are a pocket pair that hit the trip card on the board. You will often be surprised by sets at first, but after a while, you'll be able to feel it when a player has a set. (If he's a good player, you won't feel it until his check-raise.)

The players who never seem to improve are the players who simply play their two cards and hope for lucky hands. No poker room bonus can save these players from losing money. The players who make money are the players who pay the least attention to their own two cards, but figure out everybody else's.

READING THE BOARD

You must be very fast and accurate in reading the board. The first thing to look at is how the flop may have helped or hurt the strength of your hand. If your cards are a pocket pair, you are definitely interested in knowing if you've flopped a **set,** which is a powerful hand.

If your cards are suited, you must ascertain if two or all three of the flop cards match your suit. With two cards matching your suit, then you have a decent shot at making a flush on the turn or river.

If your cards are connected, even if separated by a gap of one to three cards, then you want to know if the board has given you a straight, an open-end straight draw, or even an inside straight draw. If your cards are A-K or A-Q, then you want to know not only if you made top pair, but if you have four cards to the nut straight (the highest straight possible) with the board cards.

Finally, you have to look for possible dangers. If your cards are Q-Q, and either an ace or king comes down on the flop, you will probably have to throw your hand away in a loose game with many callers.

If all three cards on the flop are suited, or if all three are connected with no more than two gaps total, then some player may already have a flush or straight. If only two cards are suited, or if only two cards are connected or separated by three gaps or fewer, then some player may be on a flush or straight draw.

Here's an example of how you must read the board and think about your hand. Let's say you are in early position with Q-Q, and the flop comes down with K-Q-6, with two of the cards suited. You have a truly strong hand right now. In fact the only hand that could beat your hand at this point is a set of kings, assuming another player was holding K-K. But both the flush and the straight possibilities are dangerous. Any player with two cards matching the suits of the two suited cards on board would make a flush if another of that suit came down.

And the straight possibilities are scary because the K-Q are right within the range of cards that many players play. Any player holding A-10, A-J, J-10, J-9, or 10-9, could make a straight if a single card came down to complete it. When you're holding trips, straights and flushes are what you most fear.

So, how do you play this hand?

You raise, reraise, and reraise again if possible. Inexperienced players will often attempt to check-raise with such a strong hand. To **check-raise** means to check, specifically in hopes that another player will bet, so that you can then raise him, extracting more money from your hand. This type of advanced play can be very effective in a higher-limit game where you are heads up with one other player, and your chance of being beaten are much slimmer. But in a loose passive game with lots of players in the hand, and such a dangerous flop, don't even think about checking here, because you could just end up giving a free card to everyone in the hand. So, bet or raise. You leave your fear of the possibility of some player holding K-K behind you, since that is the most remote possibility, and you make anyone who is drawing to a straight or flush pay to see the next card, and pay as much as you can make them pay.

If this were a no-limit game, you might go all-in just to get rid of the whole lot of players. But you can't go all-in in limit hold'em, so you do the next best thing—you charge them a price to see the next card.

Because once that straight or flush becomes more of a possibility, with three cards to the straight or three to the flush on board, which could happen on the turn or river, in a loose passive game you've got to leave your aggression behind. From that point on, should it occur, you must just check and call, hoping your set holds up.

The fact is, you will almost never have the nuts in a hold'em game, and in these loose games, some of the bizarre winning hands will amuse you. Don't be surprised if you flop a set of sevens when the flop comes down 7-5-4 and you get beaten by a player who flopped a straight because he entered the pot under the gun with 6-3 suited.

One other important factor you must bear in mind when reading the board is that any time there is a pair on the board, some player could be holding a full house (or even **quads**—that is, four of a kind). If the board pairs, you must slow down your betting if all you have is a flush or straight.

In any case, you must learn to read the board both for what it means to your own hand and what it might mean to other possible hands at the table.

BETTING ON THE FLOP

The way to make money in hold'em is to bet your strong hands aggressively in order to increase the size of the pot for your wins, and to throw your weaker hands away so that you give up less money to stronger hands when you lose. In addition to playing too many hands, weak players stay in pots—continuing to throw in more money, sometimes all the way to the showdown—far too long.

There are times, especially in the low-limit games when there is so much money in the pot, that it is correct to slow down your betting, prepared to call to the end, if you feel you have a reasonable shot at winning. You only have to win a big enough percentage of these big pots to pay for, and profit from, these appropriate calls. But if you find yourself continually just calling with marginal hands because the pot is so big, you are playing too many hands and staying in too many pots too long.

TOP PAIR ON THE FLOP

Top pair means that one of the cards in your hand is paired with the highest card on the board. For instance, you hold A-K, and the flop comes down K-8-3. Or, you hold 8-7, and the flop comes down 8-5-3. In either case, you have flopped the top pair. In the first example, your hand is very strong because no higher card can come down and ruin your hand. In the second case, your top pair (eights) is vulnerable to any player who is holding big cards, as the turn or river card could easily make your hand second best.

Generally, you should bet any premium hand, including top pair with a good kicker, as aggressively as possible. With three to a flush or straight on board, however, and another player reraising, you must slow down, and if all you have is top pair, don't be averse to throwing it away against aggressive betting with many players in the pot. Against a single player, depending on who that player is, I would probably check and call.

But almost all poker players, both in live games and online, have flush consciousness. If there is aggressive betting with three to a flush, then this betting is either coming from a player who has already made the flush, or who has flopped a very strong hand such as a set or two pair, and who wants to kill the action before someone draws out on him by making the flush if a fourth card of that suit comes down.

Never fall in love with top pair. The inability to surrender after making a pair of aces costs many poor players—who play far too many aces to start with—a lot of money. With three to a flush on board, or three to a very dangerous-looking straight—such as 9-10-J—you should always discard your top pair in the face of two aggressive bettors. With one aggressive bettor, you must make your decision based on your knowledge of that player.

AN OVERPAIR ON THE FLOP

An **overpair** is a pocket pair in your hand that is higher than any card on the table. For instance, you hold pocket jacks, and the flop comes down 9-7-4. You have an overpair to the board. Always bet an overpair aggressively, and only slow down in the face of dangerous straight or flush possibilities. If an overcard to your pair—in this example, any A, K, or Q—comes down on the turn or river, your hand may die a quick death. Even with no straight or flush possibility on the board, it is always possible that another player has flopped two pair or a set, or has a bigger pocket pair than yours, and already has your hand beat. Unless and until you can actually "read" your opponents well enough to make these types of difficult judgment calls, if you are not facing a very dangerous straight or flush possibility, you should usually play your overpair aggressively to the end.

SECOND PAIR ON THE FLOP

Second pair means that one of the cards in your hand is paired with the second highest card on the board. For instance, you hold J-10, and the flop comes down K-J-3. If you make second pair, you must be very cautious. Say you called a middle-position raiser with J-10 suited on the button, and the flop comes down, K-J-7 rainbow. **Rainbow** means all three cards are a different suit—no flush scare. If everyone checks to you, bet. It is unlikely that any player has a king. The only real danger would be a player slowplaying a set. It is possible that an early position player entered the pot with A-J and has your J-10 beat, but that player is now being penalized for playing such a hand from early position. He was afraid to bet his jacks because of the king on board, and now—with your bet—he must assume that you have a king.

It is possible that he will call your bet, hoping for his ace to hit giving him aces up, but he cannot play with any aggression at this point. You have both position and first strike aggression over him. If this is a very poor player, he may fold when you bet on the river if he doesn't hit his ace, thinking you had him beat from the start with your kings, and he never hit the card he was drawing to. Poor players are always afraid of an ace or king on board if they cannot beat aces or kings. A smarter player will call you down, especially if he recognizes you as one of the more dangerous players at the table, as he will realize that you could very well be just playing your position. In fact, you will also want to note which players play position aggressively, as these tend to be the better players.

There is also the distinct possibility that the caller has your jacks beat because he's got a bad king, possibly playing a K-3 suited or some-thing, and he was afraid to bet with his terrible kicker. In this case, he will probably call you down and take the pot at the showdown. That's life when playing against players who play crappy cards.

What if you called two early callers from middle position with A-Q, and two more players entered the pot after you? Then the flop comes down K-Q-7. This is actually an easy hand to play. If either one of the early callers bets, fold. He has a king, and you have no reason to believe there's going to be enough money in the pot to try and draw out on him. If neither of the early callers bets, then you should bet. This is the only way to find out if one of the later callers has a king. If you get raised, fold. If you get called, you get to see one more card. But you're hoping you can just pick up the pot right here.

NOTHING ON THE FLOP

What if the flop doesn't hit you at all? Let it go. Even if you're on the button, you'll probably have to check if it gets checked around to you after the flop. You might try betting on one of the rare occasions when you're up against only one or two other players, and you might even get them to fold if there's an ace or king on the board. But if there's no ace or king on the flop, and either player holds an ace or king, or any overcards to the board, low-limit players will often call you down to the end with just overcards unless there are scary straight or flush possibilities on board. Low-limit players don't go away very easily. These are just not games to try to bluff or steal in. Some players will call you down just to see what you had, especially if it's only a buck or two to call. As the limits go up, the play gets more intelligent, and you can bluff more successfully.

FLOPPING A MONSTER

What if you flop a monster, say, the nut flush, nut straight, or a full house? Is it ever wise to slow play? In my opinion, there's not much value to slowplaying in a low-limit game unless you have an aggressive bettor you know to be a smart player who is betting at you. Raising or check-raising his bet on the flop may cause him to fold and you'll only have gotten one bet out of him. By calling, he may believe you are on a draw, and he will probably bet at you again when the bets get more expensive. Aggressive players also often bet, and sometimes raise, when they are on draws. Most of the time in a low-limit game, however, you should bet and raise with every strong hand.

CONTINUE TO PUT EACH PLAYER ON A HAND

The action on the flop will likely eliminate some players from the preflop crowd, and your assessment of what each player may be holding may also change. If an ace comes down on the flop, and an ace master folds in the face of betting, then he did not have an ace this time. Nor does it matter at this point what he saw the flop with. Your only concern now is the players who remain.

Based on the cards on the board and the betting action, you want to continue to put each player on a likely hand. And again, you do this even if you are not in the pot. One of the reasons there are so many poor players online is that the online format is boring to watch compared to a live game. In low-limit live games, players who play every day tend to watch each other play simply because there is little else happening. Some of these players become quite good at beating these low-limit games simply because they become good poker players.

Online poker tends to be a duller show. The temptation is to do something else while you're waiting for a hand. If you are already a good poker player, this is fine, as there are few tells to watch for, and online play really is more mechanical, based on betting, cards, and position more than players. Professional players, in fact, play very mechanically online, often playing multiple games simultaneously and paying no attention whatsoever to their various opponents' playing styles.

This is not the way to learn poker skills, however. Whether playing in live casinos or online, you must first strive to be a good poker player, especially if you have aspirations of advancing as a player and increasing your skill.

BETTING ON THE TURN

The deeper you get into the board, the trickier it gets. As each card is added, the possibilities for premium hands become greater. Essentially, you do the same thing on the turn that you did on the flop. You consider the possibilities for your hand, and the possibilities the board cards present for other possible hands. One major difference at this point, however, is that the field may have been thinned after the flop, and you will know which players, if any, played with aggression on the flop. The betting on this round doubles, so some players can be convinced to fold if they don't hit something here.

Here's a checklist of what to look out for when considering the premium hand possibilities:

1) If there is no pair on board, then it's impossible for any player to have a full house. If you have a flush, then it can only be beaten by a bigger flush or a straight flush. Be aware, however, that with one card to come, any player who currently holds a set can make a full house (or even quads) on the river.

2) If, in addition to no pair on board, there are no more than two of any suit on board, then no player could possibly have a full house or a flush. If you have a straight, the only hand that can beat you is a higher straight.

If all four cards on board at the turn are of a different suit, then no player can even draw to a flush. With two of like suit, the flush can still show up on the river.

3) Straight possibilities are more difficult to read, but there is a simple rule. If there are any three cards on the table with less than three gaps between them in total, there is a possible straight. Example: With 6-7-8 on board, the straight possibility is obvious. There are no gaps. With 6-7-9 or 5-7-8, there is a single gap, so the straight is possible. With two gaps among three cards, such as: 4-7-8, 5-7-9, and 5-6-9, the straight is still possible. But if there are more than two gaps, no one could yet hold a straight. 5-7-10 has no straight possibility.

SLOWPLAYING THE TURN

One thing to keep in mind when playing the turn, however, is that it is impossible to have four unpaired cards on the table such that no player could possibly have a straight *draw*. This is why you must play any set aggressively on the turn. Never give a free card here unless you have the stone cold nuts and truly believe that you will get substantially more action on the river by letting other players make hands that they are likely to believe are competitive.

For instance, if you have a suited ace, and three cards to your suit are on the board, with no card on the board paired, you have the nuts. There is no hand at that point that could possibly be better than your ace-high flush. You do not have the stone cold nuts yet, however, because if any card comes down on the river that pairs the board, your flush may still be beaten by a full house or quads.

For example, if you have the nut flush, and a player bets at you on the turn, that player most likely has either a set or a smaller flush. If other players behind you have yet to act, you may be tempted to take a chance and just call here, hoping that the players behind you will also call, and that one or more will fill a straight on the river, or even make a smaller flush than yours if another of your suit comes down. These players would likely find it hard to lay down their hands on the river. The chance you take, however, is that the board may pair, giving someone with a set a chance to draw out on you.

As a matter of fact, I would raise here with my nut flush. Any player who has a set will likely call, as will any player with a smaller flush. The straight and flush draws may go away, but you want to charge those players with sets as high a price as possible to draw to a full house. And if the board does not pair, then any sets or flushes in play are also likely to call your bet on the river when you know you have the nuts.

Let me describe an actual hand that shows an example of how slowplaying can backfire. I like this example because I won this hand. I've lost so many hands trying to slowplay in low-limit games that I now know better. This is what happened to a player who tried slowplaying me.

I was in late position in an unraised pot with six players in for the flop. I had pocket eights. This is a hand I would almost certainly throw away if I did not flop a set, as the likelihood of overcards to my pair coming down was so great.

The flop was 9-3-3.

The players in front of me checked, and there was only one player to act behind me—the player on the button. I bet. This was not a bluff, but a value bet based on my belief that I probably did have the best hand at this point. There was some chance that the player on the button who had yet to act had a 9, possibly even a pair of tens, or that some player held a 3, but I felt there was a reasonable chance that I had the best hand at that point, so I wanted to charge the overcards to see the turn. And I knew, with that raggy flop, that I would get calls.

The player on the button called my bet, as did two of the players who had checked in front of me. I suspected all held overcards.

The turn card was an ace, a card I had really hoped not to see. Both players in front of me checked. I decided to take a chance here and bet. This was not really a bluff, despite the fact that the ace is a scare card. Unless the player yet to act had an ace, I probably still had the best hand at this point, and I did not want any non-ace overcards to get a free card here to try and beat me. My bet would probably be read by those at the table as a declaration that I either had an ace, or that I had an ace beaten and didn't fear an ace. If I had been in an earlier position, I could not make this bet with three players to act behind me. But with two players already checking, indicating neither had an ace, then the only ace I had to fear was one in the hand of the player on the button. If he had no ace, then I would take the pot right here. If he raised, then my betting was over, and I would give up this pot to any action at all.

The button called. The other two players folded.

I assumed the button had an ace, but that he did not like his kicker enough to raise me. I would not bet again, and if he bet on the river, I would fold. I knew my eights were no good.

To my delight, however, the river produced an 8, giving me eights full (that is, a full house with three eights and two threes). I felt that I absolutely had the best hand now, and that there would be no reason to slowplay. The button player could not possibly fear that 8, so he would at least call my bet with his aces up, even with a bad kicker. There was just too much money in the pot for him to fold now.

I bet, and he raised.

I considered the possible hands he could beat me with. I did not believe he was slowplaying pocket aces or pocket nines, though it was possible. The only other hand that could beat me was pocket threes. Was he slowplaying quad threes? I reraised, and he reraised me again.

Now, fearing he had either pocket aces or pocket nines, and a bigger full house, I called.

He showed down an A-9 for two pair—aces and nines—and I took down a nice pot.

What did he do wrong?

First, when the flop came down 9-3-3, he had my eights beat with his nines, and he should have raised. He had two pair with an ace kicker, and calling here was just downright wimpy. Even if he thought I had a 3 in my hand, he should have raised me to see if I would reraise him. It would have been more likely I had a hand like 8-9, 10-9, or J-9, and his ace kicker had me beat.

When the ace came down on the turn, he now had aces and nines, the top two pair, yet, he only called my bet again. He probably did believe I held an ace, but he also had to believe he had the best hand, because on the river, his aggressive raises and reraises showed that he had not just been playing cautiously by calling my bets, but **sandbagging,** another term for slowplaying a hand you believe to be the best hand. Unfortunately, he let me stay too long. Had he raised on the turn, I would have folded my eights in a heartbeat and he would have won that pot.

There are lots of different ways you can make money in hold'em, but as a beginner, you make most of your money by betting your strong hands aggressively. Betting builds the pots for your wins, charges players on draws a price to try and draw out on you, and folds players who won't pay the price. When you have a good hand, you rarely want to give free cards to others. Save slowplaying for the rare occasions when you have the nuts, and you truly believe you can get more money by letting other players either catch some cards to make playable hands or just take shots with the hands they have.

PLAYING THE RIVER

With five cards on the table, every possibility is now on the board. There will likely be many possible hands that can beat yours. In a higher-limit game, you can often eliminate many, if not most, of the possible hands that could be in play, simply based on how the betting has gone since the hand began. In a low-limit game, you never know.

After the river card is dealt, look at each player in the pot and see how that card may have helped or hurt him based on what you guessed him to have on the turn. If you put a player on a flush draw, for example, and the third card to the suit comes down, does he bet? Whether you are involved in the pot or not, follow the action and see if your assessments change.

Any time you feel you have a reasonable chance of winning the pot on the river, but you are unsure, then check and call. If the betting is very aggressive with raising and reraising, in a pot with three or more players in it, I would fold top pair, and might fold two pair if the board looked particularly dangerous. I would usually fold a set only if there were four to a flush or four to a straight on board, though I would definitely call one bet with my set. Players in low-limit games generally do not bluff much, so raises and reraises with four to a straight or flush are always indicative that these hands have been made.

If I truly believe my hand is the best hand, then I will definitely bet and raise on the river, even if I do not have the nuts. If I can jack up the money in the pot a few more bets before I take it down, then I will do so. If I read the situation wrong and my hand gets beat, then I'll chalk it up to education, and go over the hand in my mind to see if I should have seen the danger.

One nice feature of the low-limit games is that you so often get to see a showdown. If you are learning poker, this is invaluable to your education because you will get to see how well you are doing predicting what hand the winner holds.

POT ODDS

One concept that is extremely important in Texas hold'em is the concept of **pot odds**. This is explained most easily by example.

Here's the situation: you are in a pot with two other players. You are on the button with K-J suited, say spades, and the flop comes down with three **rags** (that is, low cards), only one of them a spade. Neither player bets on the flop. You bet, hoping to take the pot here, but both players call. No surprise in a low-limit game. On the turn, an ace of spades hits the board, giving you four cards to the nut flush, since you have the suited king. The first player bets, and the second player raises.

At this point, all you have is a nut flush *draw,* and you are certain that both players currently have you beaten. There is only one card to come, and if that card is not a spade, you will have to fold. If it is a spade, and it does not pair the board, you will definitely win the pot. Should you call the two bets?

This is just a math problem, pure and simple. The first step to answering the question is to figure out the pot odds. The concept of pot odds is very easy to understand. If I say, "What are the odds the pot is giving us for our bet?" and if you are unfamiliar with the concept of odds, you will be scratching your head. But if I first explain to you that if the pot has $100 in it, and it will cost me $10 to call a bettor and stay in the pot, then the pot odds are 10 to 1, you would have a moment of enlightenment. Suddenly, the concept of pot odds becomes clear as day.

If a pot has $30 in it, and I must bet $5 to call, what are the pot odds?

If you immediately answered 6 to 1, then you got it right. If you did not immediately realize that 30 to 5 is the same as 6 to 1, you will need to practice to get comfortable with the concept of pot odds. It'll be worth the effort because just about everything that pro gamblers ever bet on—from sports and horse racing to poker and blackjack—is based on the concept of odds.

In any case, the Internet poker rooms make it a breeze to figure out the pot odds because the total amount in the pot is displayed right there on the screen. In fact, one of the problems faced by many online players when they first start playing in live games is that there is no display of the pot amount at a live poker room table. In a live game, if you do not total up the pot as it is being built, you can find yourself at the turn or river staring at a small mountain of chips of different denominations, with no idea of the total.

The only adjustment to the Internet pot display that you will ever have to make is that you must add the current bets of active players on a round to the amount in the pot (if the pot display has not already been adjusted for these bets) before you can estimate the pot odds.

So, let's go back to our example. Let's say I am on the button with my K-J spades, and the two other players in the pot were the two blinds. Let's say this is a $6-$12 game, and preflop there was exactly $18 in the pot. The flop put another $18 in the pot, for a total of $36, when I bet and both players called.

Now, the ace of spades has hit on the turn. The small blind player bets $12, and the big blind raises to $24. The bet to me is $24, so I must bet $24 into a $72 pot. (Go ahead and add it up.) What are the pot odds? 72 to 24 is simply 3 to 1.

Can I answer the question yet of whether I should call?

Not quite. I could answer it very quickly if I just knew three very simple facts that every hold'em player should know. There are three very common drawing hands that I will have to make decisions on time and again. These hands are four to a flush, four to an open-end straight, and four to a gutshot straight.

A gutshot straight draw, also called an inside straight draw, or a one-way straight draw, is a hand which can make the straight only one way. For instance, if I have a J-Q and the board has an A-9-8, I have a gutshot straight draw. Only a 10 will make my straight. Likewise if I have that J-Q and the board has an A-K-6, again, only a 10 will make my straight. If there are two possible cards that will make your straight, then it's an open-end or two-way straight. For instance, if I have J-Q and the flop comes down 10-9-3, I can make a straight with either a king or an 8.

These are the pot odds I need to call a bet if I have four cards to a straight or flush and I'm hoping to make one of these common drawing hands:

> Flush Draw: 4.2 to 1
> Open-End Straight Draw: 5 to 1
> Gutshot Straight Draw: 11 to 1

That answers the question pretty quickly. Since I need pot odds of at least 4.2 to 1 to draw to my flush, and this pot is only giving me 3 to 1, it's a bad bet. I should fold.

Except that the *implied odds* might change that decision. What are **implied odds**?

That $72 in the pot right now might not be the whole pot by the time I take it down, if I make my flush. First off, if I call the $24 bet to me right now, there's a good chance the player who bet the $12 will also call. That extra $12 would make the pot I'd be winning $84 even if there were no other betting. And if I could squeeze one more $12 bet out of each player on the river, that would make the total I'd win for my $24 bet $108.

Is $108 enough?

Well, that would make it about 4.5 to 1, just over the threshold of what I need to make my call a good bet.

So, this is a real judgment call. If I'm really unsure about the likelihood of both players staying in the pot, and both calling another bet on the river, and if I think there's a good chance that one of the two players currently in the pot has a set and will beat my flush with a full house if a card in my suit comes down but pairs the board. And it wouldn't surprise me if the player who raised on the turn actually had a set, and raised to make it too expensive for any flush draws to call. So this is probably a bad bet. The odds against both my making my flush and winning with it are too high for me to call this raise.

Note that there are two very important concepts in this example. One, that I do not have sufficient pot odds to call this bet under the circumstances, and two, that the raiser may have raised specifically to "price me out" of it (that is, make it too expensive for me to be correct to draw to a flush). If the raiser had simply called the $12, then the pot would have had $60 in it, and the $12 bet to me would be giving me 5 to 1 pot odds. Then, if I figured I could get at least one more $12 bet out of each player on the river if I hit my flush, that would give me implied odds of at least 7 to 1, and my $12 call would be a very good bet. But that $12 raise, making it $24 to me, made it too expensive a call for me to make.

The tactic used by the raiser above, of betting to make it too expensive for another player to draw, is a tactic you will use again and again when you have a premium hand and there is a strong possibility of another player drawing out on you. By raising, you make it a mistake for him to call because you've effectively decreased his pot odds.

If a player on a draw does call when you raise, it's very important for you to know if your raise in fact made the pot odds insufficient for his call to have been a good bet. If your raise made his call a mistake, you did the right thing by raising—even if he calls and gets lucky and draws out on you.

Amateur players get very upset when this happens. When another player sucks out on their set of kings on the river with a bad flush, the hand immediately goes into their never-ending thread of bad beat stories. But professional players care little about the results of any given hand. They know that this player paid too much for his draw, and that the professional players will make money off such bad calls in the long run. It is like having a mini-ATM machine at hand. You will make lots of withdrawals from players who play without consciousness of the pot odds.

In fact, you will make most of your money at the poker tables not from being dealt pocket aces, or flopping sets, but from players who make mathematical mistakes. And the biggest mistakes, the expensive mistakes, the continual mistakes, that provide an income for the pros, are the times when players pay too much to try and make hands.

Although it's enough for you to know those three important numbers above for the pot odds you need to draw to certain common drawing hands, it's not a bad idea for you to also know where those numbers come from. Here's how we figure the odds.

COUNTING THE OUTS

If we are on a draw, first we count our total number of outs. An **out** is a card we need to get "out" of the jam we're currently in, facing a stronger hand. For an open-end straight draw, let's say a 5-6-7-8, we have eight outs— the four nines and the four fours that would make our straight. For an inside straight draw, 5-6-7-9, we have only four outs— the four eights. With four cards to a flush we have nine outs since there are 13 cards in each suit, there are nine cards left that could make our flush.

After we count our outs, we have to subtract the number of outs we have from the total number of cards we haven't seen. This number is always 47 after the flop, or 46 after the turn—that is, 52 cards (the full deck) minus the two cards in our hand and the cards on the board.

So, for an open-end straight draw on the turn, we subtract our outs from the unseen cards: 46 - 8 = 38

And the odds against our making the draw are 38 cards that are bad for us to 8 cards that make our straight. 38 to 8 is about 4.75 to 1. As a matter of fact, we are not going to calculate this number every time we have a straight draw on the turn. We will simply memorize those pot odds we need to call with the three most common drawing hands. To simplify, if we get pot odds of 5 to 1 or more for an open-end straight draw, we make the call.

There are many more complex considerations with regards to pot odds. For example, if you have a draw to a straight or flush that is not the nut straight or nut flush, you must consider the possibility that you will get one of your outs, then be beaten by a bigger hand. You may also have a straight or flush draw with an overcard to the board. You may believe that if the board pairs your overcard, this would also win the pot for you. You may have four to a flush *and* four to a straight. These types of considerations get into complexities of poker beyond the scope of this book.

At a low-limit table, the important factors to keep in mind are the pot odds for drawing to flushes and straights, gutshot and open-end. I would advise against drawing to overcards in these games, and by the same token, I would advise against counting overcards among your outs. With so many players in every pot, many playing any two suited cards, any two connected cards, and any high cards, suited or not, a lot of straights, flushes and two-pair hands are shown down.

As a general rule, if a straight or flush draw is not using both of the cards in your hand—meaning there are three to the flush or straight on the board and you hold only one of the needed cards to complete the hand—slow down. Even if you get one of the needed outs, you may be losing this pot to a higher straight or flush, or splitting it with an equivalent straight.

As an example, suppose you have an ace in hand when the flop comes down K-Q-6, then a 10 comes down on the turn. Even if the pot is offering you the 11 to 1 needed pot odds to draw to this inside nut straight, or you believe the implied odds will make the pot big enough to pay 11 to 1 or better, you are unlikely to be the only ace at the table in a low-limit game. Personally, I would abandon this hand. If the jack shows up on the river, the only bettors remaining will be the players with aces and any dreamer who may be holding a 9 and just can't let it go. You are highly unlikely to be paid full price for your call. You will end up splitting the pot with one or more ace masters, and you won't get nearly 11 to 1 for your money. And even if you do happen to be the only ace in play on this hand, over the long run, you won't be, so it's just a bad call.

6. NO-LIMIT TEXAS HOLD'EM ONLINE

The general theory of beating no-limit hold'em games is similar to the general theory of beating limit hold'em games. Be selective in the hands you play, and play them aggressively. The biggest difference in no-limit games is that you play even fewer hands while you're learning, and you play much more aggressively than in limit games.

There are two major mistakes players make in approaching the no-limit games. First, they tend to believe that no-limit games are much more like limit games than they are. In fact, everything in a no-limit game is exaggerated—the value of position, hand, chip stack, etc. Second, many players believe that a no-limit game is the same as the no-limit tournament coverage they watch on TV. The main thing that drives a tournament, however, and dictates virtually every player's strategy, is the constantly increasing cost of the blinds and the players' inability to add to their chip stacks in any way other than winning pots. No-limit hold'em in a ring game is an entirely different animal. This is a waiting game. No one is ever forced to bet by the rising blind costs. The blinds are small compared to any player's allowed buy-in, and anyone is free to buy more chips if they go below the maximum buy-in amount.

Limit hold'em games, both online and in live poker rooms, are always listed by the size of the early and later street bets—$2/$4 games, $10/$20 games, etc. The typical online poker room that offers no-limit games, however, categorizes them by the maximum buy-in amount. If an online casino lists no-limit games, you will find the choices listed as: NLH$50, NLH$100, NLH$200, etc. These descriptions indicate games where the maximum buy-in allowed is $50, $100, and $200, respectively. The blinds, in most cases, are a function of the buy-in allowed. Typically, the big blind is 1 percent of the maximum buy-in. In an NLH$50 game, the small and big blinds would be 25 cents and 50 cents. In an NLH$400 game, the small and big blinds would be $2 and $4.

This no-limit buy-in/blind structure is meant to prevent players with very large bankrolls from bullying tables where most players cannot match their chip stacks. But this only limits the degree of bullying; it doesn't eliminate it in any sense. To have 100 times the big blind is to have one hell of a lot of chips compared to what any player would have in any typical limit hold'em game. I can't even imagine a player buying into a $10/$20 limit hold'em game with $2,000. There would be no reason to sit at a $10/$20 table with so many chips in front of you.

But in no-limit hold'em, players often buy in for the maximum allowed and go all in against players with like amounts. There are occasionally some incredibly large pots given the size of the blinds. But play this aggressive does not occur all the time. Most poker rooms list the average pot size over some specified range of recent hands in addition to the players at the table. At a NLH$200 table, which has $1/$2 blinds, you will often find average pot sizes of $10 to $15. However, a NLH$200 table with an average pot size of $20 is quite a bit more aggressive than the norm.

CHOOSING A NO-LIMIT TABLE

If you are not an experienced no-limit player, choose a full 9 or 10-player table. Short-handed no-limit play is much trickier and should not even be considered by beginners.

Judge these games by their average pot size. If the average pot size is on the high side compared to other no-limit hold'em tables with the same max buy-in, then this table probably has one or more aggressive players who will take frequent shots at the wimps. These relatively few aggressive bets, though often not called, will crank up the average pot size. It's also possible that the average pot size was recently skewed upwards by a single monster pot involving two players with big chip stacks and premium hands—for example, a full house meets a nut flush at the river. You can usually tell if this might be the case by opening a table and watching the action for a while.

If the average pot size is on the low side compared to other no-limit hold'em tables with the same max buy-in, then this table likely has less aggressive players, often players with more limit than no-limit experience, and they are ripe for an experienced and aggressive no-limit player to go in and start pushing them around. If you watch one of these tables for a while, you will see that it is often possible to see a flop simply by calling the big blind. This type of table occurs online at all levels of play.

Assuming you are not an experienced and aggressive no-limit player, you'll probably do better at the table with the average or smaller than average pot size where the aggressive players are not already having their way with the wimps. If you are going to play no-limit, then you are going to have to go in and be that aggressive player who pushes the wimps around. If you can't do it, stay out of the game. It's the only way to play. But before we get into strategy considerations, let's describe how no-limit play differs fundamentally from limit play.

THE BULLY'S GAME

Doyle Brunson once called no-limit hold'em the Cadillac of poker games because everything that makes poker poker is even more poker in a no-limit game. No-limit hold'em is a bully's game. You don't need a strong hand to win so much as a good read on your opponent—and the guts to put your money where your read is. But because you can employ the strategies of poker so much more effectively in no-limit than in a limit game, it is far from an easy game to master. Many players at the table know that bullies rule, and they all fancy themselves bullies. You're going to be coming up against other players who have the same ideas you have. You don't want to bluff that river flush if your opponent actually made that flush.

PREFLOP

Do you want to try to drive other players out of the pot preflop in order to give your pocket jacks the best chance to win? This move is called "limiting the field," and it's not easy to do in a $2/$4 limit game. But it's very easy to accomplish in a no-limit game with $2/$4 blinds. Just raise the bet to $20. See how many callers come in.

You want to steal the blinds? Again, not easy in a $2/$4 limit game. You can raise the $2 big blind to $4 from the button but if that guy has any kind of a playable hand, he'll protect his $2 investment and call your bluff. In a no-limit game, just make it $40 and see how protective the big blind's feeling, knowing he'll have to throw $38 more bucks into the pot just to play you out of position. You don't get many sheriffs at a no-limit hold'em table. (Note: a "sheriff" is a common type of player found in low-limit games who tends to be overly suspicious that players are bluffing and will call suspected bluffs too often—even when his own hand is very marginal. He'd rather lose than be bluffed.) Of course, if you try to steal the $1 and $2 blinds with a raise to $40 from the button, you better pray you don't get a call. You could be betting into aces with that $40 bet, so an overbet like this may not be the wisest move. I don't want you to think I'm suggesting a strategy here. I'm just illustrating a concept.

POST-FLOP

Flop a set and you want to keep the players with straight draws and flush draws from drawing out on you? Not always easy to do in a limit game. Your bet on the flop won't often make the flush draw a bad call. But it's no problem in no-limit. With one bet you can cut the pot odds to pretty damn close to even money, usually making any draw a big mistake.

You want to bluff on the river when the third card to a flush comes down and you put your opponent on top pair? In a limit game, he'll call your raise. It's a no brainer. That bluff is useless. In a no-limit game, you can make him pay with all his chips to keep you honest. If all he's got is top pair, he'll go away mad, but he'll go away.

SIMPLE FORMULAS

I've heard of many "simple formulas" for beating no-limit hold'em games online, though I tend to regard anything that's too simple as not being worth much. Everyone seems to know someone who knows someone who is killing with a simple formula in the online no-limit games, but I have yet to actually meet the guy himself. I'll describe two of the methods you're likely to run into on the Internet discussion forums. Most of the simple formula strategies claim to work at the low buy-in no-limit games only. They differ radically from the advice found in the writings of no-limit's major authors, but then, I'm not sure Doyle Brunson or T.J. Cloutier ever played no-limit hold'em in a game with a $25 maximum buy-in and blinds of 10 cents and 25 cents. Perhaps Doyle will someday tell us his secrets for making $5 an hour in these games when he writes Super System 3...

1. Selective Aggression: Lying in Wait

This formula is the simplest of all. You pick the five top starting hands—A-A, K-K, Q-Q, J-J, and A-K—and you go all in with them whenever you get them. With this strategy, you'd be playing, on average, about one hand out of every thirty-three dealt. I presume you would also go all in over the top of a raiser if you held A-A or K-K, but would you do this with A-K or J-J? Would you call an all-in with J-J or Q-Q?

How well this strategy works in real life depends on a few of these fine points of play and on how much action you actually get when you go all in. To estimate your potential win, you'd subtract the cost of all the blinds you'd be going through without playing, then subtract the total amount of your losses from the total amount of your wins. You'd most likely win more than you'd lose on the hands you played. Unfortunately, I'm not sure you'd win enough to pay for the blinds while waiting to play, primarily because I don't think you'd get that much action. This strikes me as an attempt to win at poker without really knowing much about how to play poker. I doubt it works consistently at any level.

2. Selective Aggression: El Cheapo Version

You buy in cheap, well under the maximum. In a $50 buy-in game, you buy-in for $10. Then, your strategy is very similar to the above, except that you also enter the pot before the flop, if you can do so cheaply, with any pocket pair.

With one of the premium two-card hands, you go all-in before the flop.

With the cheap pairs, if you flop a set, or have an overpair to the board after the flop, you go all in. That's it.

This strategy will presumably make more money on the hands played because it will get more action both before and after the flop. Since the player is substantially under-chipped compared to most of the other players at the table, his all-in bets will not appear to be that threatening. Players with more marginal hands and with $50 in front of them might be more tempted to call all-ins from a $10 raiser who can't make it any more expensive for them.

One player told me he made money with a variation of this strategy for months, but then suffered some bad beats and gave back a lot of it. Again, the strategy is contrary to the general theory of no-limit Texas hold'em, which tells us that chips are power and you want as many of them in front of you as you can get in order to batter your opponents. So, instead of looking for an easy formula, let's consider actually learning how to play the game by using the Internet for the poker college that it is.

WATCH THE PROS

One of the most important things to do before you buy in at a no-limit table is watch the action for a while. You will find all of the same types of players at the no-limit games that you find at the limit games. There will be players who want to see lots of flops, and players who seem to wait forever to play a hand. You'll see players make all-in bets with hands like A-J offsuit and players who call all-in bets with hands like K-J offsuit. In fact, although these games tend to be tighter than limit games, as you gain experience you will be amazed at how often players overplay their high cards before the flop.

There will almost always be one or more players who are quite a bit more aggressive than the others and who seem to bully other players out of a lot of pots. Often, these players are sitting there with the biggest chip stacks. Watch these players. You will rarely get to see their cards, so watch how they play their position and their opponents.

These players are almost always aggressive. They rarely check or call. They generally enter any pot with a raise or a re-raise. They rarely check-raise because they don't check much to start with. But they will re-raise a check-raiser all-in, a move that more often than not wins them the pot. If you are going to be successful at no-limit hold'em, you will have to employ an aggressive style similar to this.

You will also note that these aggressive players get involved in a lot of pots. They don't sit and wait for hands. And although they generally come in with a raise or a reraise, and always a fairly substantial one, they do not usually go all in before the flop. If the pot was already raised, they might bet two to three times the size of the pot when they enter it.

If you start taking notes on these players, you'll find that they are far more likely to play from late position than from early position. You'll also note that they tend to get involved with players heads-up and are rarely in multi-way pots. (A multi-way pot is any pot with three or more players involved in it.) If a pot stays multi-way beyond the flop, they exit. You will see them fold hands suddenly against a bet, but they always seem to get out relatively cheaply.

The question you have to answer as you watch these players make money is how do they know when to get involved and when to back off? You'll also find that they seem to pick on the same players over and over again. And there are some players they rarely get involved with.

All of this should teach you something about how to win at this no-limit game, as opposed to winning at limit poker.

YOUR STRATEGY

PREFLOP NO-LIMIT STRATEGY

Playing AK, AA, KK, QQ, and JJ:

1) If you are the first player into the pot from any position, come in with a standard raise of 3 to 4 times the size of the big blind. If the blinds are $2 and $4, a $4 raise would be the minimum raise allowed, but you should come in with a bet of $16 to $20. That is, you're calling the $4 big blind, and raising $12 to $16 more. If you are reraised by any player, push all-in. If a player reraises all-in, call his all-in bet. (Note that the "standard" raise in a no-limit game is higher than the standard raise in a limit game, where you are only allowed to double the previous bet. In a limit game with $2 and $4 blinds, the maximum amount a player could bet would be $8, which would raise the $4 big blind by $4 more. One tell that a player may be new to the no-limit game is if he raises just the minimum allowed. Although this may be a tricky player with pocket aces or kings who is just hoping that some other player will reraise him, it is more often a sign of inexperience at the game.)

2) If you are not the first player into the pot, but the players who entered in front of you limped in, bet double the amount in the pot. For example, with blinds of $2 and $4, and two players in front of you who limped in for $4 each, making the pot size $16, you should bet $32. If you get reraised, push all-in, and call any all-in.

3) With any previous raise in front of you, simply push all-in.

Note that you will never fold any of these hands preflop under any circumstances. Nor will you hesitate to push all-in or call any all-in.

Playing AQ, AJ, 10-10, 99:

1) Fold these hands in early position.

2) If you are first into the pot from middle or late position, raise 3-4 times the size of the big blind, but fold to any reraise.

3) If you are not the first player into the pot, but the players who entered in front of you limped in, bet double the amount in the pot, but fold to any reraise.

4) With any standard raise (3 to 4 times the big blind) in front of you, fold in middle position, but call in late position.

Playing KQs, QJs, J10s, 88, 77:

1) Fold these hands in early and middle position.

2) If you are first into the pot from late position, raise 3-4 times the size of the big blind, but fold to any reraise.

3) If you are not the first player into the pot, but the players who entered in front of you limped in, limp in yourself from late position, but fold to any reraise.

4) With any raise in front of you, fold in any position.

Playing 10-9s, 9-8s, 8-7s, 66, 55, 44, 33, 22:

1) Fold to any preflop raise from any position.

2) Call limpers from late position only.

3) Raise 3-4 times the big blind from the button if first into the pot, but fold if either of the blinds reraises.

No fixed strategy will turn you into a sure winner online, and this is especially true in no-limit games which are the most dangerous. The above strategy for deciding on which starting hands to play is meant as a general guideline for beginners. If you are in a game where aggressive players seem to always reraise any standard raise, then this strategy will not work as they will steal from you every time you raise other than all-in. Either learn to play back at them, or find another, less aggressive, table.

PLAYING ON THE FLOP, TURN, AND RIVER

Once the flop has come down, you'll have a much better idea of the value of your hand. If you raised with pocket jacks preflop, and the flop came down with an ace and a queen, you could be in a world of trouble. If you "have position" on your opponent—that is, he must act on his hand before you—you must bet the size of the pot if he checks, but fold if he check-raises you. If he has position on you—that is, you must act before he does—you should check and fold if he bets. If he's on a straight draw, you hate the thought of giving him free cards, but the fact is this flop was about as bad for your hand as a flop could be, and you're probably going to have to give it up if you're not in position.

On the flop, turn, and river, you must look at the actual value of your hand in relation to the likelihood that your opponent has you beat with a hand he will not put down. The preflop strategy for entering pots above should get you into pots with either stronger than average cards, or position on your opponents, or a combination of both. When the cards on the board are scary, and your opponent is playing aggressively, you are usually correct to just give it up.

Winning at no-limit hold'em is really about four factors:

1) Always play with relentless aggression.

2) Play from a strong (late) position unless your hand is very powerful, so that you can see what your opponent does before you must act.

3) Pick your opponents carefully, and be ready to attack those you can push around.

4) Get out as cheaply as you can when you don't have a hand and you realize your opponent will not go away. (But note: a skilled no-limit player does not need a hand to get involved in a pot. He simply needs position and a timid player for an opponent.)

If you follow the above advice, and realize that no-limit hold'em is at least as much about aggression and strategy as your actual cards, you may turn out to be a good no-limit player. If so, then you may want to move on to the online games with six to eight players, instead of the safer nine to ten-player games. The fewer the players, the less likely it is that a premium hand will be out there in an opponent's hand, and the more aggression and smart strategy will pay off.

Never buy in at a no-limit table for more than you would be comfortable losing on a single hand. And if the thought of losing your whole buy-in on a single hand pains you, this probably isn't your game. Also, always buy in for the maximum amount allowed. If you cannot comfortably lose the max buy-in on a single hand, then play in a game with a smaller max buy-in. Chips are power in this game, so you want to have enough chips in front of you intimidate players when you want them to fold, and to maximize your win when you trap an opponent into taking a shot at you when you have the nuts. If you lose any substantial amount of your initial buy-in, then go to the cashier and replenish your stack to the maximum allowed.

Also, if you have a couple of nice wins at a no-limit table, doubling or tripling up your initial buy-in, get some of that money off the table unless you are prepared to lose it the same way you won it. Once you are well past the learning stage, and you feel you can protect your chips with your judgment, then keep stacking your winnings in front of you. There's nothing quite as intimidating to a new player entering a $100 maximum buy-in table as seeing a player sitting there with $750 in chips.

7. NO-LIMIT TOURNAMENTS ONLINE

Tournament play, whether live or online, is nothing like playing in ring games. From the moment the first hand is dealt until the last chip is won by the only player remaining, every player in the game is in a fight against time for survival.

For most players interested in playing no-limit hold'em, it's better to start with tournaments rather than with the real money cash games. Tournaments will limit your losses on any play to the tournament buy-in (plus rebuys and add-ons, when allowed). If you pay $42 to enter a tournament, that tournament will cost you $42 and no more. You know this going in. And tournaments will definitely give you a feel for the no-limit game because the increasing blinds will force you into aggressive play.

A player who has lost half his chips in the first hour is not allowed to pick up the rest of his chips, cash out, and go home. With every player at his table now eyeing that small stack of chips that's in front of him, he knows he has to make a move.

By the same token, a player who has won more chips faster than he's ever won before can't just pack it in and call it a day. It's not a day; it's only the fourth blind level. He's got hours of play before him and a minefield of desperate players taking shots at him. And he can't just sit tight and retain his fortune. He's got to double his win, triple it, quadruple it before he even gets near the final table. There are hundreds of players between him and any real money. He knows that the only thing separating him from that guy on the short stack are a few lucky hands. The whole thing could turn around at any time.

The Internet offers all kinds of poker tournaments, from one-table "sit & go" tournaments with $2 buy-ins, to monster tournaments with thousands of players and seven-digit prize pools. There are single-table satellites for winning entries into bigger multi-table tournaments, and multi-table mega-satellites for winning seats at major live tournaments like the main event at the World Series of Poker (WSOP) or a World Poker Tour (WPT) superstar event. There are even heads-up tournaments where opponents face each other one-on-one.

FREE ROLL TOURNAMENTS

Many major online poker rooms offer freeroll tournaments for their new players, and many offer them as part of their bonus programs for both new players depositing money and reload deposits. You should always take advantage of these tournaments when offered. As long as there's a real prize, every tournament is a learning experience.

EVALUATING YOUR CHANCES IN A TOURNAMENT

There are dozens of excellent books providing tournament strategies for playing in both limit and no-limit tournaments. Very few authors, however, discuss how you should choose a tournament when you have such a vast array of options. Once you understand the general theory of Texas hold'em—the value of hands, position, and aggression—you're ready to try your skill at tournaments. So where do you start?

Every tournament can be classified as fast, medium, or slow. I will define these terms more precisely below, but for now, let's agree that a single-table satellite, designed to come up with a winner in an hour or so of play, is a fast tournament. The WSOP main event, which takes the better part of a week to determine a winner, is the ultimate slow tournament.

The faster a tournament is the more likely it is that the winner will be determined by luck, as opposed to skill. This is not to say that fast tournaments require little skill to win. In fact, some pros concentrate on fast tournaments.

Many players make the mistake of assuming that it is the size of their initial chip stack that makes a tournament fast or slow. This is not the case. It's the blind structure in relation to the number of chips each player starts with that makes a tournament fast or slow.

SATELLITES

A one-table satellite is fast because each player starts with only a few hundred dollars in chips and the blinds go up fast, often doubling every ten minutes. In a satellite like this, most players quickly become short-stacked and must start taking shots with marginal hands. Luck plays a big part in determining a satellite winner because if one player happens to be dealt a few more premium hands than the other players or just happens to draw out to better hands a few times, that player will have a great shot at winning the satellite, even if others at the table have superior poker skills.

This does not mean that single-table satellites are simply luck fests. Pros play satellites and make money from them. The theory of winning a satellite is pretty simple. You take early advantage of the amateurs who don't realize from the start how fast a satellite is. If you have a legitimate hand, you play it—and with aggression. The definition of a "legitimate" hand is pretty loose in a satellite. The faster the format, and the smaller the field of players, the lower the standard gets. In a fast satellite, A-10 offsuit is often a legitimate hand to play from just about any position. Pocket sixes are a pretty good hand to go all-in with. By the time the tourists figure it out, they're short-stacked. Game over.

SIT & GOES

All major online poker rooms offer a type of single-table tournament, generally around the clock, called a **sit & go**. The term "sit & go" refers to the fact that there is no official starting time for the tournament. Players buy-in one at a time and take a seat. As soon as all seats are filled, the tournament starts. The only real difference between a sit & go and a one-table satellite is that the term satellite implies that the prize for the winner is not cash, but placement in a bigger tournament where the buy-in would be higher, usually about ten times higher, than the cost of the satellite.

There are also multi-table satellites, especially for the major tournaments, where many players, not just the winner, can earn a seat. But the most common type of satellite is the single-table event that rewards one or two winners, and these types of satellites are equivalent to the popular single-table sit & go tournaments we find online. Sit & go winners get the cash pool created by the buy-ins.

There's very little time for playing much fancy poker in a satellite or a sit & go. At the beginning, for the first couple of blind levels, you might get a bit of play in, given the right hands and situations. And if you hit some nice pots early and pull well ahead of the crowd, you might even get a short respite from play if you're just not getting the cards you like. You can let a few of the short stacks take shots at knocking each other out for awhile.

But, when it's down to two or three players, there's no time to wait for a hand. The best situation you can have at this point is to be up against amateurs who made it this far with nothing but lucky cards. Even if you're short-stacked, you've still got a chance to run over them with aggression while they're waiting for more good cards to play back at you.

When it's down to two players, if you're up against a player who knows the score, it will very soon be all-in every hand until the cards decide. It won't take long. To be heads up in a fast single-table tournament is not the same thing as being heads up at the final table of a major multi-table event. In a big tournament, when two players have all the chips, the game can go on for hours. In a satellite, even if the final two players have fairly equivalent chip stacks, both will be short-stacked compared to the blinds, and neither will be able to pay the price of sitting out a few hands.

But if luck were the sole determiner of a fast tournament, there would be no satellite pros. For every ten-player satellite, each player would win one out of ten times in the long run. But a satellite pro will win one out of every five to seven satellites he enters. If he's playing these satellites for WSOP event chips, he'll in effect be buying those chips at a discounted price, and he can sell them for full value, or use them to enter events at a discount himself.

Close to half the time, the winner of a fast one-table tournament will be whatever player got the luckiest cards, often just a few lucky hands. Pros make out when the cards are more evenly distributed, and especially when the amateurs don't know how to make money with the good cards when they do get them. A player who fails to bet aggressively with premium hands or who folds his pocket queens to an all-in bet because he's afraid of aces and kings, can get all kinds of lucky hands and still never get close to winning. Satellites aren't for wimps.

FAST SPEED STRUCTURES

Many of the small buy-in tournaments we find online have fast blind structures, similar to satellites, even when there are hundreds (or thousands!) of players. Amateurs' chances of winning are greater in these fast tournaments than they are in long, slow tournaments. But luck only lasts so long. Even a fast tournament that lasts, say, four or five hours will leave many of the rankest amateurs in the dust. The more time there is to play poker and the more chips there are to play with, the more skill becomes a factor in determining the winner.

But let's define the terms "fast" and "slow" a bit more precisely. Any tournament where you start out with twenty times or less the size of the big blind is **fast**. If blind levels increase every fifteen minutes or less, it's lightening fast. So if you get $1,000 in chips, and the blinds start at $25 and $50, you've got exactly twenty big blinds to start with. If the blinds go up every fifteen minutes, players are in desperate shape right from the start. Most of the amateurs don't know this, which means this is a good time to play with aggression. While the players at your table are thinking "survival," you should be thinking: "Attack!"

There's no time to fool around. If you've read other tournament books that tell you not to feel desperate until your chip stack amounts to only ten big blinds, forget it! Those books were written by players who assumed blind levels would last sixty or ninety minutes—or even a full two hours as in the World Series of Poker main event.

With the blinds going up every fifteen minutes, you'll be entering the fourth blind level, with blinds of $150 and $300, in forty-five minutes from the time you start. You will not have seen even twenty-five rounds of play by this point in time. So you'll need to get to work right from the start. With a lot of players in the field, this tournament could last a couple of hours, but this fast format is as luck-based as any satellite.

Also note that a slower blind structure can make a tournament with equally few starting chips much more skill-based than you might think. For example, if you have starting blinds of $25 or $50, and only $1,000 in chips to start, that's only twenty big blinds. But if the blind levels increase only once per hour, this is a real tournament and it's not all that fast. In this structure, at the end of two hours, you'd just be entering the third blind level, with blinds of $100 and $200. Even if you don't play a single hand in those first two hours, you'll still have a couple hundred in chips in front of you. (Not that I'd recommend this!)

With fifteen-minute blind levels, as described above, you'd be entering the *ninth* blind level after two hours. This would put the blinds at $600 and $1,200 with a $200 ante!

So it's the combination of starting chips and the rapidity with which the blind levels advance that defines the speed of a tournament. And fast blind levels are generally the more important factor. Note that, in these examples, I'm using the same blind levels that are used for the WSOP hold'em events. If you are in a tournament where the blinds start at $5 and $10, and you have $200 in starting chips, this would be equivalent in speed to the example above where we start with $1000 in chips and blinds of $25 and $50.

With thirty or more big blinds and twenty-minute blind levels, it's still a fast tournament, but it's a notably slower structure than with fifteen-minute blind levels, and you'll feel the difference. With this format, you might start with $1,500 in chips and blinds of $25 to $50. At the end of forty minutes, you'll be entering the third blind level, which is $100 to $200. If you don't make some money in the first hour of play, you are definitely in trouble, but at least you have an hour of being a bit more selective in choosing hands to play and/or shots to take. This slightly slower format provides the more skillful players with a bit more time to get reads on their opponents and a feel for the table.

MEDIUM SPEED STRUCTURES

With fifty big blinds to start with and thirty-minute blind levels, you've got some time to play. This is a medium-speed format. If the field of players is bigger than one hundred, and if 10% or so of those players are fairly proficient tournament players, expect these skilled players to occupy three to five of the seats at the final table. Luck will still be a factor for many players in the money, but its effect is greatly diminished. Again, the more time the talented players have to use their poker skills, the less of a factor luck becomes.

SLOW SPEED STRUCTURES

With one hundred big blinds to start with, and sixty-minute blind levels, you've got a slow structure that will weed out most of the less-skilled players the first day. This tournament will probably not end on day one unless the field of players is very small. A rank amateur will make it to the final table in a format like this once in a blue moon, and then only when there is a huge pool of amateurs to start with. Any unskilled players in a tournament like this are exactly the types of players every pro wants to see—dead money.

DEAD MONEY

The most pathetic player in a no-limit hold'em tournament is the player who gets blinded off while waiting for a hand. This player epitomizes the term **dead money**. His chips have no life to them at all. They just sit there in front of him getting eaten away slowly, as round after round goes by with him waiting for a hand. If you ever find yourself dreading the approaching blinds because they will take away so many of your precious chips, you've already waited too long for a playable hand. You've had a lot of playable hands if your chip stack is this short. You just didn't realize it. Long before this point, you should have been looking for a shot to take.

Before those blinds get around to you again, make a decision to go all-in. The cards you play are of secondary importance. Hell, they're of no importance. 3-2 offsuit? Possible straight. Go for it. If you lose, you lose. But make a resolution that you will never allow yourself to be in that position again. You must keep your chips alive on the table at all times. If this happens to you again and again, you may not have the heart for tournament play.

THE VALUE OF FAST TOURNAMENTS

In evaluating tournaments to find the ones where you have the best chance as a beginner, keep the speed factor in mind. If you are not an experienced tournament player, then you stand your best chance of getting into the money in a faster tournament. If you get the right cards, you just might make it.

And don't make the mistake of thinking you should start out in slow tournaments because you want to use and test your skill. Entering a major WSOP or WPT event, when you have very little tournament experience, is just throwing your money away. Fast tournaments are excellent to start out in because fast play is an art form in itself, and it is an art form you will use and encounter in every tournament you play, whether the overall structure is fast or slow. In a fast tournament, the desperation level starts high and never stops rising. These tournaments will force you to recognize hands of value based on the combination of your position, your chip stack, and the players you are confronting.

When you're taking a shot with a marginal hand, these are hugely important factors, and the only way to learn how to evaluate these factors is by putting yourself under pressure to do or die. Fast tournaments also force you to identify weak players and dangerous players quickly.

If you get to the point where you can win money in fast tournaments, the skills you will have developed will be invaluable in slower tournaments as well. Every tournament becomes fast for every player who ever gets short-stacked. There is an art to playing a short stack successfully, and nothing teaches this art like playing in tournaments that start out fast and never slow down.

If you never develop the art of fast play, you will also be at a disadvantage in any tournament when you encounter players who are short-stack experts. Any player who can change gears—switching from fast and loose to slow and tight, then back again—is a dangerous player. It's a general rule in no-limit hold'em that you don't go up against the player with the big stack of chips, as that player can really hurt you. If that big stack of chips is sitting in front of a wimp, however, a player who's simply had a few lucky hands, you might well prefer to take on that player rather than the short-stacked pro who's capable of putting you to a test with his all-in bet. Any player who gives no indication of whether he's playing his cards or his guts is a dangerous player. You not only want to be able to recognize that player, *you want to be that player*.

Many players who enter slower tournaments do well until they get roughly to the halfway point, then they die. They can never seem to figure out why the good cards stopped coming. In fact, their lack of success has nothing to do with the cards they were getting. Every tournament gets faster as the tournament progresses. Many players who do fine early on can't change gears for the faster play. They ought to forget about the slower tournaments for a while and get into some of these hair-raising fast tournaments. They need a crash course in speed play.

Finally, skill at fast play is exactly the talent you need to win satellites. These satellite skills are very valuable to players who want to play in the bigger tournaments but don't want to risk the big buy-ins. Satellites can get you in cheaply.

REBUYS

Many online tournaments allow players to acquire more chips through **rebuys**. In some cases, a single rebuy is allowed during the first few blind levels or during some time period such as the first hour. In other cases, unlimited rebuys are allowed during the rebuy period, provided the player is at or below some specified number of chips, usually the starting amount. In still other cases, all players may make a single rebuy called an **add-on** at the end of the rebuy period, regardless of the number of chips they have.

Generally, you should always maintain the maximum number of chips in front of you that you are permitted to have. If that means making a rebuy, make the rebuy. This rebuy period does not last long, so make the most of it. On the other hand, if you lose all your chips near the end of a rebuy period in a tournament with fast blind levels, it's generally best to call it a day and go home. It is not wise to start over in a tournament with a smaller stack than most of the players at your table when the blinds are already double or triple their first level. If you would not enter a tournament with such a structure in the first place, then rebuying into it is a mistake.

If rebuys or a rebuy and add-on provide substantially more chips than the initial starting allotment, then it might be fine to rebuy at this point. Before doing so, ask yourself what the next blind level is, how many big blinds you'll have for that level, and how far behind in chips you'll be from the average player at your table. If you believe you'll have a competitive chip stack, you might want to pay the price to stay in the tournament. In most cases, however, rebuying at the end of a rebuy period when you're down to the felt is the equivalent of buying into a tournament with a bad format and a serious chip handicap.

SUMMARY

This isn't a book on how to win no-limit hold'em tournaments. There are a dozen books on the market that discuss which hands you should play, when you should raise, how you should disguise your hands, and a hundred other topics of importance. In the space I have to cover online poker tournaments in this book, I won't even pretend to cover these strategic considerations. My major concern in this book is with Internet-specific aspects of these tournaments. The biggest difference between the online tournaments and the tournaments offered by your local casino poker room are the huge number of choices you have online.

How do you decide which tournament to enter? Is there a difference between the big ones and the smaller ones? Again, to me, the real issue you face in evaluating which tournaments to enter is the *speed of play*, and this is an area of tournament theory covered by very few authors. The slower the format, the more skill will be a factor in determining the winner. With minimal tournament experience, your chances of finishing in the money will be better in the faster tournaments. These fast tournaments will also provide you with an invaluable education in the skills required for all tournaments—especially managing a short stack and taking shots at the pot with nothing more than position and guts.

The Internet allows you to play at almost any speed you desire, so why not use these tournaments to fine-tune your game at all speed levels? The big money, of course, is in the big, slow tournaments. But these are terrible tournaments to learn in. So, get yourself into some cheap sit & goes and learn how to play when the cards aren't favoring you. The Internet is a school for tournament play, and the tuition can be cheap.

8. POKER BOTS, CHEATING, AND OTHER WEIRDNESS

There are two types of cheating that online poker players worry about. One is play by "**bots**," or non-human computer programs. The word "bot" comes from "robot" and is a common computer geek term for any program that makes decisions and interacts with preprogrammed intelligence. When it comes to a poker bot, the question is: does use of a bot to play your hands even qualify as cheating? This was never a concern in live poker rooms because it was never a possibility.

The other type of cheating online players worry about is **collusion** between two or more players sharing information about their hands via telephone or private computer messages. Collusion has always been a problem in live poker games, where colluders use secret signals to transfer information, and it's the same problem in the online games. Everyone acknowledges that collusion is possible, and that it is cheating, but how dangerous is it, and what can be done about it?

BOTS

One type of bot is a computer program designed by a player to play his hands automatically, without the other players at the table or the poker room knowing this. Is it cheating if the "player" in seat #8 is not a human being but a software program making the decisions for a human player who set up the account, deposited funds with the poker room cashier, and bought into the game, then went to dinner while his bot was attempting to earn some money for him?

I don't think most players who are skillful enough to make money from poker would be highly concerned about such a bot. Most skilled players would find it hard to believe that a computer program could beat them. And many professional players would acknowledge that their own online play—when carried out on four or more simultaneous tables, often using multiple computer monitors—is not a whole lot different from what a bot might be programmed to do. This type of assembly line play prevents the player from paying much attention to other players at the tables. Pros who employ these tactics make formulaic decisions based on their cards, their position, and the prior action in the round, just as a poker bot would do. If I am playing poker online, and I have a chart on my desk that provides the complete betting and playing strategy I will use, would this be cheating? Would it suddenly become cheating if I put that exact same strategy into a computer program, and my computer played the hands for me?

POKER ROOM BOTS

The more worrisome type of bot, and the type that just about all players feel is a serious violation of the ethics of the game, is a program employed by the poker room itself. This type of bot is identical to the type described above, that might be employed by a player, and it too gives the appearance of being just another human player. A poker room might defend its use of such bots in the way that a live casino poker room might defend its use of proposition players or shills. A **proposition player** is paid a flat hourly rate by the poker room to sit and play at a poker table. A "prop" player plays with his own money and bears the brunt of his own wins and losses. A **shill**, on the other hand, is a player who is paid a flat hourly rate, but plays with the house's money. The house bears the brunt of his wins and losses. Shills are generally required by the poker room to follow strictly defined and conservative playing styles. Some poker rooms use props and/or shills in order to keep tables in action during slow periods. Shills are virtually never employed in high-limit games—not because the pros wouldn't tolerate them, but because the poker room management knows that the pros would eat them alive. At the lower-limit games, most amateurs don't even know that some players may be props or shills. In the case of a bot being used by a poker room, this would be more analogous to a poker room using a shill than a prop player, as the bot would be playing with the house's money against whatever other human players are at the table.

I definitely have moral objections to any poker room using bots to beat its own customers. I consider this to be fraud.

Poker strategies are largely based on deception. Every player at every table employs deception and expects deception from his opponents. That's the game. But whether online or live, this battle of liars must take place on a level playing field. That means that the poker room itself—including the dealers, the cards, the rules, the procedures, the shuffle—everything must be the same for all players. One problem with an online poker room using bots is that the poker room has access to information that the other players at the table don't, including information about all of the players' hole cards. The poker room may insist that it would never employ its bots in such a devious way, but the fact that it so easily could employ such a strategy should be reason enough for the use of bots to be regarded as unethical by a poker room, and every poker room should assure its players in its terms and conditions that the use of such bots is a violation of their policies and will never be done.

Poker is about deception, but the poker room itself is never supposed to be part of the deception in any way. Everything the poker room does must be above board. Think of how easy it would be for a poker room to devise a bot to beat its players, even if the bot didn't peek at the players' cards. The poker room has the hand histories of every player at their tables. Since human players are allowed to use the hand histories they collect on the games they play or observe, would that mean it would be fine for the poker room to analyze the players based on their hand histories?

I do not believe any major Internet poker room would ever use bots to cheat the players on their own tables. The money that these poker rooms make from their rake is just too much to jeopardize. The marketing dollars they spend to attract well-known pros to their sites as endorsers and resident experts is enormous. To chance having an operation like this shut down with a poker bot scandal would be idiotic.

HUMAN BOTS

The Internet has provided a way for many skillful poker players to go from hobby level to full-time pro, even on a relatively small starting bankroll. A $10/$20 player who is capable of earning $10,000 per year in live casino poker rooms can't really afford to quit his job and play poker full-time. $10,000 a year might be a nice supplemental income for a retiree on a pension, but it's a poverty level existence for anyone without another income source.

If this same $10/$20 player moves his game online, he'll often find that he can earn $12,000 to $15,000 annually. He'll lose a part of the win rate he was getting from his ability to read his opponents' body language, but this loss is more than made up for by the speed of online games, savings on tips to dealers, lower house rake, and easy home access to play at all hours. He's able to play more hours per week, at a faster clip, and with lower expenses.

And as soon as this player discovers that he can play two tables simultaneously just as easily as one, then four tables almost as easily as two, his day job is likely to start taking a back seat to poker play. Without increasing his strategic skills one iota, he's seen his game go from a potential $10,000 per year income to a real $50,000 to $60,000 plus per year.

In live casino poker rooms, he dreamt about the day he could move up into the $20/$40 games, then the $30/$60 games. This might have remained a fantasy forever. Now, he's thinking in terms of getting another computer monitor, wondering if he can handle six tables, then eight. He doesn't feel a need for any more poker skill. He wants hardware!

Prior to the Internet, most poker players thought of $10/$20 hold'em games as entry-level games. If you could make money at $10/$20, you had a shot at moving up to where the big bucks were.

With the online poker revolution, many online players make a living without ever worrying about moving up from the $10/$20 games, because this level of skill in itself can generate an income of $75,000 plus per year.

Lucrative as this online multi-table play may be, it's not really high-level poker. Although it takes some real knowledge and intelligence to design the strategy, the application comes down to formula. This type of player is similar to a speed chess player who takes on twelve simultaneous opponents, beating most of them, hour after hour. Pit him against one grandmaster and he's toast, but he can beat the public till the cows come home.

Personally, I have no moral objections to any player creating a bot to play the way he plays, and using his bot in public poker rooms. I'm sure there are some players who have done this, and I admire them for their ingenuity. Unskilled players have to learn to play poker, and whether they are schooled in the fundamentals by a bot or a human who plays like a bot makes very little difference. The lessons cost the same.

There's a popular software program called *Turbo Texas Hold'em,* and another called *Poker Academy,* that are collections of poker bots that you can play against. They are training programs, designed to teach the game. There are dozens of different cyber-players you can choose from, all set to play with varying degrees of skill, aggression, passivity, looseness, or tightness.

The main problem with learning to play hold'em with *Turbo Texas Hold'em,* however, is that the players have no memory. They can play their position aggressively. They can even do tricky things like bluff, slowplay, and check-raise. They can decide on how to play based on the prior action in a round. But they pay no attention whatsoever to who made the action. If you steal the blinds from a passive player 100 times in a row, he doesn't remember the next time you make your move.

So after a while, it's not hard to beat these players. You know which players are tight, loose, passive, etc., which players try to steal pots, which ones will call you down. And none of them ever know anything about you. Poker bots without memory, whose strategies never change to fit specific players, just aren't scary. No matter how good they are, they're predictable.

Poker Academy, on the other hand, allegedly employs an artificial intelligence (AI) program which allows its bots to remember the way you play your hands and to play their own hands based on their assessment of your play.

It's not really difficult to beat the players in either *Turbo Texas Hold'em* or *Poker Academy.* The *Poker Academy* games do have more of a real feel to them, but in many ways it's easier to beat their games precisely because their players have more intelligence in their decisions.

There are websites right now that are advertising poker bots for sale, with claims that their bots can earn hundreds and sometimes thousands of dollars per day in the online games. Because these bots are being touted, I'm sure there are players who have tried them. I myself have not, so I have no idea of whether or not the advertisers claims are legitimate. After thirty years of studying gambling systems and watching the new fads come and go, I have a natural inclination to mistrust any claims about any gambling system that makes it sound too easy, and I suspect that the bots being hyped online have very limited applications and are not nearly as profitable or successful as the sellers claim.

I think the main worry players have about bots is the fear that as artificial intelligence advances, bots might be able to beat more and more players at ever-higher levels, and gambling conglomerates might start to maintain armies of bots to get rich in online poker rooms. Should this occur, online poker as we know it might disappear. These bots could be used cheaply to dominate tables at all levels.

So, despite the fact that I would not categorize a player using a poker bot as immoral or illegal, I know many poker players who dislike this trend, and not a few professional gamblers who are seriously looking into the possibility of making a few quick million with such bots. But I don't know any who have succeeded yet.

COLLUSION

Recently, I was sitting at a tournament table in a popular Las Vegas casino poker room, and the subject of online play came up. One player said he would never play online for any serious amount of money because it's too easy for players to collude with each other. Another player said he didn't worry about that because the online poker rooms all have software for detecting collusion between players at the same table. The first player said he and his buddies never got caught when they did it! Then, a third player piped in and said he'd done it as well with some of his friends, but they never were able to make any money with this strategy!

So far be it from me to tell you there's no collusion happening online. If two players sitting at a live poker table would discuss it so cavalierly in front of strangers, I suspect it's been tried a lot. I guess some players just don't see it as cheating.

Let me just point out that collusion is wrong. It is cheating. It is not poker, but an attempt at theft.

Most players who attempt collusion cannot beat poker with skill. Thankfully, they are often just as bad at crime as they are at poker.

It is much easier for players to collude online than it is for them to collude in live games. In live games, they need finesse, subtle signals, timing, and no small amount of nerve. Online, two players can be on the phone with each other telling each other exactly what their cards are every hand. That doesn't take a lot of finesse.

But online games also make it easier for colluding players to be caught *after the fact*. In a live game, once those cards hit the muck, everything about a hand is lost except for what players remember. Online, there is no muck. The poker room has a history of every hand, every card every player was dealt, and every action on every game.

If you suspect collusion between two players, you can contact the poker room management and ask to have the hand histories reviewed. And collusion is not difficult to detect if you can see all of the hands and the way they were played. Let's look at how collusion works, what it looks like, and how it can be exposed.

HOW DOES COLLUSION WORK?

Two players working in collusion can steal a lot of pots by raising and reraising each other to get opponents with marginal hands to fold. Usually, one player will have a strong, or at least a playable hand, and the other will simply be in there to jack up the bets to the point where everyone else folds.

Once the competition is gone, the weak hand folds to a raise, and the strong hand picks up the pot. The strong hand can also voluntarily show his cards at this point to make his aggressive play look good. If the strong hand is truly a monster, the weak hand can stay in the pot for the purpose of building the pot and keeping other players in it. He can throw in calls to give others the incentive to stay in the pot. And if other players are aggressively betting or are obviously not going to go away because they have so much already committed to the pot, the weak hand can go into the raising/reraising routine with the monster hand to suck more bets out of the players who aren't going to go away. The only important thing the weak hand must do in order to pull off this scam is never show down the cards he was playing.

But there are other advantages to collusion. Just knowing two other cards that are not available to be dealt on every round is an advantage. If I'm dealt an A-J and my partner has a J-8, I know the value of my jack is greatly diminished. If I've got pocket sevens, and my partner has J-7, I'll throw my sevens away before the flop since my chance of flopping a set has been cut in half.

If both colluding players have strong hands, the weaker hand can fold if another player is aggressively contesting the pot. The colluders do not mind winning each other's money, since they split up their spoils at the end anyway, but they will not give a third party any chance to beat both of them. For example, if I'm holding A-K, and my partner has A-Q, and an ace comes down on the flop, the A-Q will fold fast. If my aces get beat because an opponent makes a set, the winner of that pot will only get my money, not my partner's. In an honest game, the A-Q might not fold, and the winner would be getting double what he got from me.

Many of these types of plays will not be seen or even suspected by players at the table since they cannot see the cards of the colluders. But the strongest plays colluders make generally involve raising and reraising each other to steal and build pots. These plays definitely stick out as unusual the second and third time you see them.

In the live poker rooms of Las Vegas, this type of amateur collusion is most commonly seen in the low-limit games, up to $6-$12, and it would never pass unnoticed in the tougher or bigger games where a lot of pros and semi-pros are working. Collusion teams do not want to play against a poker room's regulars. They want to skin neophytes and tourists for a few hundred bucks, then move on to a new table. Poker collusion today is primarily a **short con**, a scam designed to be pulled off quickly for a small amount of money that will not be noticed, then done again and again against different suckers in a different location. Whether in live games or online, it's a poker room version of three-card monte.

In addition to an online poker room's ability to look at complete hand histories for their games, another problem colluders face on the Internet is that the poker room can see if two players always show up together or move table to table together. And the hand histories of these tables can also be examined. So, although the online games make collusion easier to pull off, the technology also allows colluders to be caught after the fact in ways that are impossible in live games.

So don't hesitate to report suspected collusion if you see unusual betting patterns, like those described above, among two or more players. And definitely don't fall for the misconception that colluders only work the big games because that's where the big money is. Crooks don't necessarily go for the big money. A lot of them go for the easy money.

PART III

End Matter

AFTERWORD

The Future of Online Gambling

If you've ever entertained notions of becoming a professional gambler, now is an exceptionally opportune time to put your money where your dreams are. The Internet has created profit opportunities for inexperienced gamblers in greater quantity, and of greater value, than we have ever seen.

Many of the most successful gamblers of all time got their starts because they recognized unique opportunities to make money and they seized the day. Some of the most prosperous blackjack players of the past quarter century were just college kids when Atlantic City introduced the first East Coast casinos in the late 1970s. The casinos opened with a unique new rule—early surrender—a rule that gave blackjack players the advantage over the house. The rule, in fact, was an "accident." The New Jersey Casino Control Commission mandated the rule but didn't know the math. By the time the casinos got rid of the rule a year later, these college kids—the Tommy Hyland team, the MIT team, the Czech team, and hundreds of other solo players—had won millions of dollars to finance lifelong careers in gambling.

I knew a college kid in the late 80s who today is one of the most successful professional gamblers in Las Vegas. He owes his career and his starting bankroll to a single rule option the Nevada casinos experimented with 15 years ago called the "over/under" rule. The few smart players who knew how to beat the rule made a killing. Over/under games lasted for a couple years until the casinos realized there were some pros making a fortune off it, and they added betting restrictions that reduced the profit potential for the wise guys. But by the time this kid graduated from UC Berkeley, he had a bankroll. He never had to look for a job. He was a professional gambler, and very few professions are as much fun, or as financially rewarding.

The single greatest obstacle to entering the gambling profession is money. Even gambling with an advantage entails financial risk in the short term, and for a player to gamble at a level where he can not only afford to play, but also support himself, he needs a substantial bankroll. For most people, this is not easy to come by. When an opportunity arises for a gambler to make a lot of money on a relatively small bankroll, it's the type of opportunity that can launch a career in gambling by providing a modestly-funded player with the bankroll he needs.

See you online...

— Arnold Snyder

email: arnoldsnyder@blackjackforumonline.com

GLOSSARY

Ace Master: Derogatory term for a hold'em player who will play any hand in any pot from any position if one of his cards is an ace.

Aces Up: In hold'em, to have two pair, one of which is aces.

Action: General casino slang for the total amount bet by players. In poker, any betting by the players on a round is the "action."

Add-On: In poker tournaments, an option to buy a specified number of chips at the end of a specified time period.

Affiliate: A web site that carries Internet casino or poker room advertisements, and receives payment from the advertiser for players who come to them through that site.

Aggressive: In poker, a player who raises and reraises frequently is aggressive. In gambling in general, any betting strategy based on placing large bets is an aggressive strategy.

All In: In no-limit hold'em, a bet of all of a player's chips.

Backdoor: In hold'em, to make a straight or flush by drawing to it on both the turn and river. Often an accidental improvement, as when a player with top pair backdoors a flush.

Bad Beat: In poker, to have a very strong hand beaten by an even stronger hand.

Bank/Bankroll: The total amount of money a player has to gamble with.

Banner: A graphic advertisement on the Internet that, if clicked on, is a link to the advertiser's webpage.

Banner Farm: A website that is primarily a collection of banner ads, used especially for websites that advertise Internet casinos and poker rooms, with little other content.

Basic Strategy: In blackjack, the mathematically correct strategy for lowering the house advantage. Also used for other casino games where a mathematically correct strategy exists.

Blackjack Switch: A hybrid form of blackjack where players play two hands, and have an option to "switch" the top cards of each hand.

Blind: In hold'em, a bet that must be placed preflop instead of, or in addition to, an ante.

Blind Level: In tournament hold'em, where the amount of the blinds increases as the tournament progresses, each succeeding increase is a different blind level.

Bluff: In poker, to place a bet with a weak hand in order to win a pot by causing other players to fold.

Bluff Master: A derogatory term for a poker player who bluffs too frequently.

Board: In hold'em, the face-up community cards on the table.

Boat: A full house.

Bonus: In Internet casinos and poker rooms, money added to a player's account in return for some specified deposit and action in the site's games.

Bonus Abuser: Online casino slang for a player who plays primarily to exploit bonuses.

Bot: A computer program that plays poker or other casino games online.

Bottom Pair: In hold'em, to have a pair by matching the lowest card on the board with one of your hole cards.

Browser-Based (software): Online casino game software that does not require a player to download playing software onto his computer, but allows the player to play games directly on the casino's server.

Build (a pot): In poker, to increase the amount of money in a pot by betting and/or raising, encouraging other players to stay in.

Bust: In blackjack, to go over a total of 21.

Button: In hold'em, the disk that rotates clockwise from player to player, indicating which player has the "dealer" position and bets last.

Buy-In: To obtain chips for playing any casino or poker game. In a tournament, the amount you pay to obtain your initial chips for playing the tournament.

Call: In poker, to match a bet in order to keep your hand alive in a pot, without raising.

Calling Station: In poker, a derogatory term for a passive player who rarely raises, but often calls with any hand.

Camouflage: In blackjack, or online casino gambling, playing or betting in such a way as to appear like a regular (losing) gambler when you actually have the advantage.

Capped Pot: In poker, a pot which has reached the limit of raising and reraising allowed by house rules on a given betting round.

Card Counting: In blackjack, keeping track of the cards played in order to get an advantage over the house.

Caribbean Stud Poker: A popular house-banked casino game that has a high house advantage, approximately 5.22%.

Carny Game: Any popular casino game that has a high house advantage and cannot usually be beaten with any intelligent playing strategy.

Cash Back: A type of online casino bonus in which a player has a portion of his loss returned to him if he loses some specified amount.

Cash Out: To withdraw your funds from a casino.

Catch: In hold'em, to make a hand by "catching" a card or cards on the flop, turn, or river.

Change Gears: In a poker game, to play more (or less) aggressively than you have been playing.

Charge: In poker, to bet in order to make other players pay to stay in a pot.

Chat: In poker rooms, the feature that allows players at the table to converse with each other by typing messages on a chat screen. Some Internet casinos also have "chat" support rooms for solving customer problems.

Check: In poker, to stay in a pot in which no bet is required, and without betting yourself.

Check-Raise: In poker, to reraise a player who bets, after having checked to him in the same betting round before his bet.

Chip Leader: In all poker and gambling tournaments, the player who currently has the most chips.

Chip Position: In poker, the relation a player's current chip stack has to others at his table. Also used in all gambling tournaments to indicate a player's current standing.

Click-Through: To enter a website by clicking on a banner ad.

Collusion: In poker, to cheat by surreptitiously sharing information with one or more other players at the table.

Committed (to a pot): In poker, to be in a position where you have already placed so many of your chips into a pot, that you must call any bet.

Community Cards: In hold'em, the face-up cards on the table that all players may combine with the cards in their hands to make the best possible five-card hand.

Comp: Casino slang for "complimentary." Any freebie given to a player in return for his action in the games.

Counter: In blackjack, a card counter.

Cryptologic: A popular major brand of Internet casino software.

Cut-Off Seat: In hold'em, the seat to the right of the button.

Dead Money: In poker, any poor player who has little chance of winning.

Deposit: Money placed with a casino or poker room cashier for the purpose of playing the games.

Deuces Wild: A popular form of video poker.

Double Down: In blackjack, to double the bet on the table, receive one card, and forfeit the option to hit again.

Draw: In blackjack, to take another card, or hit. Also, a once popular form of poker in which players had the option to discard from their initial hands and be dealt replacement cards.

Drawing Dead: In hold'em, to draw to a hand with no chance of winning because another player already has a hand ranked higher than any hand you could make.

Draw Out: In hold'em, to beat a player who had a better hand prior to the card(s) that appeared on the flop, turn, or river.

Early Position: In hold'em, the players who must bet first (generally the first four betting positions in a ten-handed game).

Entry Fee: In a gambling tournament, the amount a player pays to the house that does not go into the prize pool.

Fast: In gambling in general, any aggressive betting is "fast" play. In tournaments, any playing structure that requires players to bet aggressively to stay competitive is a "fast" tournament.

Fifth Street: In hold'em, the fifth community card. Also called the river.

Final Table: In a tournament, the last table of players remaining at the end.

Fish: In poker, a poor player who is expected to lose.

Five-Card Charlie: In blackjack, a five-card hand that automatically wins. Not common in regular casino blackjack, but a standard rule in the popular Internet casino game of Pontoon.

Flop: In hold'em, the first three community cards dealt onto the table after the first betting round.

Flush: In poker, a hand with five suited cards.

Flush Draw: In poker, a hand in which it is possible to make a flush with a card (or cards) to come.

Flush Master: A derogatory term for a hold'em player who will enter any pot with any two suited cards, and who will stay in any pot as long as his flush draw is alive.

Flux: Common gamblers' slang for fluctuations, the inevitable winning and losing streaks caused by good and bad "luck," as opposed to any actual advantage or disadvantage in the games.

Fold: In poker, to discard a hand by refusing to call a bet.

Fourth Street: In hold'em, the fourth community card dealt face-up onto the table. Also called the turn.

Free Card: In hold'em, a turn or river card that any player can see for "free," because no betting occurred on the prior betting round.

Free Roll: Common gambler's slang for any bet or game that costs nothing but has a real money prize.

Full House: In poker, a hand consisting of a pair and three of a kind. Also called a boat.

Full-Pay: In video poker, a payout schedule for any of the popular variations that is considered the best payout schedule for that variation.

Full-Ring Game: In hold'em, a 9 or 10-handed game.

Gaff: Common gamblers' slang for any cheating device.

Gutshot: In poker, an inside straight draw, or any straight draw that can only be made on one end.

Hand History: In online poker, a feature that allows players to review the hands at the tables where they played after the play is through.

Heads Up: Common gamblers' slang for any betting that occurs between only two players. In blackjack, this would also mean a player who is alone at the table with the dealer.

Hit: In blackjack, to take another card.

Hold Up: In poker, for a hand that is not a premium hand to win the pot.

Hole Card: In blackjack, the dealer's face down card. In hold'em, any of the players' first two cards.

House: The casino.

House Edge: The advantage that is built into a casino game.

Implied Odds: In hold'em, the mathematical relationship of the current bet you must make to the total you might ultimately win if you take the pot, assuming the probable betting action after your bet.

Inside Straight Draw: In poker, a hand in which you have four cards to a straight, but need a card which falls between two of your cards to make the straight, as opposed to needing a card on either end. Also called a gutshot.

Insurance: In blackjack, a side-bet that the dealer has a ten in the hole when he shows an ace up-card.

Jacks or Better: A popular form of video poker.

Kelly Criterion: A betting model used by many gamblers to lower their risk and increase their long term win rate by betting according to the actual percentage advantage they have.

Kicker: In poker, a card that a player holds as the next highest card in his hand, and that will be used to determine a winner if two players otherwise have identical hands.

GLOSSARY

Late Position: In hold'em, the last players to bet on a round, the button being the latest position.

Let It Ride: A popular house-banked casino game that has a high house advantage, approximately 3.51%.

Limit: In poker, a game in which bets are limited to a specified betting structure.

Limit the Field: In hold'em, to raise in order to discourage marginal hands from entering a pot and possibly drawing out on you.

Limp In: In hold'em, to enter a pot on the first betting round with the minimum bet allowed.

Loose: In poker, a player who plays a higher percentage of hands than normal. A loose table is one where many players consistently enter the pot. A loose call is a call with a marginal hand that does not have the mathematical odds to call.

Loss Rebate: In casino gambling, a rebate of some percentage of a player's loss by the casino, usually as a form of "comp" to high rollers.

Maniac: In poker, a very loose and aggressive player whose bets seem to have little relation to his cards or chances of winning.

Marginal Call: In poker, to call a bet when the odds of winning the hand are very close to the odds needed to make the call a profitable bet.

Matchplay: In casino gambling, any matching of a player's bets with house money.

Microgaming: One of the biggest providers of casino gambling software for the online gaming industry.

Middle Position: In hold'em, any of three seats located halfway between the first betting positions and the button, the central positions to act on their hands.

Mix Up: In poker, to play the same hands in different ways at different times in order to keep competitors from figuring out your hands.

Monster: In poker, any highly ranked hand that is unlikely to be beaten, such as a full house, a straight flush, etc.

Neteller: An online banking service popular with players in online casinos and poker rooms.

No-Hole-Card: In blackjack, a rule common in European casinos (as well as in some European Internet casinos), in which the dealer does not take a hole card until after the players have completed the action on their hands.

No-Limit: In poker, a betting structure in which the only upper limit to the amount a player can bet or raise is the amount of chips or money that player has on the table.

Non-Sticky (bonus): An Internet casino bonus added to a player's account that a player may withdraw as cash after meeting a wagering requirement.

Nuts: In poker, a hand that cannot be beaten by any other possible hand in play.

Odds: The chances against something happening.

Off-Suit: Two cards that are not of the same suit.

On Tilt: In poker, to play erratically and poorly, usually as a result of a bad beat or a lengthy losing streak.

Open-end (straight draw): In poker, four consecutive cards to a straight, which can be made with one more card on either end.

Out: In poker, a card that will increase the value of your hand to a winner.

Overbet: In poker, to bet an amount that seems very big based on the size of the pot.

Overcard: In hold'em, a card in the hole that is higher than the highest card on the board.

Overpair: In hold'em, a pocket pair that is higher than the highest card on the board.

Overplay: In poker, to bet too aggressively with a marginal hand.

Over-the-Top: In poker, to raise a bet or raise is to go over-the-top of the bettor.

Passive: In poker, a non-aggressive playing style or table with mostly checking and calling, and very little raising.

Penetration: In blackjack, the depth to which a dealer deals out a deck or shoe between shuffles.

GLOSSARY

Playtech: A widely-used brand of online casino software.

Pocket: In hold'em, the hole cards, mostly used to describe a pair in the hole, such as "pocket pair," or "pocket jacks," etc.

Pocket Rockets: In hold'em, two aces as hole cards.

Pontoon: A hybrid version of blackjack, popular in Internet casinos, in which the player sees no dealer upcard.

Portal: A website with banner ads that lead to other websites.

Position: In hold'em, the players' betting order in relation to the button.

Pot: In poker, the total amount bet by all players in a hand.

Pot Limit: A form of hold'em in which the largest bet that can be made is the size of the current pot.

Pot Odds: In poker, the ratio of the total amount in the pot to the amount of the current bet required to keep a hand alive.

Preflop: In hold'em, the action that occurs based on the players' hole cards before the flop.

Prize Pool: In a tournament, the total amount of all prize money to be awarded to the winners, based on the total buy-ins of all players in the tournament.

Property Group: The management/ownership company that oversees a group of online casinos.

Proprietary Software: Any Internet casino software that has been created for the exclusive use of a single online casino or property group, and is not available to other online casinos.

Protecting a Hand: In hold'em, betting with a made hand to keep others from drawing out.

Pseudo-Sticky (bonus): In Internet casinos, a type of bonus that players may not withdraw, but may play with until they lose it, even if they withdraw their initial deposit and winnings.

Push: In blackjack, to tie the dealer's hand. No money exchanges hands.

Quads: In poker, four of a kind.

Rag: In hold'em, a low card (usually 2-8).

Rainbow: In hold'em, cards of all different suits on the board.

Raise: In poker, to increase the bet from the previous bet.

Rake: In poker, the percentage of money the house takes from the pot.

Read (a player): In poker, to figure out the strength of a player's hand by his actions, betting, or physical mannerisms.

Read (the board): In hold'em, to figure out the possibilities presented by the community cards in assessing the strength or weakness of your own hand and others.

Real Time Gaming (RTG): A widely-used brand of online casino software.

Rebuy: In poker tournaments, to purchase more chips after a tournament has begun.

Red Dog: A popular house-banked casino game that has a high house advantage, approximately 3.20%.

Reload: In online poker rooms, to deposit more money to play after an initial deposit.

Reload Bonus: In online poker rooms, a bonus offer to current (not new) players, to entice them to deposit more money to play.

Reraise: In poker, to raise a prior bettor's raise.

Ring Game: In poker, a full-table non-tournament game, usually with 9-10 players.

River: In hold'em, the fifth and last community card to be dealt. Fifth street.

Rock: In poker, a very tight, conservative player.

Rogue Casino: An online casino that is suspected of cheating customers, either by using unfair software, or by failing to honor bonus terms, or by failing to promptly pay players when they cash out.

Royal Flush: In poker, the highest ranking hand, a straight flush to the ace.

Runner-Runner: In hold'em, to make a strong hand by catching needed cards on both the turn and river.

Run Over: In poker, to bully opponentss with very aggressive play.

Sandbag: In poker, same as slow play.

Satellite: A poker tournament played to win a seat in a bigger tournament.

Scare Card: In hold'em, a card that appears on the board that makes premium hands possible.

Semi-Bluff: In poker, a bet where you do not yet have a strong hand but which might improve to a strong hand if the right card falls.

Set: In hold'em, to make trips by holding a pocket pair and getting the third card on the board.

Sheriff: In poker, a player who will call down suspected bluffers, often to the detriment of his own bankroll.

Shoe: In blackjack, a card holder that sits on the table top designed to allow the dealer to deal from more than two decks, most often 4, 6, or 8.

Short Bank: In gambling, a bankroll for playing that is dangerously small.

Short-Handed: In hold'em, a game in which there are fewer than eight players.

Short-Pay: In video poker, an undesirable payout schedule which pays less than the normal amount for that type of game.

Short Stack: In poker, a small amount of chips to play with.

Showdown: In poker, the revelation of the hands after all betting is completed, to determine the pot winner.

Sit'n'Go: A popular type of online tournament that has no scheduled starting time, but begins as soon as the required number of seats are filled with players.

Slow Play: In poker, to deliberately refrain from playing aggressively when you have a very strong hand, usually to keep other players in the pot in order to draw more out of them by not revealing your strength.

Split (a pair): In blackjack, an option to make two separate hands when you are dealt two cards of the same denomination.

Split Pot: In poker, a pot that is divided between two or more players who have identical hands.

Stackable: In online poker rooms, a type of bonus that is available to players who are already playing on another bonus offer in that poker room.

Standard Deviation: A math term that describes the normal amount of fluctuation in results just due to "luck."

Steal: In poker, to take a pot by betting when you have no hand of value.

Sticky Bonus: An Internet casino bonus added to a player's account which a player may use for wagering purposes, but may not withdraw.

Straight: In poker, a premium hand that consists of five consecutive cards with no gaps, such as 9-8-7-6-5.

Straight Flush: In poker, one of the highest ranking hands. It consists of five consecutive cards, all of the same suit.

Suck Out: In hold'em, same as draw out. To beat a player who has a better hand by making a superior hand with cards that come on the board.

Suited Connectors: In hold'em, two hole cards that are suited and consecutive, such as 7-8 or J-Q.

Surrender: In blackjack, an option to give up your hand and half your bet. In poker, to fold.

Table Limits: In casino games, the minimum and maximum bets allowed on a table.

Take a Shot: In poker, to bet at the pot, usually hoping to win it with no callers or raises.

Take Down: In poker, to win the pot is to take it down.

Tap Out: Common gamblers' slang for losing all funds.

Tell: In poker, a player's unconcious action or mannerism that reveals something about the player's hand.

Ten-Play: In video poker, a program that allows the player to play ten simultaneous hands on screen.

Terms and Conditions (T & C): In online casinos, the statement that defines all rules and procedures for players.

Three-Card Monte: A con game played by hustlers to extract money from the gullible.

Three-Card Poker: A popular house-banked casino game that has a high house advantage, approximately 3.37%.

Tight: In poker, a player who plays relatively few hands, also said of a table where there is little action because of the presence of many such players.

Top Pair: In hold'em, to have a card in the hole that matches the top card on the board.

Tournaments: Any gambling games that are set up with a formal structure for eliminating players until one (or some few) players remain and share a prize pool composed of all players' buy-ins.

Trips: In poker, three of a kind.

Turn: In hold'em, the fourth community card dealt on the board. Fourth street.

Under the Gun: In hold'em, the first player to act on his hand pre-flop.

Under-Chipped: In poker, to have few chips relative to the size of the bets in a game.

Unraised Pot: In hold'em, a preflop pot in which any active players simply called the big blind without raising.

Upcard: In blackjack, the dealer's face-up card.

Variance: A math term that denotes the amount of fluctuation in results that is normal for a game.

Viper: A Microgaming software program that aids players in their decision in blackjack and video poker games.

Wagering Requirement (WR): In online casinos and poker rooms, a total dollar amount of wagering that a player must meet in order to qualify for a bonus.

Watchdog: A website that monitors players' reports on online casinos as a consumer service.

Win-Required (bonus): A type of deposit bonus that requires that a player win a specified amount of money from the casino before the bonus funds can be cashed or used.

APPENDIX

Blackjack Switch Basic Strategy
(For Multiple Decks, European No-Hole Card Rule)

	2	3	4	5	6	7	8	9	X	A
STAND										
17	S	S	S	S	S	S	S	S	S	S
16	S	S	S	S	S	H	H	H	H	H
15	S	S	S	S	S	H	H	H	H	H
14	H	S	S	S	S	H	H	H	H	H
13	H	S	S	S	S	H	H	H	H	H
12	H	H	H	S	S	H	H	H	H	H
DOUBLE DOWN										
11	D	D	D	D	D	D	D	H	H	H
10	D	D	D	D	D	D	D	H	H	H
9	H	H	H	H	D	H	H	H	H	H
A8	S	S	S	S	S	S	S	S	S	S
A7	S	S	S	D	D	S	S	H	H	H
A6	H	H	H	D	D	H	H	H	H	H
A5	H	H	H	H	D	H	H	H	H	H
A4	H	H	H	H	H	H	H	H	H	H
A3	H	H	H	H	H	H	H	H	H	H
A2	H	H	H	H	H	H	H	H	H	H
SPLIT										
AA	$	$	$	$	$	$	$	$	$	
99			$	$	$		$	$		
88	$	$	$	$	$	$	$	$		
77		$	$	$	$	$				
66			$	$	$					
33				$	$	$				
22				$	$	$				

INSURANCE: NO

S = Stand   H = Hit   D = Double Down $ = Split

The House Advantage in Internet Casino Games

Blackjack (with Chapter 7 basic strategy)	0.50%*
Jacks or Better Video Poker (with Chapter 11 strategy)	0.52%**
Blackjack Switch (with Chapter 8 strategy)	0.10%
Pontoon (with Chapter 9 strategy)	0.19%
Baccarat (banker bet)	1.06%
Baccarat (player bet)	1.24%
Craps (pass bet)	1.41%
Craps (don't pass bet)	1.36%
Roulette (single-0, even money bets with en prison)	1.32%
Roulette (single-0, bets other than even money)	2.63%
Roulette (double-0)	5.26%
Three-Card Poker (pair plus bet only)	2.32%
Three-Card Poker (ante/play with best strategy)	3.37%
Red Dog (single-deck with best strategy)	3.20%
Let It Ride (with best strategy)	3.51%
Caribbean Stud Poker (with best strategy)	5.22%
Slots (advantage varies by machine/casino)	5.00%***

* Approximate. See Chapter 7 for precise advantage based on rules and number of decks.
** Approximate, assuming full-pay pay table (See Chapter 11).
*** Approximate.

INDEX

INDEX

CARDOZA POKER BOOKS
POWERFUL INFORMATION YOU MUST HAVE

CHAMPIONSHIP HOLD'EM *by T. J. Cloutier & Tom McEvoy.* Hard-hitting hold'em the way it's played *today* in both limit cash games and tournaments. Get killer advice on how to win more money in rammin'-jammin' games, kill-pot, jackpot, shorthanded, and other types of cash games. You'll learn the thinking process before the flop, on the flop, on the turn, and at the river with specific suggestions for what to do when good or bad things happen plus 20 illustrated hands with play-by-play analyses. Specific advice for rocks in tight games, weaklings in loose games, experts in solid games, how hand values change in jackpot games, when you should fold, check, raise, reraise, check-raise, slowplay, bluff, and tournament strategies for small buy-in, big buy-in, rebuy, incremental add-on, satellite and big-field major tournaments. Wow! If you want to win at limit hold'em, you need this book! 392 pages, $29.95.

CHAMPIONSHIP NO-LIMIT & POT-LIMIT HOLD'EM *by T. J. Cloutier & Tom McEvoy.* This is the bible of winning pot-limit and no-limit hold'em tournaments. You'll get all the answers here —no holds barred—to your most important questions: How do you get inside your opponents' heads and learn how to beat them at their own game? How can you tell how much to bet, raise, and reraise in no-limit hold'em? When can you bluff? How do you set up your opponents in pot-limit hold'em so that you can win a monster pot? What are the best strategies for winning no-limit and pot-limit tournaments, satellites, and supersatellites? Rock-solid and inspired advice you can bank on from two of the most recognizable figures in poker. 304 pages, $29.95.

CHAMPIONSHIP OMAHA (Omaha High-Low, Pot-limit Omaha, Limit High Omaha) *by T. J. Cloutier & Tom McEvoy.* Clearly-written strategies and powerful advice from Cloutier and McEvoy who have won four World Series of Poker titles in Omaha tournaments. Powerful advice shows you how to win at low-limit and high-stakes games, how to play against loose and tight opponents, and the differing strategies for rebuy and freezeout tournaments. Learn the best starting hands, when slowplaying a big hand is dangerous, what danglers are and why winners don't play them, why pot-limit Omaha is the only poker game where you sometimes fold the nuts on the flop and are correct in doing so and overall, how can you win a lot of money at Omaha! 296 pages, photos, illustrations, $29.95.

HOW TO WIN NO-LIMIT HOLD'EM TOURNAMENTS *by Tom McEvoy & Don Vines.* Learn the basic concepts of tournament strategy, plus how to win big by playing small buy-in events, how to graduate to medium and big buy-in tournaments; how to adjust for short fields, huge fields, slow and fast-action events, plus how to win online no-limit tournaments; manage a tournament bankroll, and tips on table demeanor for televised tournaments. See actual hands played by finalists at WSOP and WPT championship tables with card pictures, analysis and useful lessons from the play. 376 pages, $29.95.

NO-LIMIT TEXAS HOLD 'EM: The New Player's Guide to Winning Poker's Biggest Game *by Brad Daugherty & Tom McEvoy.* Two world champions give you a crash course in how to beat no-limit hold'em tournament winners and cash game players. You learn the winning principles and four major skills of how to: evaluate the strength of a hand; determine how much to bet; understand opponents' play; plus bluffing and when to do it. 74 game scenarios, two betting charts for tournament play and sections on essential principles and strategies show you how to beat live and online tournaments. 288 pages, $24.95.